DATE DUE

MY 12 99			
MY 27 99			
MY 30 00			
SE 8 00			
MY 1 '03			
MY 21 03			

DEMCO 38-296

···

American Finance
for the 21st Century

R

· ·

American Finance for the 21st Century

Robert E. Litan

with

Jonathan Rauch

Brookings Institution Press
Washington, D.C.

ofit organization devoted to research,
~~education, and publication on important~~ sues of domestic and foreign policy. Its
principal purpose is to bring knowledge to bear on current and emerging policy
problems. The Institution maintains a position of neutrality on issues of public
policy. Interpretations or conclusions in publications of the Brookings Institution
Press should be understood to be solely those of the authors.

Copyright © 1998 by
The Brookings Institution
1775 Massachusetts Avenue, N.W.
Washington, D.C. 20036

Library of Congress Cataloging-in-Publication Data
  Litan, Robert E., 1950–
  American finance for the 21st century / Robert E. Litan with
Jonathan Rauch.
      p. cm.
  Includes bibliographical references and index.
  ISBN 0-8157-5288-1 (alk. paper)
  1. Finance—United States. 2. United States—Economic conditions.
3. Banks and banking—United States. I. Rauch, Jonathan, 1960– II.
Title.
  HG181 .L628 1998
  332'.0973—ddc21   98-8988
                                                                       CIP

9 8 7 6 5 4 3 2 1

The paper used in this publication meets the minimum requirements of the
American National Standard for Information Sciences—Permanence of Paper
for Printed Library Materials, ANSI Z39.48-1984

Typeset in Garamond

Composition by Cynthia Stock
Silver Spring, Maryland

Printed by R. R. Donnelley and Sons Co.
Harrisonburg, Virginia

Contents

Preface

IN THE Riegle-Neal Interstate Banking and Branching Efficiency Act of 1994, Congress directed the Secretary of the Treasury to take a broad look at the strengths and weaknesses of our financial services system. To assist us in fulfilling that mandate, the department called upon leading experts outside the government on the variety of issues that would have to be considered. The advisory commission that was appointed in 1995, consisting of people with a broad range of experience in financial services, has certainly served that objective well, and I am grateful for their participation and support

For the task of drafting the study, we turned to Bob Litan and Jonathan Rauch, both of whom have extensive experience with financial regulation and financial markets.

Deputy Secretary Summers and I, together with a number of members of the Treasury staff, spent many hours with the authors, and among ourselves, discussing drafts of the study. While each of us might have our own way of expressing our views on the many complex issues covered in the study, we are in agreement that the study presents an extremely useful analytic framework for considering issues confronting the financial services system of the twenty-first century.

Riegle-Neal also requires the Secretary of the Treasury to develop and submit to Congress recommendations for legislative changes to improve the operations of the financial services system. In June 1997 the Treasury Department transmitted to Congress a draft legislative proposal intended to make the system more effective in serving the needs of users by eliminating outmoded barriers to competition. Our proposal addresses many, but not all, of the issues raised in this study, and we hope the study will serve as a basis for further policy discussion and debate.

This Congress has an opportunity to pass landmark legislation in this area that will be of enormous benefit to consumers of financial services, and it is my hope that this study's look into the needs of the financial services system of the twenty-first century will be of value to Congress as it confronts that task.

Robert E. Rubin
Secretary of the Treasury

Introduction and Summary

AS RECENTLY as thirty years ago, Americans lived in a financial world that today seems a bygone era. Investment choices were meager. If you valued safety above all else, you could invest in a government savings bond or in a federally insured savings account that could pay no more annual interest than the mandated ceiling rate of just over 5 percent. If you wanted to take a little more risk, you could buy "whole life" insurance, with a cash surrender value that would increase over time; you could buy mutual fund shares, but only a few funds were available; you could buy stock, but only from a brokerage firm that charged high commissions at fixed rates. If you had a pension plan, you probably did not control its investments, and when you retired you hoped that the company you worked for was still around to honor its commitments. Even so, you probably stored much of your wealth in your house—its value and that of its furnishings.

When Americans borrowed money, they also faced what today seems a stark poverty of choices. Shopping for credit, for most people, was virtually synonymous with shopping for a bank. And when you did borrow from the bank, you probably filled out lots of forms, pledging as collateral whatever assets you may have owned—if, that is, you were lucky enough to get the loan at all.

Or take the most basic financial service of all, making payments. If you paid in cash for the goods and services you bought, you almost certainly filled your wallet only after standing in line at a bank and waiting for a teller to cash your check (or, in some cases, waiting for the supermarket clerk to do it for you). You probably made most of your payments by check, drawn on accounts that, by federal dictate, could not pay interest. You may have used a credit card—if, that is, you were one of

1

the relatively few people who qualified for one—but probably just for a few purchases. Millions of Americans who today use credit cards just as readily as they use cash are old enough to remember when "charge it" was a phrase for special occasions.

To say that finance has changed in only thirty years would be an understatement. That stolidly reassuring world of 1967, which had remained comparatively stable over the postwar period, now seems part of a quaint past. Interest rate controls have collapsed, and the array of options available to ordinary savers has grown beyond all recognition: derivatives markets and securities firms have invented whole new categories of financial instruments, cash is rapidly losing ground to plastic, and checks are yielding to electronic exchange. A wide and increasing array of mutual funds allows small savers to invest in broad stock indexes or, just as easily, to invest narrowly in Asian equities, high-technology firms, health companies, or any number of other specialized sectors. A large and growing number of Americans now control their own retirement destinies by managing their own pension plans.

Borrowers, too, enjoy more choices than ever before, and at lower cost than they would pay if not for the innovations of the past several decades. Home buyers enjoy cheaper access to credit, thanks to the transformation of mortgages into financial commodities that are now routinely bundled into securities and sold to investors and institutions around the world. Consumers enjoy wide access to credit cards. Indeed, people can and do start their businesses using credit cards without filling out forms and enduring painful credit interviews. Medium-sized companies and consumers can turn for credit to such large and growing finance companies as GE Capital and Green Tree Financial, rather than banks. Large firms now generally shun middlemen altogether, borrowing instead by issuing their own commercial paper directly to investors. And all this activity, which so recently involved so many trips to other people's offices, is often taking place in "virtual space," the realm of telephones, on-line services, and the Internet.

Change is not without its difficulties. Arguably, the new world of finance is somewhat more treacherous for investors who are uninformed or underequipped, those who assume, erroneously, that their money-market fund is federally insured or who lack the equipment or know-how to log on to the World Wide Web. And surely the world is becoming more treacherous for the men and women in Washington and in the state capitals who seek to regulate and support the country's financial system. If they regulate the financial services industry too tightly, they may smother it at a time when innovation is, more than ever, its life-blood. If they are clumsy in their efforts to stabilize it, they may instead disrupt or undermine it. And if they try to protect the small investor from its hazards, they may deprive him or her of its opportunities as well. Some would argue, indeed, that the job of financial regulators is becoming not only harder to perform well, but harder to perform at all. Today a sum equivalent to about two months of the American economy's output is exchanged in the foreign currency markets *every day*. In a world where capital crosses borders in the blink of an eye, what is a mere national regulator to do?

The world of financial services has changed more in the past thirty years than in the thirty before that; and the rapid pace of innovation suggests that over the next few decades the transformation of finance will be even more dramatic. As far away as the world of the 1970s may seem to today's saver or investor, the 1990s will seem more remote still to consumers or investors twenty years from now and to their financial service providers. And the transformations now beginning raise any number of questions. With the growth of electronic commerce, will the middleman role of financial institutions—matching buyers with sellers, savers with investors—give way to direct dealings between those who want financial instruments and those who create them? Will it still be possible to draw boundaries meaningfully between the types of financial institutions—banks, securities firms, insurers, mutual fund providers—whose distinctness Americans have long taken for granted? What will constitute money and who will coin it? Will financial markets be more stable or less so? How much leeway will regulators have in which to operate? Will the continuing changes in the financial world be harnessed in a way that brings maximum benefits to consumers? And what should be the main goals and tools for American policymakers as they seek to sort through the dozens of complex issues that will come flying their way?

This report was called for by Congress in the Riegle-Neal Interstate Banking and Branching Efficiency Act of 1994, which directed the Treasury Department to prepare a study of "matters relating to the strengths and weaknesses of the U.S. financial services system in meeting the needs of the system's users." Congress directed this study to consider, among other things, changes in the financial services industry during the next ten years and beyond, and to review the adequacy of existing statutes and regulations.

The Treasury Department asked us to prepare a report that responds to this challenge. We have worked closely with the department to do so.[1] In the process, we have taken the opportunity to scan an even broader horizon: to look out at least to 2010, and in some cases beyond. Our goal has been to identify the most important forces that are transforming the financial services industry and the products and services it offers, to suggest what policy issues those developments may raise, and to offer a framework for meeting new policy challenges. Of necessity, the report is selective. It does not in this short space try to fulfill all these goals. But by drawing on the best available information from industry and academic sources, as well as on the government's knowledge and its long experience of regulating national financial institutions, it identifies and brings into focus some of the most important themes and questions that federal policymakers will be called upon to address over the next decade and beyond.

If the pace of change in financial services is so rapid, why take the risk of peering so far ahead? Certainly, much will happen that no one can now foresee. Yet it is precisely the rapidity of change that requires a long view. Too often in the past, policymakers have legislated and regulated to prevent a crisis that has already occurred. Both the industry and its regulators would be better served if the general direction of policy, at least, were set in *advance* of market change instead of lagging behind it. By looking a decade or more into the future, toward new financial developments and the policy issues they may raise, this report inevitably makes forecasts that may not turn out to be correct. But to confess the possibility of error in no way diminishes the importance of looking ahead. A long-term view can not only help policymakers escape crisis thinking, it can help refine their thinking on what should be done in the short run. It may help them reduce, or at least identify, some of the uncertainties that could otherwise frustrate progress toward new products and services that could be provided to more people at lower cost.

This report assumes one further reason to think ahead. Current policy is based on a view of the world developed primarily to prevent another Great Depression; and in doing so it relies on a mix of practices that can and should be improved. That is not to say that all of federal financial policy as it now stands is unsound and needs to be replaced. Far from it. America now has the world's strongest and most dynamic financial sector, an achievement that is in no small measure a result of having rightly framed many major elements of policy. But times change, and as they do, adjustments in the organizing philosophy of financial policy are inevitably necessary. This report attempts to sketch, at least in broad outline, a model for financial regulation in the coming century.

Over the past 200 or more years, American policy for financial services has been created within two major frameworks. One prevailed through the nineteenth century and the early years of the twentieth century. Apart from some safety standards and some strictures designed to prevent financiers from becoming too powerful and big banks from growing too big, the nineteenth-century model mostly left markets to their own devices. When the Depression came, this comparatively laissez-faire approach collapsed, and its successor radically changed the path of American finance. To the old fear of concentration was now added a new fear of instability. And concentration and instability were both believed to be products, in large part, of an excess of competition, which (supposedly) allowed financial companies to take too many risks and to force their way into too many markets.

Starting in the 1930s and extending through the 1970s, three hallmarks of a different paradigm were enacted. First, financial markets were distinguished and segregated by product line, provider, and geography. Banks could not offer nonfinancial products, could not own (or be owned by) nonfinancial companies, and could not expand across state lines. Those constraints, it was thought, would keep competition within carefully limited and safe bounds. Second, the government set about attempting to make financial failure a rarity by fencing off financial institutions from marketplace pressures, imposing capital requirements (which to a significant extent, however, were neglected in practice during the 1980s), and establishing a federal safety net that gradually expanded. Third, Washington did not shrink from micromanaging the financial sector or applying broad uniform standards across its conspicuously diverse makeup.

A major theme of this report is that the time has come for financial policy to emerge at last from the shadow of the Depression. To wit: whereas the Depression-era model relied on market segmentation and failure prevention—often pursued using very broad measures—the model for the next century needs to emphasize instead competition and failure containment, pursued by more targeted means.

That means the time has arrived for federal policy to embrace competition in financial services wholeheartedly and open-mindedly. It is no longer necessary or desirable to view competition as the enemy of marketplace stability or to preslice and segregate entire markets to protect consumers or investors. Indeed, competition is a simple yet powerful tool that federal policy has embraced in virtually every economic sphere *except* in some important sectors of finance. True, a good deal has been done in recent years to open financial services to competition and innovation. But policy change has lagged behind market change, and there is more left to do. In making this case, the report does not suggest that freewheeling competition is by itself the solution to all marketplace problems. Rather it argues that for too long government policies have deprived consumers of the full benefits of an innovative, robustly competitive marketplace, and that the goal of policy in the coming century should be to encourage rather than to suppress competition and innovation in finance.

In today's quicksilver financial marketplace, new institutions and instruments crop up constantly, and the richest returns flow to companies that innovate, not merely to the ones with the deepest pockets or the longest experience. The growth of competition driven by rapidly advancing technology and rapidly dissolving financial borders thus has a further implication: policies that try to make the financial system safer by tying the hands of institutions will inevitably put a damper on innovation, at considerable cost to the economy as a whole and potentially to America's world leadership in financial services. Moreover, such policies will generally fail and can, indeed, imperil markets instead of protecting them.

All of this became painfully evident in the savings and loan crisis of the 1980s, a fiasco largely attributable to a series of policy mistakes spanning several decades. Having been confined by government to a narrow market niche with little freedom to manage their risks, savings and loans were at a loss to meet the demands of market forces when interest rates soared and new competitors emerged. Washington, struggling to prevent a wave of failures, failed to respond when the higher interest rates caused the market value of the thrifts' assets to plunge far below their book value. Instead, policymakers sought to keep large numbers of insolvent or weakly capitalized thrifts open by letting them sink billions of dollars of taxpayer-backed money into investments in which they had no experience (commercial real estate, for example). In the end, the attempt to prevent (or defer) failures helped turn a $15 billion problem in the mid-

1980s into a disaster roughly ten times that size by the end of the decade. The attempt to sidestep market pressures finally undercut the very goals—financial stability and failure prevention—that policy had sought to pursue.

Even if failure-prevention strategies based on market segmentation and one-size-fits-all standards once did work tolerably well, such strategies will only become harder to sustain as new products and producers emerge. For example, many kinds of companies other than traditional banks are now involved in making loans, and telling a bank that it cannot provide information services at the same time as it gives customers the ability to bank on-line makes little sense and frustrates innovation, particularly given that nonbanks may not be operating under the same constraints. Simple standards are less easily applied in complex markets, and the attempt to divide the financial world into discrete segments is becoming hopeless. Meanwhile, the remaining legal barriers between the banking, insurance, and securities industries are quickly being eroded by regulatory and judicial circumventions, driven ultimately by the desire of many firms to offer one-stop shopping for their customers. None of these trends is likely to reverse itself.

To discuss the disadvantages of what we call in this report the twentieth-century paradigm is not, it should be emphasized, to suggest throwing all prevention strategies out the window. Government will always need to make sure that financial institutions take reasonable precautions, just as cities need fire codes. Rather, it is to suggest a shift in emphasis. But toward what?

The report suggests a subtly but importantly different model of financial policy for the twenty-first century, one that shifts gradually away from regulation designed to prevent the failure of each and every institution, and toward making the market in which all institutions operate less vulnerable. To use a transportation analogy, the twentieth-century model of financial policy has, for the most part, set a slow speed limit, specified a few basic models for cars, separated different kinds of cars into different lanes, and demanded that no one leave home without a full tank of gas and a tune-up. Better suited for the mercurial financial world now emerging is a model that, while not abandoning all that went before, focuses less on preventing mishaps and more on ensuring that an accident at any one intersection will not paralyze traffic everywhere else.

A number of specific policy ideas flow from this approach. They are briefly summarized later in this introduction and are discussed in greater detail in the body of the report. But all of the ideas share a common premise: in an increasingly competitive financial world, periodic upsets in financial markets—sometimes very large ones—are inevitable, and the foremost goal of policy should be not to prevent such upsets but to *contain* them. That means, to the greatest extent possible, identifying, isolating, and disposing of trouble spots so that they do not endanger the stability of the whole system, and doing so without at the same time requiring the federal government, and thus taxpayers, to extend blanket guarantees against loss. The latter qualification is critical. If market participants know that the government will always be there to bail them out if they make mistakes, they have nothing to lose and everything to gain by taking reckless risks.

In recent years, policy has already begun quietly moving toward relying more on containment of stress and less on a government safety net. Regulators have been required by statute to "promptly correct" bank misbehavior by gradually imposing more severe sanctions as a bank's capital dwindles. This early-intervention strategy encourages banks to manage themselves better, so as to prevent a loss of capital in the first place, and it contains the loss to the economy and taxpayers should a bank nevertheless fail. In addition, the law now makes it more difficult for government authorities to bail out all depositors of large institutions, a change that has sent a powerful signal to participants in the financial markets to behave more prudently.

But more can and should be done to move toward a containment policy, most notably taking steps to further reduce, if not eliminate, risks that the systems for clearing and settling payments among banks and securities firms could break down because of the failure of one or more parties to honor their obligations. The containment strategy is far from foolproof; but, combined with continuing supervision, it can make the financial market as a whole safer, with more room for competition and innovation—and for failure—than the prevention model allowed.

Financial policy for the next century should change in another respect. The twentieth-century model has relied too heavily on broad solutions for what often have been rather narrow problems. Because Washington has been primarily concerned about runs on banks, it adopted a regime that, until it was recently reformed, had gradually evolved into a federal guarantee of *all* deposits, or at least of all deposits held in large banks. Depositor runs were stopped, but the result was to create a giant taxpayer liability that extended far beyond the boundaries of the original problem. Similarly, because Washington was concerned about keeping banks in touch with local communities and with preventing so-called excessive competition that could be damaging to banks, it banned interstate branching and limited interstate banking (expansion by bank holding companies). And because Washington was concerned that financial power might become excessively concentrated, it used the law to segment entire markets while creating a regulatory apparatus marked more by its fragmentation than its coherence. Here again, such scattershot policies proved far more expensive and less effective than their architects had expected.

To be fair to policymakers, in the days of adding machines and file cards, technological and institutional limitations often required broad-brush solutions to fine-grained problems—and, to no inconsiderable extent, they still do. But information technology and institutional sophistication have come a long way. For example, some of the same information technologies that could in principle spread a financial shock across the globe in minutes can also be used to provide regulators and markets with up-to-the-minute information that will help them avert shocks in the first place. And modern financial markets boast a variety of specialized financial instruments and institutions—asset-backed securities, catastrophe futures, commercial paper, community development financial institutions, hedge funds, mortgage banks, and many others—that were unknown to the framers of the financial policies we have inherited.

Another recurring theme, then, is that policy in the future should target particular areas of need rather than try to micromanage whole sectors. That idea is applied in various ways throughout this report. Targeting implies, for instance, more intensive use of specialized institutions and focused federal initiatives to help make sure that additional credit and financial services flow to underserved neighborhoods. It implies providing a strictly bounded safety net, rather than promising investors a federal rescue anywhere on the high seas of finance. And it implies using discrete antitrust tools rather than wholesale market segmentation to prevent undue concentration.

The approach advocated here is not one easily captured in slogans about smaller government or bigger government; the question, rather, is one of *better* government. Finance is a good example of a sector in which to oppose market forces is becoming an increasingly futile task, yet in which government's core functions remain as essential as ever. The government's basic commitments in financial policy—to protect taxpayers and consumers (especially the most vulnerable) and to help ensure that the financial system is sound—are not negotiable. But in a world in which particular businesses and consumers will be able to perform more tasks for themselves and to customize more of their transactions, regulators must be especially wary of policies that inadvertently construct a cage for markets rather than a foundation for them. In short, government has no choice but to regulate financial markets, but it must do so in a way that gives markets plenty of space for innovation and adaptation. "Big government, small government" rhetoric is of little help in financial services, and is best checked at the door. If ever there were a need for "smart government," it is in today's kaleidoscopically dynamic world of finance.

Chapter 1, "The Financial Services Industry Today," lays the groundwork for this view with a snapshot of the financial services industry and a discussion of the three core functions of finance: operating the payments system, intermediating between lenders and borrowers (savers and investors), and spreading risk. Then it traces the development of financial regulation up to the present, first with a look at the (comparatively) laissez-faire approach of the nineteenth century, then with a more detailed discussion of the complex web of policies and ideas that have so decisively shaped American finance in this century. Finally, it takes up the erosion of the twentieth-century model under steady pressure from market forces, a process that culminated in the savings and loan crisis of the 1980s. Fundamentally, the chapter argues, the basic flaw of past policies was that, when they were subjected to stress by a rapidly changing marketplace, they undermined rather than supported each other.

If anything, change in financial markets will only accelerate. Chapter 2, "Tides of Change," turns to the forces that are reshaping the financial services industry: primarily, but not only, globalization and advances in information technology. Already those forces are creating many new products and providers, eroding national boundaries, and heightening competition in all parts of finance—indeed, obliterating many of the industry's traditional boundaries. The chapter discusses the benefits that innovation may bring to each of finance's major functions. Payment will become both more flexible and convenient as electronic transfers and digital money gain ground; intermediation will become less costly and indeed less necessary as information technology lets the users and suppliers of financial services get directly in touch with each other; and the dispersion of risk will benefit from markets' growing ingenuity in using such tools as financial derivatives. Those changes, the chapter argues, are likely to put particular pressure on traditional banks and brokerages, which, to survive, will become (and indeed are becoming) a good deal less traditional. Finally, after considering the waves of consolidation and restructuring already under way, the chapter sets forth some principles for policy: hospitality to innovation, use of market mechanisms to pursue policy goals, avoidance of micromanagement in pursuit of stability, and a preference for targeted policies over expansive and uniform mandates.

Inevitably, the financial market is becoming a more competitive place; but competition itself raises questions for taxpayers, financial providers, and consumers. Chapter 3, "Energizing Competition," argues that government first needs to be supportive of competition. Already it tries to be, but there remain important impediments to competition that only Congress can remove. In the process, consumers of financial services stand to reap significant gains, especially as firms currently in different segments of the financial services industry bring best practices and new ways of doing business to other segments.

At the same time, government needs to ensure that as depository institutions gain more freedom to launch other financial ventures, the taxpayers who insure bank deposits neither underwrite risky adventures nor end up stuck with the bill for them. That will require, among other things, taking further steps to make sure that a bank's assets cannot be tapped by creditors if its affiliate or subsidiary fails. The government should not, however, dictate the organizational chart for diversified organizations. Private actors should choose where to place nondepository financial activities, either as bank subsidiaries or as affiliates (owned by a common holding company).

Another question taken up in chapter 3 is what sort of rules the government should set for providers of electronic money (e-money), the newest vehicle on finance's digital highway. Although digital payment as yet poses few problems for the soundness of the financial system as a whole, an important issue is whether government should lead or follow the market in regulating e-money.

Meanwhile, what about protecting consumers from monopoly power and market concentration as the financial industry consolidates, and as big companies are allowed to cross into new lines of business? In the

main, chapter 3 argues, existing antitrust tools—intelligently targeted—
are up to the job of preventing abuses of market power. Indeed, digital
finance promises consumers more choices than ever. But in the coming
years a particular sort of antitrust problem may surge to the fore: that of
so-called gatekeeper and keyholder companies that control vital networks
or technologies.

Competition and innovation are all well and good, but *soundness* is
essential. Chapter 4, "Containing Risk," turns to what is arguably the
government's single most vital job in finance: preventing systemwide
meltdowns, or, in the jargon, reducing systemic risk. The discussion first
takes up the major sources of systemic risk: cascades through the financial
system, notably through the mechanisms for the payment and settlement
of transactions; contagions that happen when financial failures spark broad
panic or flight; and asset-value implosions, when prices fall faster than
people and institutions can adjust. How to deal with these? Not, the chapter contends, by seeking to prevent failures, but by seeking to contain
them.

To that end, the chapter offers several strategies. First, impose early
quarantine on troubled institutions, isolating them before they can damage the rest of the system, as is required by the Federal Deposit Insurance
Corporation Improvement Act of 1991, an important first step toward containment. Second, reduce information gaps about financial risk, disseminating information more quickly and steadily, ideally on something close
to a real-time basis, to make sure that regulators and markets learn of, and
thus can adjust to, bad news before it piles up too high. Third, rely increasingly on market-tailored buffers that enlist markets themselves to set
and enforce safety standards to bolster government-imposed rules and
supervision. Fourth, move further toward instantaneous settlement of transactions, a step that would reduce or eliminate the lags that could turn the
payments system into an echo chamber for financial shocks. Finally, given
the enormous growth in the use of derivatives in recent years, the appropriate level of margin requirements for derivatives traded on and off the
exchanges deserves further scrutiny.

The particular paths toward containment of risk are many, and the
measures offered here are intended as a starting point, not an ending
place, for discussion. Less important than the details of the strategy is the
regulatory philosophy that they embody: by making particular failures
less dangerous for the system as a whole, containment lets regulators

open new doors to competition while making the financial system stronger. Although the measures we suggest are neither perfect nor complete, they can work with, rather than against, both each other and the markets. And so containment is likely to be both more effective and more sustainable than the regime that preceded it.

Government's job, however, does not end with promoting competition and safety. Chapter 5, "Expanding Financial Opportunity," argues that the government also has a vital role in opening financial doors to all Americans. In the main, marketplace competition serves consumers well—dazzlingly well, in fact. But some poorer neighborhoods and citizens may be left behind at just the time when digital media offer the capacity to bring more services to more people than ever. Existing measures to extend credit to minorities and the less affluent—notably the Community Reinvestment Act and the Home Mortgage Disclosure Act—have for the most part worked well. In fact, great strides have been made in recent years toward extending credit to women, minorities, and other traditionally underserved populations. But more targeted approaches, notably reliance on specialized lenders such as community development financial institutions, will increasingly be needed, since the tools that policymakers now mainly rely on will diminish in power as the marketplace evolves and traditional lenders are elbowed aside. Moreover, a potentially greater problem for vulnerable populations is obtaining reasonably priced depository services (services that let them cash checks and perform other basic financial operations). Chapter 5 concludes with an assessment of this important but often overlooked problem and notes that the government's decision to replace nearly all federal checks with electronic transfers offers a valuable opportunity to bring many of the unbanked into the ambit of affordable and reliable payment and deposit services.

America's financial industry is the world's most advanced. It has long been, and continues to be, a leader in the race of American competitiveness: a source of opportunity at home, a magnet for investment from abroad. Policy must be committed not only to maintaining the soundness and vitality of the industry, but also to strengthening its greatest asset: its ability to innovate and thus to make more capital available to more people more efficiently. Financial policy needs to minimize the risks of a system-wide financial crisis, but it should do so in a way that allows new products and new market participants to bubble quickly to the surface. It needs to help ensure that the benefits of financial services flow broadly to American consumers, yet it must avoid heavy-handed rules that twist financial markets into perverse or anachronistic shapes. And it needs to meet all its goals in the context of a world that is giving governments ever less time to react.

This report outlines, in broad themes, the kinds of policies that can help American financial regulation meet the challenges of a new era. We envision not a radical reversal of policy's course but a steady adjustment: a series of discrete policy changes to be enacted under the support of an organizing framework that differs fundamentally, if sometimes subtly, from the ideas in this century, but that in no way compromises the vital objectives of safety and soundness. Many of the details of the next regime for American finance remain to be devised. But the core principles—competition, containment, and targeting—are already in view.

1

· ·

The Financial Services
Industry Today

NO INDUSTRY is more important to a thriving economy than financial services; and for centuries none has been so greatly mistrusted and misunderstood. "Neither a borrower, nor a lender be; / For loan oft loses both itself and friend, / And borrowing dulls the edge of husbandry," warned Shakespeare's Polonius in *Hamlet*, dispensing advice that, if generally heeded, would bring commerce, and for that matter "husbandry," to a rapid halt. In Europe, lending money at interest was for many centuries often considered a dirty business in which the uncharitable gouged the needy. In America, mistrust of big banks and financial tycoons was a staple of nineteenth-century politics and remained a strong influence on policy, sometimes to ill effect, when today's banking laws were framed in the middle third of this century.

Yet to call the work of financiers essential is no exaggeration. Their importance to the functioning of a healthy economy, indeed, could hardly be overstated. The work of the financial services industry—or, perhaps more properly, industries—is rich and complex. Three functions stand out.

What Financial Services Do

First, financial companies—banks and, increasingly, credit-card providers—*process payments and settlements*. It is easy to overlook the importance of this seemingly mundane task. For people to carry all of their money in their pockets would hardly be a good idea, even if it were possible. Payments systems, whether paper (checks), plastic (credit cards), or electronic, dispense with the need for settling transactions in cash. In the process they quietly but efficiently make possible the bustling, far-flung commercial life that people now take for granted.

Second, the financial services industry *intermediates* between those who have money and want to earn a profit on it (savers and investors) and those who need it (borrowers and entrepreneurs). In a small community, investors and borrowers could find one another efficiently just by asking around. But in an economy of hundreds of millions of people, each with a variety of saving and borrowing needs, putting every dollar of capital to efficient use is a vastly complex yet enormously important job. By issuing claims on themselves in the form of deposits (banks and thrifts), commercial paper (finance companies), contracts (insurers), or shares (mutual funds), *financial intermediaries* bridge the gap between countless borrowers and lenders. The more effectively they do this, the more efficiently capital will be allocated to its most productive uses, and the faster the economy will grow.

Intermediaries exist because they can take advantage of economies of scale in obtaining and processing information. By knowing how to extend credit efficiently and with minimal losses, a bank typically can lend much more cheaply to a borrower than can any individual or group of individuals. Insurers take advantage of similar economies (in assessing and pooling risk), as do operators of mutual funds.

But, as will be discussed in greater detail throughout this report, more and more business borrowers are finding it easier and cheaper to obtain their funds directly by issuing claims on themselves rather than by going to an intermediary. In these cases, *markets* bridge the gap between savers and investors by providing a place—once physical and in the future likely to be virtual—where millions of borrowers and lenders can match up. Brokers and dealers, who are part of the financial services industry, help them.

Whether through institutions or markets, the financial services industry is crucial to matching the hopes and dreams of the most inventive participants in our economy with those who have capital and want to put it to work. The importance of this matching function is perhaps best demonstrated by the failure of state-managed economies, in which governments rather than markets do the matching. No centrally planned economy has come close to the efficiency that the financial marketplace achieves as a matter of course.

Finally, the financial services industry helps to *spread risk*. People who live prudently need to plan for trouble. Whether any particular person or business will be stricken by calamity is difficult or impossible to know, but the frequency with which disaster may strike a very large pool of people or companies is not so hard to assess. That fact provides the foundation for the business of insurance. For a fixed regular payment, insurers give their customers the right to collect potentially much larger sums if the events insured against—fire, theft, sickness, or some other calamity—occur. The insurer uses the premiums it collects to invest productively elsewhere in the economy, thus performing an intermediary function as well. Mutual funds also perform double duty. On one side, they provide an important vehicle for investing in the instruments of companies that seek financing; on the other, they let investors diversify their holdings more cheaply and effectively than they could ever do by buying and holding individual securities. Stock index funds, for instance, now let an investor buy what amounts to a share of the entire stock market—not an easy thing to do on one's own.

Just as they intermediate between savers and investors, financial markets also spread the costs of risk. So-called derivative instruments, whose values are derived from an underlying asset, carry out this risk-sharing function. Derivatives come in many forms. Two of the simplest, as well as the earliest, are options and futures contracts. Options give the buyer the right to buy or sell a commodity, and more recently a financial instrument, at a fixed price. Futures contracts perform similar price-locking functions. The common feature of both instruments is that they allow those who are worried about price movements to transfer their worry and their risk to someone else. More exotic forms of derivatives—currency swaps, interest rate swaps, and so forth—do the same thing, but for different types of risk.

It is sometimes said that these financial instruments, or intermediaries, only move risk around, without eliminating it. That is true, but it also misses a crucial point. Markets and institutions allow those who wish to avoid risk to do so, while enabling those most willing and able to bear risk to assume it. In the process the financial services industry helps make the business environment less unpredictable and hazardous, reducing the cost of developing, producing, and delivering products and services.

In all of these functions, financial institutions and markets act as middlemen, and middlemen tend to have a bad name. But the reality is that in many or most cases there would be no deal at all without the middleman's work; or, to be more precise, there would be some other deal of lesser economic value. A hundred-ton pile of unsorted books is not much more useful than a hundred tons of scrap metal, but those same books, carefully indexed and shelved, constitute a library, an information resource of enormous value. Between the piles of books and the library lies the work of a middleman, a librarian, whose job is to organize and catalog information, then create a place where information and reader can meet.

In like fashion, financiers create places where borrowers and lenders can meet. More than that, they analyze and organize countless bits of economic data: credit records, corporate balance sheets, stock prices, recent market activity, the effects of floods and famines, and much more. By doing so they sort and catalog investment opportunities and capital needs, creating wealth in the form of information, much as a librarian does. In that respect, the financial industry acts as a kind of computer, but a more powerful one than any cyberengineer has yet devised. Every securities deal or insurance contract processes facts, figures, estimates of risk, hopes for future earnings, and gut instinct into marketable packets of information. Other things being equal, then, the more efficiently the financial industry does its job, the more Americans know about their economic world and the opportunities it affords. Finance thus not only makes markets, it makes value. No less than agriculture or manufacturing, it creates wealth. An efficient financial services sector is essential to prosperity.

Through all three of its major functions, finance connects Americans with each other and the world. By rating a person's credit and providing a quick and reliable payments mechanism, the company issuing his credit card allows him to make purchases by telephone from companies that know nothing about him and are located thousands of miles away. Mutual funds give each American the ability to invest in products and services being provided by millions of diverse economic agents without actually requiring any two of those agents to do so much as converse with one another. And by providing vehicles for saving, markets and intermediaries allow each generation to bequeath a wealthier future to its children. In short, the financial services industry connects Americans to each other, not only today but across decades.

A Snapshot of the Industry Today

By conventional statistical measures, how important is the financial services industry? Figure 1-1 shows that the financial services sector, broadly defined to include depository institutions, securities firms, insurers, and mutual fund providers, contributes a significant portion of the nation's $8 trillion output. Measured in real terms (that is, after adjusting for inflation), financial services account for over 6 percent of GDP, today about $500 billion.

The financial services sector also employs a little less than 5 percent of the roughly 125 million Americans who work. Yet the share of total employment accounted for by finance has been falling steadily since 1987 (figure 1-2), in contrast to the relatively stable share of finance in overall

Figure 1-1. Share of U.S. GDP Originating in Financial Industry, 1977–94

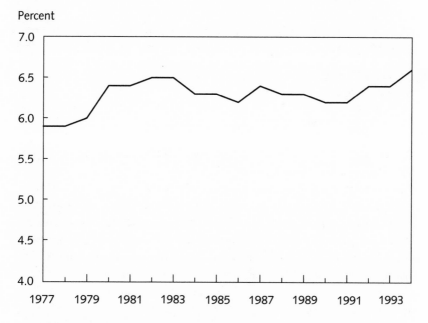

Percent

Source: Bureau of Economic Analysis, gross product by industry (constant 1987 dollars). Data include SIC codes 60–64 and 67.

Figure 1-2. Finance and Insurance Employment as Share of Total U.S. Employment, 1972–96

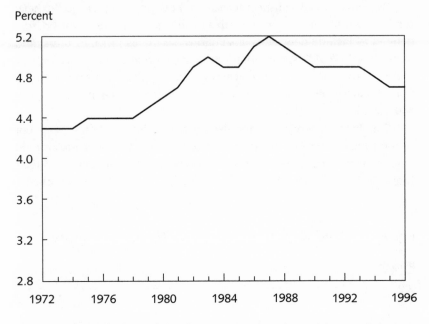

Percent

Source: Bureau of Labor Statistics data on national employment hours and earnings. Data include SIC codes 60–64 and 67.

national output, a fact which reflects significantly more rapid labor productivity growth in finance than elsewhere in the economy (although
measurement problems cloud the issue somewhat).[1] Productivity is growing in finance in large part because of the rapid diffusion of information
technology throughout the industry: from automatic teller machines for
consumers to sophisticated computer programs for processing ever growing volumes of information in the offices of banks, securities firms, and
insurers. The impact of this information revolution on financial services
has been so significant that it is the subject of a much more extensive
discussion in chapter 2.

It is worth noting that such bare statistics do not and cannot fully
capture the importance of the financial services sector. By processing
transactions, matching savers with investors, and diversifying and spread-

ing risk, financial service providers lower the cost of business for everyone. Finance is the lifeblood and circulatory system of our economy.

The U.S. financial services industry nonetheless has undergone significant transformations in recent decades. Measured by their control over financial assets, banks have been steadily losing ground, replaced primarily by mutual funds. At the same time, banking itself is becoming less asset intensive and increasingly consists of various off-balance-sheet activities, most notably dealing in derivatives. All of the segments of the industry, meanwhile, are being reshaped by the rapidly growing influence of information technology and computers, as well as by the increasingly global scope of financial and economic activity. Each of these trends will be explored in this report, beginning with an in-depth look in chapter 2 at the recent past, the present, and likely future.

Linchpins of Policy

Precisely because it is so important, finance has been supervised and regulated by governments for centuries, not only in America but all over the world. Governments have tried to accomplish many kinds of ends with their oversight of finance. Very broadly stated, however, government's proper role in finance can be summarized as follows: to foster a financial system that provides the financial services and products that individuals and businesses demand and that does so with a maximum of efficiency, safety, and accessibility. This broad objective can be broken down into three more specific goals. Not only markets but governments are best served when they keep their eyes mainly on these three goals, as opposed to all the others that may seem appealing from one day to the next.

—*Protecting consumers.* This responsibility has several aspects: promoting the efficient and competitive operation of all segments of the financial service industry, so that its services and products are delivered at low cost; ensuring that consumers are dealt with fairly when they cannot reasonably protect themselves; and helping vulnerable consumers secure reasonable access to basic financial services. To a great extent, of course, consumers are more than capable of looking out for their interests. On that score, indeed, they are usually a good deal shrewder than any distant bureaucrat. Nonetheless, policy needs to help ensure that consumers have the information they need, that the marketplace is as free as possible from cheats and extortionists, and that no monopolist or syndicate is able to shut out competitors and dictate terms to the market. Government also has a legitimate role in bringing vital financial lifelines to consumers who may lack them and so may be cut off from the larger economy.

—*Reducing systemic risk.* Government has a vital stake in helping the markets and the economy ward off a large-scale financial crisis. A loss of confidence in the financial markets can have grave economic consequences, whether through liquidity crunch, marketplace gridlock, capital flight, draining of consumer confidence, or a combination of those and other problems. From the earliest days of central banking, governments around the world have accepted a role as lender of last resort, supervisor of depository institutions, and backstop against wholesale panic.

—*Protecting taxpayers.* Finally, government has a fiduciary duty to keep taxpayers' exposure to a reasonable minimum if it is called upon to come to markets' or insured investors' rescue. To whatever extent government stands behind the financial markets, it inevitably puts taxpayers' wallets on the line, as the savings and loan disasters of the 1980s made plain. The government's job is to make sure taxpayers' money is neither abused nor called upon unnecessarily.

Although none of those goals is unique to finance, all can pose special challenges in financial markets. The exceptional complexity of some financial markets, combined with the essential role of financial services in connecting citizens to the broader economy, may create the need for more watchfulness on consumers' behalf than is exerted in some other sectors. Systemic risk is not generally regarded as a problem for most manufacturing industries, because the failure of even a very large company is unlikely to induce a panic among shareholders generally. In financial markets, however, failure may under certain circumstances rapidly spread if panicky depositors or investors simultaneously run for safety. The failure of one or more large banks or securities firms could also bring down others that belong to common clearing and settlement networks, or it might even impair the operations of the settlement system itself, causing still larger marketplace disruptions. As for taxpayer risk, it is not an issue when nonfinancial firms fail unless the government explicitly decides on a bailout (as it did for Chrysler in 1980); but *every* federally insured depositor may, in principle, require taxpayer protection.

In its pursuit of those goals (and others besides), American policy in finance has availed itself of many different tools, ranging from obscure regulations to sweeping legal prohibitions. And for the most part policy has largely been reactive, aimed at cleaning up one or another crisis or plugging a leak in the legal framework that innovative actors have attempted to exploit. Thus any generalization in characterizing policy must admit of many particular exceptions. Nonetheless, even in as complex a policy geography as that of finance, one great Continental Divide stands out, unmistakable in its broad contours. In essence, this country has had two major regimes for regulating finance, with the Great Depression of the 1930s marking the dividing line between them.

The Nineteenth-Century Landscape

There is not much new under the sun, but certainly there are new mixes of things. All of the major financial institutions with which we are now familiar—banks, savings and loans, mutual funds (then called investment companies or trusts), insurance companies, and pension funds— had been developed before the 1930s, and in fact before the twentieth century. But in those days, to speak of finance was to speak for the most part of banks. Depository institutions (banks and savings and loans) dominated the financial landscape, accounting for the majority of assets held by all financial intermediaries. And the current regulatory framework did not exist. There was no central mechanism for controlling the amount of money or credit in circulation or for providing liquidity to the economy in times of peril. Not until 1914 was the Federal Reserve System created to fill this void, seven years after the banking crisis of 1907 when one man, J. P. Morgan, personally arranged for loans to help keep many endangered banks afloat.

In that era financial policy was largely laissez-faire, at least by comparison with today's world. Banks and insurers were supervised for "safety and soundness" to ensure that they had sufficient capital to withstand losses. The federal government, however, regulated only banks that had federal charters; state-chartered banks and all insurers were regulated at the state level (as they still are today). No deposits in banks or savings and loans were insured, despite Congress's frequent attempts, dating from 1886, to adopt an insurance scheme. Securities firms were virtually unregulated. Although a few of the nation's banks—about 500 out of the 25,000 in business before the Depression—had affiliates that underwrote securities, they did little more than underwrite bonds. And until 1927 the federal government placed no restrictions on the geographic reach of banks. States, however, were more restrictive, fearing that a few banks might come to dominate local credit markets. Many states thus limited their banks to doing business out of one or only a few offices. Not until the McFadden Act in 1927 did the federal government explicitly bar depositories from operating offices in multiple states.[2]

Bank lending was sorely limited, at least by today's standards. Loans were made primarily to businesses for short-term purposes such as financing inventory, and to a lesser extent to investors who wanted to finance their purchases of stock (putting up as little as 10 percent of the purchase price of the stocks they bought). Banks provided virtually no credit for consumers, who had to turn to loan sharks or pawn shops, once fixtures of everyday American life. Nor would a bank lend to individuals so that they could buy their own homes. Savings associations, which dated from the 1800s, filled the gap by extending residential mortgages, but the loans were generally for five years (in sharp contrast with the typical thirty-year mortgage today). As a result, before the Depression fewer than half of the country's households owned their homes, compared with 65 percent now.

The Twentieth-Century Regime

Then came the stock market crash of 1929 and the Great Depression. Roughly 9,000 banks failed in a four-year period. Many depositors raced to their banks to withdraw their funds; many who did not run, or who showed up at the teller's window too late, lost their life's savings. Investors who had purchased stocks on margin, putting up only a small fraction of the purchase price, lost their investments.

As an earthquake reveals fault lines, the Depression revealed deep flaws in the regulatory system. Certain features of the pre-1930s landscape aggravated rather than mitigated the initial damage done by the stock market crash, and thus probably made the Depression worse than it would otherwise have been. For example, the restrictions on branching forced many banks to concentrate lending on borrowers in a single local industry, such as agriculture. When agricultural prices tumbled, thousands of rural banks collapsed. Low margins fueled the downturn in stocks as investors or their brokers, frantic to stem their losses, tried vainly to sell out. Perhaps worst of all, the Federal Reserve compounded the economic damage by failing to provide liquidity as uninsured depositors grabbed their money from banks and stuffed it in mattresses at home. Low on both confidence and capital, banks pulled in their horns and all but quit lending to businesses and individuals. Credit dried up.

Devastated by the Depression and its aftermath, policymakers resorted to a battery of measures aimed at restoring the health of the financial industry and the wider economy. For convenience, we combine all these steps taken since the Depression under the label of the twentieth-century model of financial policy, which has had several objectives.

One goal, naturally enough, has been to keep financial crises, once begun, from feeding on themselves—what would today be characterized as measures to *prevent contagion.* A second goal has been to avoid another systemic crisis by *preventing failure*—that is, preventing particular institutions and markets from ever again getting into trouble in the first place. A third objective, unrelated to the causes of the Depression but responsive to concerns that arose during it, has been to *widen the availability of credit*, initially for housing and later for disadvantaged areas and customers. Finally, policymakers have continued to block the *concentration of economic power* held by financial institutions in general and banks in particular. Financial concentration was a long-time worry, and indeed the dominant focus of financial regulation in the nineteenth century. But the focus widened after the Depression era, and found expression in the fragmented way the nation regulates not just banks but all financial institutions. Because that is a complicated story involving many industries and their regulators, in some cases with overlapping federal and state jurisdictions, interested readers are referred to the appendix to this chapter for a brief guide to the subject.

Taken as a group, the Depression-era measures, together with the reactions and modifications that they sparked, have defined the outlines of financial policy for six decades. A brief inventory follows.

Limits on Competition

From the vantage point of the 1930s, markets understandably looked anything but robust and financial institutions far from safe. Having seen banks and markets collapse all around them, policymakers drew what seemed an obvious conclusion: when many financial institutions fail, they can all too readily drag the marketplace and even the whole economy down with them. At the core of twentieth-century policy, then, has been a determination to prevent failures, in significant part by limiting competition in finance, even at the cost of penalizing consumers.

Thus until this strategy began to break down in the 1970s (for reasons to be discussed shortly), Congress placed ceilings on the interest that depository institutions could pay their depositors: for demand deposits, or checking accounts, interest was flatly prohibited, a restriction that technically continues to this day. The idea was to prevent what was regarded as dangerous competition for deposits, which might push banks beyond the edge of solvency in their efforts to attract customers. In addition, until regulators' attitudes changed in the 1960s, entry into the banking industry was tightly limited. Restricting competition, it was thought, would assure banks of reasonable profits and thus minimize the danger that any could fail. The Securities and Exchange Commission used a similar rationale in allowing the New York Stock Exchange to maintain a system of fixed brokerage commissions for many years, a system that lasted until the mid-1970s, when it was picked apart by market forces and then abolished by government mandate.

Policymakers also limited competition by restricting the activities in which banks could engage. The Glass-Steagall Act of 1933 limited commercial bank affiliations with securities underwriters. To be sure, this was not the first time that legislators had restricted bank activities—banks historically had been prohibited from engaging in merchandising and manufacturing—but it was the first express limitation on mixing two related *financial* activities, namely lending to borrowers and underwriting their securities. Later, the Bank Holding Company Act of 1956 took additional measures to keep owners of banks out of nonbanking activities as well. Moreover, the Bank Holding Company Act barred companies from owning separate banks in more than one state (without states' express permission, which was not expected to be given). This was meant to block a device that banks had found for circumventing the McFadden Act's restrictions on branching. Yet, somewhat oddly, Washington left untouched other financial service firms—in the securities and insurance industries, for example—that could continue to be affiliated with each other or to be owned by a single firm, whether financial or nonfinancial. The resulting playing field was far from level.

In fact, there was neither then nor now any compelling evidence that excessive competition among financial institutions, and banks in particular, had contributed to the collapse of the financial system during the Depression. Nor was there evidence that restrictions on price competition among securities firms were ever necessary to protect their financial health. To the contrary, the restrictions on interstate banking and branching impinged directly on safety and soundness by preventing institutions from diversifying their portfolios, so that they were unnecessarily and sometimes tragically vulnerable to shocks in local or sectoral markets. But so fearful were policymakers of financial concentration, and so worried were they by the specter of financial titans dragging each other to ruin, that they plunged ahead all the same. Other factors were at work as well: evidence suggests that the 1933 Glass-Steagall Act was largely a punitive measure aimed at several large banks that had engaged in securities abuses (as many securities firms that were unaffiliated with banks had also done) rather than a device for assuring bank safety. None other than Senator Carter Glass, one of the bill's principal authors, repented two years after it was enacted and called for its repeal—to no avail.

Deposit Insurance

Perhaps the best-known policy measure introduced in the wake of the Depression has been deposit insurance. Before the Depression, not only had Congress failed to create insurance for bank deposits, but Franklin Roosevelt himself had actively opposed the idea, denouncing it as an invitation to unsound banking. The sight of panicky depositors fleeing banks in 1933 changed the new president's mind. With his support Congress promptly created the Federal Deposit Insurance Corporation (FDIC). Initially, deposit insurance covered $2,500 of each account, but coverage has since been gradually raised to its present level of $100,000 (the most recent increase in coverage having been adopted in 1980). In addition, the federal government has on occasion expanded its protection even to technically uninsured depositors and unsecured creditors.

Capital and Margin Regulation

Even before the Depression, banks and insurers were subject to capital regulation, meaning supervision aimed at ensuring that they had a deep enough cushion of shareholders' equity to ride out some bad times. But even the best of capital standards, designed to protect individual institutions from failure, could not protect the financial system in the face of the massive crash in asset values that characterized the Depression. As a result, it is perhaps not so surprising that despite the travails of the Depression neither Congress nor the regulators tightened capital requirements, which typically required banks to finance at least 10 percent of their assets with shareholders' equity (deposits constituting the balance of their funding sources). More important was that regulators later failed to maintain effectively the capital rules that existed. In the long postwar period when financial institutions seemed invulnerable, capital ratios steadily eroded, and in the case of thrift institutions in the 1980s, they essentially vanished (when calculated using market values rather than book values of thrifts' assets).

Congress did call for new capital requirements for securities firms and investors. In 1934 it created the Securities and Exchange Commission to oversee the industry, with a mandate to prevent manipulation of prices and dissemination of false or misleading information, and to require that securities firms maintain a reserve of capital to support their activities. For investors, margin requirements—or the percentage of a stock purchase that must be financed with the investor's own money rather than with borrowed or promised funds—are the counterparts of capital requirements for banks. Having put up as little as 10 percent of the cost of their stock purchases, investors were quickly wiped out when prices fell sharply in October 1929. Moreover, by allowing investors to reap large gains when the market was rising before the Depression, low margins contributed to the buying stampede that sent prices to unrealistic heights in the first place. One of the lessons that Congress drew from those events was that margins that are too low can aggravate financial instability. Rather than setting margins in legislation, which can be inflexible and difficult to change, Congress delegated authority to set margin requirements to the Federal Reserve. Since the end of World War II the Fed has kept securities margins at or above the 50 percent level.[3] One issue that regulators and policymakers must wrestle with now and in the future is whether margins for derivatives are sufficient to prevent financial instability.

Disclosure

Another inference that policymakers drew was that poor information had played an important role in the stock crash. If investors had had more and better information about securities issuers, they might not have bid up prices so inordinately and instead of dumping their holdings left and right might have been more discriminating when prices of some securities began to fall. As a result, the new Securities and Exchange Commission was empowered to impose disclosure and registration requirements on issuers of securities and on securities brokers and dealers. Among other things, the SEC requires financial statements of issuers of securities to be prepared in accordance with generally accepted accounting principles (GAAP), which are determined by a private organization, the Financial Accounting Standards Board (FASB), that the SEC oversees.[4]

The main purpose of requiring disclosure by corporations, however, is not so much to prevent excessive market turbulence as to help the market work efficiently so that the scarce capital in the economy is allocated by the combination of many individual private decisions toward the most productive uses. Timely disclosure of the financial condition of corporations also aids the market in disciplining companies that take excessive risks. The fact that corporations can and do fail does not mean that the disclosure policy has failed. Instead, disclosure simply enables companies and other investors to know what they are doing when they assume risk.

Precisely because society is so much less tolerant of risk taking by financial institutions—especially, of course, taxpayer-insured ones—than by other types of companies, policy historically has relied much more heavily on government supervision of financial institutions than on market-based disclosure. As the nation's financial markets grow increasingly complex and fast-paced, a crucial question is whether policymakers should continue to rely so heavily on the supervisory model or whether government might be aided by the discipline of the market to help police excessive risk taking. That subject is addressed more fully in chapter 4.[5]

Credit Availability and Specialized Institutions

Massive unemployment during the Depression wreaked havoc with Americans who owned their homes, leading to a wave of mortgage defaults, which in turn triggered the failure of roughly 600 of the nation's 12,000 state-chartered savings institutions. In response, Washington adopted measures designed to widen access to credit without leading to another round of thrift failures. As it turned out, these policies, as refined over subsequent decades, proved to be far more successful in achieving the first of their objectives than the second.

Congress began in 1934 by creating a federal charter for savings and loans, extending federal deposit insurance to them, and creating new institutions to provide thrifts with liquidity, the Federal Home Loan Banks. At the same time, however, Congress wanted to be sure that thrifts would stick to providing mortgage finance, so it limited them almost exclusively to investing their deposits in long-term fixed-rate residential mortgages. Such restrictions may have appeared sensible at that time, but they also planted the seeds for the thrift disaster of the 1980s.

Congress did more. In 1934 it created the Federal Housing Administration (FHA) to provide insurance to homeowners (and their lenders) against mortgage defaults, thus considerably expanding access to credit by allowing people to buy homes with smaller down payments. In 1938 Washington launched the Federal National Mortgage Association (Fannie Mae) to support a secondary market in FHA-insured mortgages. After World War II, Fannie Mae was allowed to expand its support to mortgages insured by the Veterans Administration. Eventually Fannie Mae was converted into a privately owned but government-sponsored enterprise (a GSE) and in 1970 was allowed to purchase conventional mortgages as well.[6] That same year Congress added another GSE, the Federal Home Loan Mortgage Corporation (Freddie Mac), to deepen the secondary market in conventional mortgage loans. Freddie Mac did this by "securitizing" mortgages, buying them from thrifts, packaging them as securities, and reselling them (Fannie Mae has since done the same thing). The resulting instruments, mortgage-backed securities, made mortgage credit more widely available than ever before by linking the capital market to the residential mortgage market.

Finally, beginning in the 1970s Congress began taking other steps to help ensure credit availability by prohibiting lending discrimination (the

Equal Credit Opportunity Act), requiring banks to serve the credit needs of their local communities (the Community Reinvestment Act), and requiring disclosure of mortgage lending patterns (the Home Mortgage Disclosure Act). In combination, these measures have done much to improve the access to credit enjoyed by the least advantaged.

The Twentieth-Century Model in a New Financial World

The twentieth-century regulatory structure today presents a paradox for policy. On the one hand, the philosophy on which it was built continues in many respects to be central to financial policy, and at least structurally many of its key elements remain in place. On the other hand, in real-world practice the Depression-era structures have begun to crumble, battered by a combination of market-driven forces and technological advances (discussed in greater detail in the next chapter). That can hardly be unexpected, given the vast changes in the environment in which financial institutions and markets must operate, including episodes of inflation, multiple recessions (although none rivaling the Depression), and the breakdown of the postwar system of fixed exchange rates. Today, therefore, American policy in financial services is in transition, halfway between the world of the Depression-dominated era and the world that is now dawning.

If markets demand that financial institutions find ways around regulatory restrictions, and if stopping such circumventions becomes too difficult or costly, it is only a matter of time until regulations lose their bite. That has been the case in varying degrees with three important regulations of the Depression-era financial landscape: price controls (on stock brokerage commissions and deposit interest rates), the prohibition on interstate banking, and the sequestration of banks from other financial activities.

The first restrictions to be removed were those on stock brokerage commissions, which the New York Stock Exchange had maintained for nearly 200 years. As with any cartel, this one could last only as long as market forces did not emerge to challenge the arrangement. But when large institutional investors and traders began to trade increasingly among themselves or on regional exchanges that did not restrict competition in setting commissions, the exchange could not withstand the pressure. Fixed commissions were abandoned in 1975.

The demise of controls on interest rates took longer, stretching out for nearly two decades. The first cracks in the edifice began to appear in the mid-1960s, when inflation pushed up market interest rates. To keep their large depositors (corporations and wealthy individuals) from deserting them for the higher rates offered in the market, banks offered off-shore Eurodollar accounts that paid essentially equivalent rates. That, however, was a minor blow compared with the next one. The introduction of money market mutual funds in the late 1970s (made possible by innovations in computer technology) eventually undermined deposit interest rate controls completely. Money market funds let *small* depositors do what the wealthy—those who could afford to purchase Treasury bills in their (then) minimum denominations of $10,000—had been doing for years: buy government bonds that, depending on market conditions, paid higher interest rates than savings accounts could. The funds managed this trick, of course, by buying government bonds in bulk and then, in effect, splitting them up into much smaller units so individuals could invest small amounts. Moreover, by investing only in riskless short-term instruments, money market funds assumed virtually no credit or interest rate risk. Thus they were able to offer accounts payable at par (with interest), just as banks did.

In 1978, when Merrill Lynch introduced a "cash management account" that combined a money market fund with a bank account, the collapse of rate controls became only a matter of time. As it turned out, the time arrived more quickly than perhaps even the developers of the new accounts had imagined. In 1979 the revolution that brought down the Shah of Iran triggered a sharp increase in the price of oil, which led to double-digit inflation rates and double-digit interest rates. Suddenly, money market accounts offered far more than the 5 percent return that depositors could earn at their banks and thrifts. Money market assets exploded from less than $10 billion in 1978 to $240 billion in 1982. Congress had little choice but to allow depositories to offer so-called money market deposit accounts, free of interest rate controls, that could compete with money market funds. Today, although demand deposit accounts are still barred from paying interest, so-called negotiable order of withdrawal (NOW) accounts, which were developed by New England thrifts in the early 1970s and are the functional equivalent of demand accounts, can and do pay interest.[7]

It has taken even longer for the restrictions on interstate banking to be phased out. And as with the removal of interest rate controls, the elimination of these restrictions was driven much more by markets than by federal policy. Americans were more mobile than ever and wanted their bank accounts to move with them. Banks wanted to meet the needs of their customers, who, if unhappy, could often turn to finance companies, which labored under no restrictions on where they could do business. Actually, neither the McFadden Act nor the Bank Holding Company Act completely barred banks from providing *some* services in other states. Banks could, for example, write loans and run nonbanking operations in more than one state. What they could *not* do, however, was open full-service banking offices (offering both deposits and loans) in other states, unless those other states allowed them to do so. Beginning in the 1980s, states began to take advantage of this escape clause. They began opening their doors selectively to banking organizations from certain other states, some on a unilateral basis and others reciprocally (meaning that one state opened up only to banks from other states that also opened up to its own banks). In this fully legal way, and without any need for congressional intervention, bank holding companies began to expand across state lines, producing the rise of super-regional banking organizations such as NationsBank and Banc One. It was not long before the new super-regionals began to challenge the large "money center" banks in size.

Still, no state allowed banks from other states to enter by branching, which could have compromised local regulators' ability to retain supervisory jurisdiction over banks from other states. Banks argued, however, that they could expand more efficiently if they could branch across state lines instead of being forced to set up and run wholly separate banks (owned by a common holding company) in each state. In 1994 the Riegle-Neal Interstate Banking and Branching Efficiency Act accepted this argument and set up a schedule for phasing out the interstate branching limitations. By the middle of 1997 most were dead.

The gradual removal of interstate restrictions has unleashed a wave of bank consolidations that is steadily reducing the numbers of banking organizations nationwide, a development hardly confined to banking, since mergers and consolidations continue apace in other parts of the financial services industry. Although consolidation inevitably will increase the concentration of bank assets as measured nationwide, many banking services and markets remain local or statewide, and in some of these markets users of financial services may face limited choices. That is where the antitrust enforcement agencies will need to look first to prevent consolidation from harming competition.

Provided this is done, the demise of interstate banking restrictions is good news for those concerned with the safety and soundness of the banking system. In the turbulent 1980s, when parts of the country were rocked by recession, industrial restructuring, tumbling commodity and real estate prices, or all of the above, many single-state depositories failed because they kept all their eggs in one basket. Few who lived in Texas during the 1980s will forget the failure of nine of the state's ten largest banking organizations, an episode that would not have occurred had some of those banks been part of nationwide organizations.

As for the segmentation rules dating from the Depression and from the Bank Holding Company Act, their fate is somewhat more complex. On the one hand, they have been weakened in some important ways; yet on the other, they remain very much a continuing force. Challenges to them have been mounted primarily (but not exclusively) by firms *outside* the banking industry that seek to add banking services to their other products and services, thus offering one-stop shopping to their customers. Mainly, this has been accomplished by offering products that are similar to banking products—such as money market mutual fund accounts, credit cards, and the like. Another way some nonbanking companies have found of entering a near equivalent of the banking business is to use the "unitary thrift holding company" vehicle in the Savings and Loan Holding Company Act, which allows organizations owning only a single thrift to compete without restrictions on their activities or affiliations. Commercial companies such as Sears and Ford Motor Company entered the business in this way (although both have since abandoned the effort). More recently, several insurers have announced their intention to enter the thrift business.

Understandably, nonbanks' invasion of banking has prompted banks to seek the freedom to counterattack by entering other financial businesses, such as securities and insurance. To date, Congress has not acted on this situation, creating a void that to a limited extent states and bank regulators have filled by using their discretion to gradually allow banks more freedom. Many states, for example, now allow the banks they charter to engage in such financial activities as brokering insurance, securities and real estate, and in some cases acting as an underwriter for securities and insurance. Meanwhile, the Comptroller of the Currency has permitted national banks to broker securities, offer mutual funds, sell insurance nationwide (out of offices located in small towns), and, most recently,

engage in a potentially broad range of financial activities through separately capitalized subsidiaries (a rule discussed elsewhere in this report).
For its part, the Federal Reserve has used authority under section 20 of the
Glass-Steagall Act to permit bank holding companies, through subsidiaries separate from their banks, to underwrite some municipal bonds, corporate bonds, and equities.[8] Several major banking organizations have
taken advantage of the Fed's rulings, increasing competition in both the
underwriting and advisory activities that investment banks once had to
themselves.[9]

The last time the Treasury Department issued a major report on the
financial services industry was in 1991 (*Modernizing the Financial System*). That report urged Congress to make three reforms: strengthen the
deposit insurance system, principally through stronger capital standards;
eliminate restrictions on interstate banking and branching; and end the
enforced sequestration of banks from other types of financial enterprises.
The first two of these objectives have now mostly been achieved, although not as quickly as the original report may have desired or envisioned. The third, ending banks' sequestration, has repeatedly been on
the legislative agenda but so far with no resolution. Accordingly, although
regulators and states have eroded some of the barriers to full competition
among finance service providers, banks still labor under limits on what
they can do, with whom they can be affiliated, and by whom they can be
owned. Correspondingly, nonbanks cannot own or be affiliated with banks.

In sum, the long-standing restrictions on banks' ability to affiliate and
enter new lines of financial businesses are alive but not well. Regulators
are cautiously but steadily letting banks do more and more, and are gradually expanding the circle drawn around bank holding companies. Banks
continue to be treated separately from other financial enterprises, but the
walls separating them are becoming more porous.

Responsibility Rediscovered

Meanwhile, to an extent that would have surprised an earlier generation, the past two decades have reawakened the financial world to the
danger of moral hazard—the danger that people who are offered blanket
protections or indemnities will take foolish risks, thus inflaming the very
perils that the protections were meant to avoid. Deposit insurance has

enjoyed unwavering public and government support since its creation and has successfully achieved its major objective of preventing bank runs, thus stabilizing the banking system in times of stress and providing a safe vehicle for savings. Even during the darkest days of the savings and loan crisis of the 1980s, no federally insured thrift experienced a deposit run, and no insured depositor at such an institution ever lost money. But this success has come at a cost, as we will see.

Still, recent events show that fears of moral hazard are not ungrounded: protections against loss will indeed lead to unsound banking practices as lenders play roulette with taxpayers' money—*if* the government does not also require the owners of insured depository institutions always to place significant amounts of their own money at risk. Supervision of insured depositories is not enough to make certain that taxpayer support is not abused. Also important, although only recently as well appreciated, is the need for sustained, meaningful capital standards: that is, for requirements that shareholders of depositories—who, unlike the federal government, benefit from any profits earned by the institutions—also bear some significant risk of losing their money if their institutions fail.

The most vivid (and expensive) illustration of this principle was the savings and loan crisis. But thrifts were not the only institutions to demonstrate the dangers of moral hazard in finance. There were problems in commercial banking as well.

Technically, deposit insurance does not protect accounts above the insured ceiling of $100,000. However, until Congress changed the rules in 1991, depositors and banks alike tended to assume that large accounts would be somehow protected, at least as long as the accounts were held in banks that were deemed "too big to fail"—a phrase that is technically wrong because large banks do fail, but that refers to the practice of regulators granting full protection to uninsured depositors and possibly other creditors. Several events seemed to validate investors' complacency, such as on various occasions when small banks failed, uninsured depositors received full de facto protection as regulators arranged for the failed institutions to be purchased by healthier ones.

Clearly, however, the most visible example of the "too big to fail" policy was the 1984 rescue of uninsured depositors and creditors of the Continental Illinois Bank and its holding company. Continental failed largely because of losses on its loans to developing countries. The banking authorities had few qualms about allowing Continental's shareholders to lose their stakes, but they nonetheless ignored the $100,000 insurance limit. One reason was that they feared that uninsured depositors at other large banks with similar exposure in developing countries would run if Continental's big depositors were not protected; another was the concern that many smaller banks with deposits held at Continental could fail if they, too, were forced to swallow losses.[10]

In retrospect, while analysts may continue to debate whether it was necessary to protect Continental's uninsured depositors to prevent a run on other large banks, it is clear that such protection was not necessary to forestall the default of Continental's correspondent banks, which would have lost only a small fraction of their balances had they been unprotected. Moreover, few observers would now defend the protection accorded to the creditors of Continental's holding company, whose health was not linked to that of other banks or, even indirectly, to other banks' depositors. In any event, by rescuing Continental's uninsured depositors and creditors, federal policymakers sent a strong signal to other big banks and to the market at large that even technically uninsured depositors at *all* major banks would be protected by taxpayers. Later, regulators broadened the implicit commitment still further by stepping forward to protect uninsured depositors of the Bank of New England (with $22 billion in assets held by its subsidiary banks at the time of failure in 1991) and the MCorp Banks in Texas ($16 billion in assets in the subsidiary banks that failed in 1989), both of which were considerably smaller than Continental.

It is difficult to escape the conclusion that by extending the federal safety net so broadly, policymakers weakened the incentives for depositors and even creditors to discipline banks against unwise risk taking. And it is unlikely that, if uninsured depositors and creditors of large banks in particular had known they were risking loss, they would have stood still in the 1970s and 1980s as their banks poured money first into developing countries and then into commercial real estate and leveraged buyouts. Perhaps the best evidence of this is that finance company lenders, which do not enjoy access to insured funds, either avoided making such risky loans altogether or were careful not to make too many of them.

The moral is that too much protection, or poorly designed protection, can make the financial system more dangerous, not less so, and not just in America. For a while the United States seemed to be unique in the depth of its banking problems. But within the past fifteen years 133 of the 181 countries that belong to the International Monetary Fund have also experienced significant problems among their banks, with 36 suffering "crises," according to a recent IMF study. That is a record significantly worse than in earlier decades of the postwar era. In many of these countries, notably Japan, Finland, Mexico, Norway, Spain, and Sweden, the costs of banking problems in relation to overall economic activity have rivaled or exceeded those of the United States. More recently, banking crises have emerged in Southeast Asia, and most notably in South Korea. In many of these cases, too, the government has either implicitly or explicitly backed all, or virtually all, depositors. Moral hazard has reasserted itself—expensively—around the world.

In America that reassertion has come with a renewed focus on responsibility and discipline in finance. In this regard, a number of measures have put the United States well ahead of much of the rest of the world.

—First and most important, capital standards for thrift institutions and banks have been strengthened legislatively (in 1989 and again in 1991) and through regulatory actions coordinated with other industrial countries under the auspices of the Basle Committee. In recent years regulators have strengthened the initial risk-based capital standards promulgated by the Basle Committee by adding specific requirements relating to the concentration of credit risk, interest rate risk, and market risks from trading activities.

—Second, in a related measure the Federal Deposit Insurance Corporation Improvement Act of 1991 (FDICIA) requires regulators to impose progressively sterner sanctions if the capital ratios of the institutions they supervise fall below the mandated minimum. Significantly, regulators are authorized to seize control of a weakened bank or thrift even before it is economically insolvent (and to provide compensation to the owners if there is any real capital left after the institution is sold to another party). These "prompt corrective actions" reverse the failed policy of "regulatory forbearance" practiced in the 1980s and send a powerful signal to the owners of banks and thrifts that they will pay a price if they extend their risk taking further than their capital will safely allow.

—Third, the FDICIA required the FDIC to vary the insurance premiums that it charges depository institutions according to each institution's risk of failing. Risk-related premiums impose a clear and direct charge on managers and owners for taking chances.

—Finally, the FDICIA imposed a series of procedural hurdles that regulators must overcome if they ever again take measures to protect uninsured depositors from loss. Although regulators may still resort to such a bailout if they believe it is necessary to prevent a broader crisis, the awareness that such hurdles now exist puts large depositors on notice that they stand to suffer if their banks should fail.[11] The law thus adds an additional source of discipline against excessively risky bank behavior.

In the few years since the changes have been in effect, the financial health of the banking industry has improved dramatically as the economy has prospered. Failures are down markedly since the dark days of the late 1980s, as shown in figure 1-3. At the same time, figure 1-4 shows that the profitability of depository institutions also has recovered. Indeed, the banking industry's resurrection has been so complete that in mid-1996 the FDIC eliminated deposit insurance premiums for all but the riskiest banks because the bank insurance fund had by then more than reached its statutory minimum (1.25 percent of insured deposits).

Figure 1-3. Depository Institution Failures, 1975–96

Number

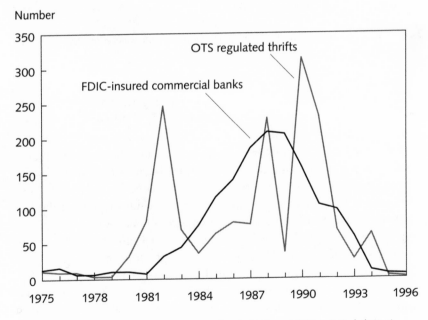

Source: FDIC statistics on banking (historical and 1996); and RTC statistical abstract.

Figure 1-4. Profitability in the Financial Services Industry
(Return on Equity), 1980–95

Percent

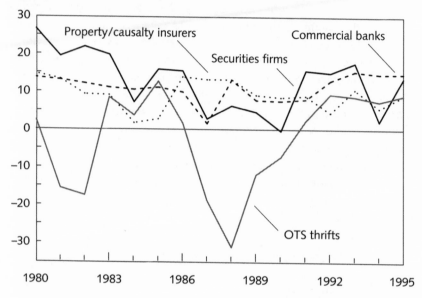

Sources: FDIC statistics on banking; OFTS, *Insurance Information Institute 1996 Fact Book*; and SIA.

To be sure, the failure of many industry laggards has contributed to the turnaround; only the healthy have survived. In addition, as the next chapter discusses in more detail, since 1990 a wave of mergers has dramatically reduced the number of banks in business, helping to wring out excess expense. Most important, the easing of monetary policy by the Federal Reserve in the early 1990s opened a large gap between short-term and long-term interest rates, allowing the industry during the first part of the decade to earn greater margins on its loans. A steadily improving economy thereafter reinforced the beneficial effects of the upward sloping yield curve. Nonetheless, the new regulatory regime has played its part in the recovery by compelling banks to hold more capital on their balance sheets. In fact, since 1991—the year the FDICIA was enacted—capital in the banking industry has jumped from $232 billion to more than $400 billion. And whereas in 1988, when a large portion of the assets in the industry was held by banks with capital-to-asset ratios of less than 6 percent, today virtually all banks are well capitalized. In short, the new capital and regulatory regime is an important, although not foolproof, bulwark against future backsliding, one that will help ensure that insured depositories do not play "heads I win, tails you lose" gambles with taxpayers' money.

The Limits of the Twentieth-Century Model

Much then has been done to repair, patch, and in some respects dismantle the twentieth-century model of financial regulation, bringing policy to its present transitional state. But in transition to what? To see the way forward, it is important to understand the limits of the current framework. By no means were all of the policy instruments and goals pursued by policymakers earlier in this century misguided, and by no means should all of those tools be junked. To the contrary, capital standards, deposit insurance, disclosure, and some other elements of the twentieth-century system were and are sound and should be maintained.

However, it is vital to distinguish between flawed tools and flawed projects. At bottom, the largest problem with the twentieth-century approach lies not in its instruments but in the fact that those instruments were used incoherently. In some respects—preventing bank runs and broadening access to credit, for example—the twentieth-century project has been a smashing success. But the project has been seriously compromised, too, by the extent to which its methods worked against each other. In good times, the internal contradictions rarely have risen to the surface, although the restrictions on competition exacted a price from consumers in the form of higher prices, dampened innovation, and limited choice. But the contradictions were always there, and in periods of stress they have become more apparent.

The first and most fundamental conflict has been between *preventing failure* and *preserving market discipline*. Twentieth-century policymakers have tended to assume that risk in the microcosm translated into risk in the macrocosm, that the failure of any one important institution or venture *always* would lead to a domino-like series of failures throughout the financial system. Of course, this sort of contagion is a real worry, as chapter 4 will discuss. But if the Federal Reserve provides timely liquidity in a crisis (as it notoriously failed to do in the 1930s), contagion is not as overwhelming a concern as policymakers have often believed, and in any case it need not be addressed by planting each domino in glue. In seeking to insulate institutions from failure and depositors from loss, the twentieth-century model also insulated them from market forces and from the discipline that market forces supply.

Policymakers have understood at least the latter problem and have attempted to substitute government supervision for marketplace vigilance. They have been right to recognize the need for regulatory oversight, but wrong to think oversight alone is sufficient. And indeed, the goal of failure prevention cuts against the goal of effective supervision, because a policy framework that seeks *as a principal goal* to head off failures, rather than to mitigate the systemic consequences of failure, inevitably exposes policymakers to a constant temptation to keep open institutions that should be allowed to die. This can easily undercut the incentives of supervisors to close weak institutions before the bleeding spreads. In the end the result may be too little discipline from markets and regulators alike.

The determination to prevent institutions from failing reinforced a tendency of the New Deal period and the years thereafter to micromanage finance. One reason policymakers set out to presort and delimit the activities of financial services firms was, of course, simply that they were afraid these businesses would get their fingers in too many pies and thus accumulate too much power. Another reason, however, was that if banks were on the one hand insulated from failure and on the other hand subject to a battery of restrictions on their activities, they could hardly be expected to compete fairly with other kinds of financial companies.

A further contradiction thus arose between *market management and competition.* In most areas of American economic policy, allowing—indeed encouraging—free and open competition is seen, rightly, as a cornerstone of innovation and consumer protection. No country in the world places a higher premium on opening its doors to competition. In the Depression-era paradigm, however, stabilization and competition became enemies instead of partners. Federal authorities backed themselves into a corner by creating narrowly focused, geographically dependent financial institutions that held sometimes hazardously narrow portfolios—institutions that were not well suited to withstand the rigors of rough-and-tumble markets. So the government came to believe it had little choice but to limit the competition to which finance's one-legged runners were exposed.

In time many policymakers began to take for granted that robust competition, far from strengthening the financial industry, would weaken it. Yet, of course, in the long run the opposite was true. Restrictions on competition made banks less able to meet the needs of their customers, and other providers—money market funds, for instance—moved in to fill the gap.

So, finally the two primary contradictions—between failure prevention and market discipline and between market management and competition—reacted with each other to produce yet further conflict. Government policy was all too often weakening financial institutions where it sought to strengthen them, to the detriment of providers and consumers alike. Thus the failure-prevention model wound up pitted against itself. Reasonable regulatory administration did much to iron out the wrinkles but could not remove the flaws in the fabric. Until the 1980s the flaws were not disastrous. But their potential to become so was realized in the savings and loan crisis, which illuminated with unfortunate vividness how the twentieth-century model's contradictions could interact with each other to produce a financial debacle.

The Savings and Loan Disaster

The roots of the S&L crisis grow from deep within the financial mindset of the 1930s—a mind-set that saw the risk of systemic crisis in any major failure; that tended to see competition as the enemy of safety; and that viewed financial institutions as static creatures rather than as rapidly evolving species. The same policies that so successfully encouraged home ownership built walls around the institutions—savings and loans—that were designed to finance it. S&Ls were required to invest their deposit funds, which could flee at any moment, almost exclusively in thirty-year mortgages, which were written at fixed rates of interest. Policy thus put the thrift industry at the mercy of the yield curve—the relationship between short-term and long-term interest rates. At the time this seemed a sure way to provide a stable source of home lending. Normally, after all, short rates were lower than long rates. And so the interest income that thrifts earned from their portfolio of long-term loans would more than cover their interest expenses in attracting short-term deposits. Moreover, deposit interest rates were capped at rates allowing thrifts to pay slightly higher interest than banks. This, it was presumed, would help S&Ls attract deposits. The result was to create an industry that was hedged in on every side, one whose income, expenses, and activities were all strictly constrained in ways that seemed guaranteed to produce profits.

The 1970s and early 1980s, however, proved to be anything but normal. Inflation and interest rates soared into double digits, and depositors began scrambling to find investments that would pay well above the interest ceilings allowed for banks and thrifts. In an earlier day, ordinary depositors would have had nowhere to run, but by the late 1970s money market mutual funds were thriving. So money began draining out of the depository system.

Thanks to the policies they had inherited, regulators were now faced with an impossible dilemma. If banks and thrifts were not allowed to pay higher interest rates on savings accounts, depositors would keep fleeing, potentially crippling the banking sector. But if depositories were allowed to pay higher interest rates, S&Ls would face deep operating losses; the short-term rates they needed to offer in order to attract deposits were well above the rates they were earning on their locked-in portfolio of fixed-rate mortgages. Regulators, having little choice, picked the second horn of the dilemma, deregulating interest rates. Sure enough, the market value of the typical thrift's mortgage portfolio plunged by more than enough to wipe out the value of the thrifts' equity. The first stage of the thrift crisis had arrived: virtually all of the 4,000 thrifts then in business became insolvent.

Taxpayers, of course, stood behind the thrift system. To liquidate all those insolvent institutions and pay off the depositors would have cost the government more than $100 billion. The insurance fund backing thrift deposits had nowhere near that kind of money. Moreover, the whole point of the policy structure was to prevent financial failures from being recognized as such. Faced with pleas from the industry for a second, third, and fourth chance, Congress and the regulatory agencies decided to encourage the thrifts to "grow out" of their problems. In laws passed in 1980 and 1982, they gave the thrifts authority to diversify into lending for business and commercial real estate, fields in which S&L operators, having been restricted to home mortgages for decades, had no experience. President Reagan called the passage of the 1982 Garn–St Germain Act, which opened the door to thrifts that wanted to jump into new activities, the "most important legislation for financial institutions in the last fifty years."

Perhaps it was, but not in the way he meant. Portfolio diversification can be an important financial stabilizer if it is embarked on from a strong capital base and with the support of time and experience. But thrifts knew virtually nothing about high-risk commercial mortgages, many of whose borrowers defaulted, and they had essentially no capital to back their investments. Indeed, measured in market-value terms, many had *negative* capital. So a long-sheltered industry was suddenly set loose to gamble in an alien market for its very survival without any capital of its own at stake. Instead, many thrifts gambled taxpayer money because they could draw on their base of federally insured deposits.

The crisis now entered its second stage. By the early 1980s, inflation and short-term rates had fallen, so that had Congress and the regulators done nothing but prevent insolvent thrifts from growing until they attracted new capital, many S&Ls would have returned to solvency. Indeed, by the mid-1980s, the estimated cost of removing insolvent thrifts from the marketplace had dropped to $15 billion. But by the time the yield curve had stopped squeezing them, the thrifts had embarked on their hapless excursion into commercial real estate. Their losses mounted rapidly.

Policy was now hopelessly entangled in contradictions, crossing its own path at every turn. All the options were bad. In principle, deposit insurance might have been withdrawn or reduced, forcing thrifts to gamble their own money if they wanted to survive. But insolvent or near-insolvent thrifts had no money of their own, and ending or curtailing the taxpayer guarantee would have sent depositors fleeing, bringing on precisely the failures that policymakers sought so desperately to avoid. Indeed, just a few years before, seeking to help the industry hold onto its deposits and thus stay afloat, Washington had *increased* federal guarantees, raising the deposit insurance ceiling from $40,000 to $100,000 per account. In principle, another possibility would have been to require thrifts to increase their base of capital. But that would have driven many undercapitalized institutions into receivership. Alternatively, and most prudently, policymakers could have prevented weak thrifts from growing until the market value of their capital base (the economic net worth of the institutions) had returned to a healthy level. Instead, by various means Congress and the regulators effectively waived the pre-1980 standards that required savings and loan associations to back at least 5 percent of their assets with capital as measured by book values, while totally ignoring any measures of the institutions' market values.[12]

The government's imperative to prevent failures was now openly at war with its imperative to ensure safety and soundness. Desperate thrifts, many of which were already technically insolvent, discovered that they could attract deposits and so keep income flowing in by offering high interest rates that were effectively subsidized by deposit insurance, since the insurance let depositors put their money in shaky S&Ls without risk to themselves. The high rates offered by deeply insolvent S&Ls—thrifts that used their federal insurance to attract depositors who otherwise would have steered clear—added to stress on healthy institutions, which were under pressure to match the rates offered by the insolvent institutions. The system now was undermining the prudent to indemnify the reckless. While policymakers failed to act, hoping that the sun might yet shine tomorrow, the bankrupt thrifts accumulated many billions of dollars of additional losses through negligence, and in many cases fraud, allowing a $15 billion problem to grow to nearly ten times that size. The downward spiral finally ended with a $130 billion taxpayer bailout, concluding easily the most expensive financial debacle since the Depression.

No doubt policymakers, like thrift managers, made many poor decisions. But even the most agile of regulators could not have made sense of the incentives and conflicting goals built into the policy regime. In the end, making failure prevention and sectoral management work on a broad scale proved an impossible mission.

The End of an Era

The thrift crisis, of course, was not the only challenge presented to financial policymakers in recent times. The October 1987 stock market correction posed a severe test. A somewhat milder challenge was offered by the losses sustained by a number of banks or their customers in the derivatives markets during the 1990s. Those were important episodes, and their implications for financial regulation in the future are taken up in subsequent sections of this report (primarily chapter 4). But the S&L debacle represented a watershed. Much as the Depression brought to light the inadequacies of the nineteenth-century paradigm for financial regulation, so the savings and loan fiasco showed the deep fissures and irreconcilable contradictions of the twentieth-century paradigm. Fortunately, the thrift crisis remains unique in its scope. But many of the problems that the crisis exposed, and the self-feeding dynamic it unleashed, are inherent in a world view that sees failure as the enemy of stability and competition as the enemy of robustness.

And so, although many particular elements of the twentieth-century model can and should be brought forward into the next century, the overall approach of that system is dying on its feet and should be finally laid to rest. The old public policies in finance tended to assume that the industry would more or less stand still while the government hedged it in with supports, protections, and prohibitions designed, so it was hoped, to make the system safe. So policy set out to make markets competitive but not too competitive, to let service providers become large but not too large, to give consumers choices but not too many choices. As policy has already begun to recognize, that approach is doomed. For, whatever else finance may be doing, it is not standing still.

Appendix: A Summary of the Financial Regulatory Structure

Regulation of the U.S. financial system is divided among many different agencies. For the most part financial regulation is institutional, and for depository and securities industries it involves agencies at both the federal and state levels. In banking, the so-called dual system of federal and state regulation is a historical outgrowth of the fact that state banks came first, and national (or federally chartered and regulated) banks were not authorized until 1863. As for the securities industry, when federal regulation came in the 1930s, it was simply superimposed on the existing state system. In contrast, insurance has always been regulated only at the state level, which means that an insurer doing business in all fifty states is regulated by fifty separate state authorities (although many state regulators rely heavily on regulators in leading states, notably New York and California). At the other end of the spectrum, investment companies (which offer mutual funds), pension funds, and futures trading have been regulated primarily, if not exclusively, at the federal level.

Except for companies that own banks, any firm that owns one or more financial activities faces no overarching "super" or consolidated regulation. In contrast, bank holding companies, as shown in figure 1-5, are typically regulated by multiple agencies: the Federal Reserve at the holding company level and at the bank level by one of three federal bank

Figure 1-5. Bank Holding Company Regulation

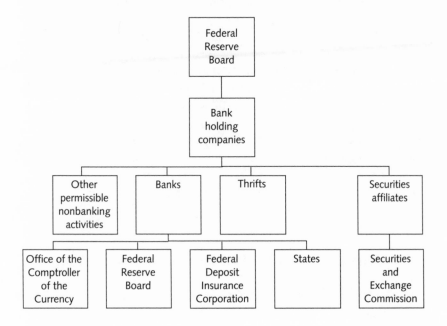

regulators and (for state banks) one or more state regulators (if the holding company owns state-chartered banks). For those bank holding companies that now are allowed to engage to a limited extent in securities underwriting, the securities subsidiary is also regulated by the Securities and Exchange Commission.

Moreover, whether or not a bank or a thrift is part of a holding company, it may be regulated by both federal and state authorities, even if it is state-chartered. This is because all bank deposits have federal deposit insurance, and in some cases state "member" banks belong to the Federal Reserve System. Accordingly, while all state banks are supervised by the regulators in the states where they are chartered, the Fed also supervises about 1,000 state member banks (as well as their holding companies, if relevant), while the FDIC supervises approximately 6,000 state banks that do not belong to the Federal Reserve System. Further, if they have holding companies, the Fed supervises those as well.

There is overlapping regulatory jurisdiction at the federal level also. A national bank owned by a holding company faces regulation by both the Comptroller of the Currency (at the bank level) and by the Fed (at the holding company level). When banks or their holding companies want to merge, both the banking agencies and the Justice Department review the transaction for anticompetitive effects. And both the banking regulators and the Justice Department review banks' compliance with antidiscrimination laws.

To be sure, the various federal and state regulators have worked out arrangements to minimize duplication where the agencies have overlapping jurisdictions. Still, the United States is unique among major industrialized countries in the extent to which its regulation of financial services—banks in particular—is fragmented. In most other countries, regulatory responsibility for banking is concentrated in a single department, whether the central bank or the finance ministry.

2

. . . .

Tides of Change

TO SPEAK of finance is still, for many people, to summon up images of pinstripes, gray hair, brass nameplates, and high-columned institutions with names such as "Guarantee," "Permanent," "Surety," "Fidelity." And all of that is no coincidence. The currency of the financial services industry, particularly in its dealings with consumers, is first and always dependability. In the face they present to the public, financial institutions emphasize their constancy above all.

Yet that imperturbable public face of finance belies another very different and sometimes, of late, bewildering one: the face of change. All American industry is rich with innovation, sometimes liberating, sometimes disorienting, often both. Finance is no exception. Indeed, in some respects it is in the vanguard. Inherently, finance is an industry organized around information: the daily collection of billions of bits of knowledge about where money is, who wants to lend it, who needs to borrow it, what all these people seek to do with it, how risky their ventures are presumed to be. The industry is, almost literally, a vast economic computer. Inevitably, its future is intimately connected with—is in fact at the mercy of—the revolution in information technology.

By now, most people have at least a broad idea what that revolution is all about. Certainly anyone who has logged onto the World Wide Web knows. As recently as a couple of decades ago, the information horizon of ordinary people extended only as far as their morning newspaper, local library, and television set. Individuals knew a few hundred or a few thousand people personally, but the rest of the world they knew only as large clumps sorted by location, nationality, or profession. What they did learn about the world outside their circle of acquaintance was likely to be a day or a week or even (at the library) several years old.

50

Today, everyone's binoculars are potentially more powerful. Anyone with a personal computer and modem can read that morning's job listings in local newspapers in Phoenix or Sacramento, browse for university courses in Chicago or London, and look down on a hurricane in the Atlantic through the eye of a satellite. Messages that not long ago cost several hours' pay to send to the other side of the globe can now be dispatched for pennies, as cheaply to Moscow or Cairo as to the pharmacist down the block. Instead of knowing foreigners only in large clumps, anyone who is "wired" can know them, almost as cheaply, as individuals.

Once the world was a place of families, clans, tribes; then of city-states and principalities; then, at last, of nation-states. People extended their horizons of trade and knowledge by aggregating other people into ever larger blocks. Now the scale economies of acquaintanceship are collapsing, disaggregating those same blocks as the cost of learning about and talking to particular individuals falls. Search engines and cross-tabulators allow individuals to sort and select each other however they please. It is becoming intelligible to speak of a world in which individuals may know millions instead of hundreds of other individuals—virtually, if not personally. All this is happening because in brief the costs of gathering, processing, and exchanging information are falling exponentially.

Finance is one sector of the economy in which the mutually reinforcing trends of the information revolution and of globalization are meeting head-on. Unlike goods, which must be physically transported from seller to buyer, or services, which often need to be delivered up close and personal, much of what we call finance—the movement of money or financial instruments that are exchangeable for money—can be and is sent around the world instantaneously and cheaply by phone, computer, and modem. Yet in finance as in so many sectors, the conventional wisdom about the information age and globalization sheds little light on what the future will bring. It would be unwise, to say nothing of immodest, for this report to pretend to clairvoyance. What it can do, though, is try to peer through the fog by sketching the forces that are now reshaping finance and by drawing some tentative conclusions about what those forces portend. Life will change, potentially very quickly, for consumers, financial firms, and not least policymakers who face the arduous task of minimizing the hazards of change while encouraging innovation, or at the very least not stifling it.

The most sensible place to begin foretelling the future is in the present.

Most of the forces reshaping the financial services industry over the next decade or two are already clearly visible. Although a brief account of those forces must necessarily be incomplete, four especially important trends stand out: advances in information and communication technology; globalization; financial innovation; and stronger competition unleashed by the removal of counterproductive restrictions. After discussing each of these forces, this chapter will consider their effects for consumers, the industry, and makers of policy.

The Digitization of Finance

In ordinary life, of course, the effects of new information technology are readily apparent in millions of American homes, where the computer is connected to the Internet, the television receives dozens of cable channels, and even the telephone is a high-technology wonder. In business the effects of information technology and ever cheaper communications are likely to be felt still more quickly. The personal computer (PC) and modem are, as a standard combination, little more than a decade old. Yet hardly any but the very smallest companies today do business without them.

Predictably, until now the computer revolution has had its most noticeable impacts on the most sophisticated providers and users of financial services. To see those effects, one need only enter any commercial or investment bank's trading room, which is likely to be lined with pricey computer technology that uses cutting-edge software to exploit complicated trading strategies. At least as important, computer processing power has allowed both investment and commercial banks to combine vast quantities of individual loans into pools and to issue securities representing interests in those pools. As this chapter will show, securitization has transformed the financial services industry, reducing the cost of credit in the process. To no small extent securitization is a triumph of data processing.

The information age is also benefiting individual consumers of financial services. Automated teller machines (ATMs)—of which there are now more than 120,000 around the country, almost ten times more than in 1979—have accustomed Americans to using a video display terminal as a banker. No longer need people fidget in long teller lines merely to fill their pocketbooks with cash. ATMs, however, are just one step in a continuing transformation not only of consumer banking but also of money itself.

The best known means of electronic payment, far from being exotic, is plastic: credit cards, which over the past several decades have become essential for most Americans. Visa, MasterCard, and all the rest are yet another testament to the power of computerized data processing, by means of which countless transactions are sorted, collated, and billed to millions of consumers every day. The market for credit cards, however, is being gradually invaded by debit cards, which subtract money directly from a consumer's checking or savings account at the time of purchase, and are used by consumers at the point of sale as substitutes for checks.

For the average American, two features of the information revolution—one physical, the other virtual—are likely to change the nature of money itself. Physically, money will increasingly be stored on portable computer chips rather than in accounts held by faraway computers that must be phoned up before transactions can be finished. The physical embodiment of the information revolution in finance, now in its embryonic stage, is the so-called smart card, or (as it is known in the industry) the general-purpose stored value card. Limited-purpose smart cards for subways or phone service are already common in many parts of the country. But general-purpose smart cards, accepted (like credit cards) by any number of merchants, are now used widely in some European countries and were introduced in the United States most visibly at the 1996 Olympic Games in Atlanta (and at this writing are being tested in New York).

Smart cards contain memory chips, onto which is loaded value in its most elemental form, that of information. Once card readers are common, holders of smart cards will be able to charge them up at banks, gas stations, restaurants, and, perhaps most important, at home through their telephones or PCs; then the cards could be used interchangeably with cash. Calls on public telephones, bus fares, taxi rides, and drinks from vending machines might all be bought without a harried search for the correct coins; "exact change only" signs might at last become relics.

The introduction of smart cards raises a number of contentious policy issues, some of which are discussed later in this report. How (and how quickly) those issues are resolved will affect the speed with which the cards penetrate the market and replace some means of payment (cash and travelers' checks) or are combined with others (credit and debit cards).

Nevertheless, independent of any policy decisions that must be made, it is important to keep the smart-card phenomenon in its proper perspective. For one thing, it is not clear how many Americans will want such a card, which may be easily lost or stolen, when they can already put debit cards in their pockets. Moreover, because the stored-value feature of smart cards is likely to be used only for small transactions—riding the subway, buying sodas from vending machines, or paying for restaurant meals—the typical American is likely to carry no more than $100 or so on the card at any one time. Thus even if every one of the country's 250 million men, women, and children carried a card with an average $100 balance, obviously an unrealistic number, but useful nevertheless to help illustrate the point, the total balance outstanding would reach only $25 billion. By comparison, checking account balances today exceed $700 billion.

Smart cards may turn out to play a far more important role, however, once they are capable of being read by personal computers and thus used to authenticate bank-to-bank transactions over the Internet. Home-based banking, long one of the holy grails of the American banking industry, is still in its infancy, accounting for only 1 percent of all transactions after more than a decade of forecasts that it would soon become ubiquitous. But the growing penetration of personal computers, modems, and the Internet should change all that, and rapidly. Already, roughly 25 million American households reportedly have access to the Net, a number that should double in just a few short years. Booz, Allen & Hamilton projects that by 2000 the number of households doing banking business over the Internet will mushroom from roughly 100,000 now to more than 16 million, in the process producing 30 percent of all retail banking profits.

The Internet not only allows customers to deal directly with their bank on-line, it also lets them do business that way with a wide variety of vendors, whether paying by credit card (which many individuals do already) or by directly debiting their bank accounts (a service banks are working hard to offer). As security issues get resolved, so-called digital cash should become a more popular means of making payments. E-money, as it is sometimes known, remains for the moment somewhat vexed by questions of security. In time, however, digital accounts or their equivalents should be commonly used for doing business on the Internet.

Given that much or even most of what banks do by way of routine payments can be digitized, why not digitize whole banks? America's first federally insured virtual depository, Security First, opened in October

1995. More will follow, including, of course, established banks, hundreds of which already maintain Internet sites and many more of which will soon do so.

Banking is by no means the only financial sector in which technology is changing the way business is done. In principle, most financial products can and will be sold easily over the Internet, because they tend to be standard instruments or contracts and consumers are most interested in only one thing: their price. Consumers can now use websites to locate the cheapest mortgages and home or auto insurance policies and apply for them on-line. They can also monitor their stocks from their living room, thanks to various stock-quotation services operating on the Internet. Taking advantage of this electronic gateway to consumers, more than two dozen discount brokerages offer stock trades over the Internet, making trades for fees well below traditional rates. A number of banks are in the process of offering similar services. A study released by Forrester Research in September 1997 estimates that 3 million stock accounts are on-line, double the level the year earlier. A related study by Piper Jaffray indicates that on-line trading commissions account for almost 30 percent of the discount-brokerage market, more than double the year before. In response, traditional brokerages, including some of the industry's largest, have been moving to reduce their rates and to go on-line themselves.

Even the core function of investment banks—underwriting the securities offerings of corporations—may be threatened by continuing developments in information technology. In just the past year new small corporations have marketed their securities to investors directly over the Internet. This kind of direct marketing could well grow.

Finance without Borders

Electrons know no nationality, and it is not much harder to move them around the world than to dispatch them next door. *Globalization* has become something of a buzzword recently in American popular economics, and often its importance is overstated. The vast bulk of what is consumed in America is also produced here, and what is often striking about foreign companies doing business on American shores is how closely they resemble homegrown ones. Skeptical economists point out that cross-border financial flows, as shares of national product, were greater in the last century than at any time since. For all the press that globalization gets, foreign transactions remain a fraction of the total, and cross-national interest rate differentials persist, suggesting to some economists that the age of a single worldwide capital market remains more a dream than a reality.

Still, the fact remains that the growth of transnational finance has been nothing short of remarkable during the 1980s and 1990s. One particularly dramatic indicator of the trend is the foreign exchange market, which has grown not only to accommodate expanding trade but also to satisfy investors' growing ability and desire to bet on other countries' currencies. In the 1980s, when world trade grew by little more than a factor of two, foreign currency transactions grew by a factor of fourteen. The foreign exchange markets now process about $1.2 trillion daily. That is double the value of foreign exchange deals in the late 1980s, and roughly twenty times the value traded in the early 1980s.

Other indicators of cross-border activity show similar leaps. Banks in Japan, the United States, and western Europe are becoming more closely linked across national boundaries. According to the Bank for International Settlements, international interbank lending reached an estimated $5.8 *trillion* in 1995. The value of bonds and securities traded across American borders has also risen dramatically, from 9 percent of GDP in 1980 to 135 percent in 1993 (a trend duplicated in other industrialized countries, especially Great Britain, where the volume of cross-border trading in 1993 exceeded that country's GDP tenfold). U.S. pension funds, which are hardly high-flying investors, held less than 1 percent of their assets in foreign securities in 1980; by the early 1990s the figure was 6 percent. A particularly direct sort of globalization happens when firms merge across national lines, as has occurred increasingly in the financial sector.

It is not just financial institutions and their corporate customers that have gone global. So, increasingly, have many American individuals. Perhaps the best evidence is growth in assets held in international equity mutual funds (figure 2-1). In 1985 such investments were negligible, but by 1996 they had grown to $250 billion, an amount equivalent to about 20 percent of the total investment in purely domestic funds. More broadly, according to one recent study, whereas foreign stock accounted for less than 2 percent of all equity holdings in the United States in the mid-1970s, Americans now hold about 10 percent of their equity in foreign stocks. The levels of foreign stock ownership are even higher in Canada, the United Kingdom, and Germany.

Figure 2-1. Net Assets in Equity Funds, Domestic and International, 1985–97

Billions of dollars

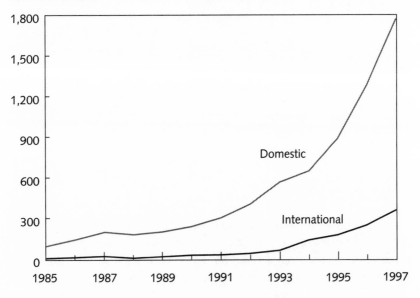

Source: Investment Company Institute.

Americans also are doing more of their banking business with foreign institutions. That is especially true of corporations, which have turned increasingly to foreign-owned banks to meet their borrowing needs. Indeed, foreign banks now supply about the same amount of credit to U.S. companies as do American banks (although almost all of the growth in the foreign bank share is accounted for by lending to offshore operations of U.S. corporations).

All of this means that, whether most Americans realize it or not, their financial fortunes are linked closely to financial systems abroad. The upside, as we discuss shortly below, is‘ that the willingness of foreigners to invest here reduces our interest rates (while bolstering the value of our dollar). The downside is that when institutions and markets abroad catch cold, so can ours. For example, the troubles that Japanese banks have experienced have caused them to shrink their lending not only to their domestic customers but to those in the United States. Similarly, when large U.S. banks encountered difficulties in the 1980s, they too pulled back from other overseas activities.

More recently, the turmoil in Asian stock markets in late October 1997 triggered a moderate (albeit sudden) drop in stock prices here, despite much talk about the United States being a "safe haven" for investors around the world (which clearly was demonstrated by the influx of funds into our government bond market at the time). Similarly, when stock prices collapsed in October 1987 they did so around the world, not just here.

In short, it is becoming less and less accurate to speak of capital markets specific to single countries, and more realistic to think of finance as operating on a global stage.

Financial Innovation

Although technological advances and globalization have unquestionably contributed to the inventiveness and competitive ferocity of America's financial markets, another force not to be underestimated is simply the native creativity of Americans who are mining that richest of natural resources, Yankee ingenuity.

Of all the financial innovations of the past several decades, the most important is probably *securitization*, the transformation of individual assets into marketable securities. Securitization is accomplished by commercial and investment banks that package many different loans into large bundles of assets held in trust. They then issue securities representing indivisible interests in the trust. The investors who buy these securities receive, on a proportional basis and minus a small transaction fee, the interest paid by the borrowers whose loans make up the trust. In an age when government is often criticized, it is noteworthy that the federal government helped launch securitization in the 1970s by guaranteeing the interest and principal payments on Ginnie Mae securities that were backed by residential mortgages. Today, more than $1 trillion is outstanding in mortgage-backed securities, a sum that is growing rapidly because almost all fixed-rate residential mortgages are now packaged into securities and sold to investors.

Just as significant, private-sector institutions—investment banks and commercial banks—have developed ways of securitizing other kinds of loans, such as automobile loans and credit card receivables. Thus far, securitization has required that the loans packaged together have standard features (maturities, interest rates, and collateral) and that the creditworthiness of the loan bundle be "enhanced" by third-party insurers or by overcollateralization of the securities (so that, for example, every $100 of securities is backed by $105 of loans). Next, banks hope to securitize loans to small businesses, which are not standardized. Legislation enacted in 1996 should help reduce some of the legal and tax-related barriers to securitization of such loans, as should continued advances in credit scoring (computerized methods of assessing loan risk). While not all small business loans are likely to be turned into securities, many will, and, like borrowers of residential mortgages, small businesses that qualify will benefit from the cost savings that securitization should generate.

The other key financial innovation of recent years is the rapid proliferation of a family of instruments that are lumped together under the name *derivatives*. In its broadest sense the term derivative covers any financial contract that derives its value by reference to some financial contract, index, or commodity that is traded in the cash (or underlying) market. Some derivatives, such as options and futures contracts, are hardly new. Flemish traders used forward contracts in the twelfth century, and contracts much like today's futures and options were used widely in seventeenth-century Amsterdam. In the United States, commodities exchanges were set up in Chicago and New York in the mid-nineteenth century to enable farmers and their customers to lock in the prices they were receiving or paying for food. What is new, though, is the increased variety and complexity of many derivative contracts, as well as the remarkable growth in transactions. For a guide to the various types of derivatives now used in financial markets, see the appendix to this chapter.

Significantly, it is not just private actors that can be innovative in the financial arena. So can the government. In 1996 the Treasury Department announced its plan to issue inflation-indexed bonds, and in January 1997 the first such bonds were sold. These bonds provide a new way for investors to protect themselves from the risks of inflation. Although the market itself will provide the verdict on whether this new product will be in strong demand, the government has a history of pioneering important new financial instruments. Inflation-indexed bonds may indeed prove eventually to be as important an innovation as was the mortgage-backed security, pioneered in the 1970s with the federal government's direct support.

Growing Competition

Two of the trends mentioned above—globalization and technological change—have created new paths for competition in finance: globalization because strong companies are increasingly able to compete in any lucrative market; technology because, for example, start-up expenses and transaction costs may be modest for some virtual firms, although for some lines of financial business, the technological sophistication required for success may only be affordable for the very largest firms. Still, on the whole, the world of finance, once securely nestled in its glass office towers, is rapidly growing less cozy.

As discussed in the last chapter, policymakers at both the federal and state levels have helped this process along by gradually letting competition work and removing restrictions that prevent firms from following customers. Of course, freedom can mean change and banking is a prime example: the gradual elimination of interstate barriers has already had a marked effect on the structure of the industry. Although the federal liberalization of branching authority has yet to take full effect, the ability of bank holding companies to acquire banks in other states was given broad scope by actions of various state legislatures. Figure 2-2 illustrates the dramatic results. Whereas in 1980 multistate, multibank holding companies accounted for about 4 percent of the assets held by banking companies, by 1994 they accounted for 70 percent. Sometime after the interstate branching restrictions largely end at the close of 1997, this country will finally, for the first time in its history, have numerous nationwide banks competing alongside many other regional and community-based institutions.

Another source of new competition is more fundamental. It is indeed one of the defining trends in financial services today: the blurring of traditional boundaries as firms in what were previously regarded as different industries invade one another's markets. Regulation and technology have both been important contributors to this trend. As shown in Chapter 1, American regulatory policy has, for most of this century, taken pains to distinguish and disentangle what were viewed as different sorts of financial businesses. Mixing businesses was seen as both destabilizing, because disruptions in one market might be too easily transmitted to another, and anticompetitive, because powerful companies might achieve enough integration to become financial octopuses. Banks in particular, it was feared, might use their customer bases to take over large segments of the securi-

Figure 2-2. Assets in Banking Companies, by Type, 1980–94

Billions of dollars

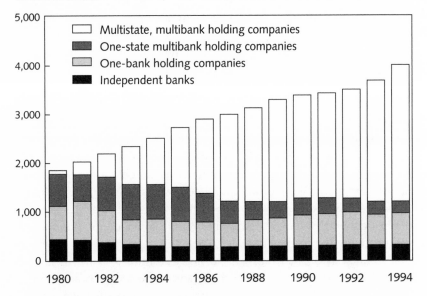

Source: Office of the Comptroller of the Currency.

ties or insurance business and use their economic power to dominate other markets unfairly. That concern, some economists believe, was over-wrought: cross-sector competition, if anything, probably increases the amount of competitive dynamism in individual markets, not only by put-ting pressure on established players but by cross-pollinating staid indus-tries with new ideas from other fields.

In any case, as chapter 1 showed, old-style partitions between sec-tions of the financial industry have begun to collapse of their own weight. Although essentially no action has been taken by Congress to tear down the walls between banks and other financial businesses, regulators and the states have gradually taken matters into their own hands. The result has been a wave of cross-competition. Securities firms and insurers now offer business loans; mutual funds have become major competitors for savers' deposits; life insurers now offer contracts that are linked to the performance of the stock market; and finance companies have become formidable competitors as lenders.

Finally, as chapter 1 noted, various sorts of price controls have been removed. Fixed brokerage commissions have been eliminated, unleashing discount brokers, a powerful new part of the securities industry, to compete with conventional full-line securities brokers. Deposit interest ceilings are gone. Only the regulation of rates charged by various lines of property-casualty insurance remains, and then only in some states.

Implications of Change

In sum, a survey of financial services yields a picture of an extraordinarily vibrant industry that is already hip deep in a current of rapid change. No one doubts that the sorts of innovations just described, already so well under way, will make life both more complex and more rewarding for financiers (and perhaps only more difficult for policymakers). No one doubts, either, that technological change and globalization and the rest will continue. But leading to what?

Technology will obviously allow financial firms to make their deals faster than in the past and to spread their services over broader areas. That is true already. But that in itself might merely mean that familiar sorts of institutions may, in a decade or two, be doing familiar sorts of things, only faster. In the 1950s and 1960s, technological optimists (and science fiction writers) predicted a world transformed by computers, which supposedly would supplant human brains in offices, on assembly lines, and behind the wheel of the family car. In fact, computers have contributed much to modern life, but they have hardly sent workers home to lead lives of leisure. In the world of finance, today's technological optimists might be similarly disappointed. Reasonable people cannot dispute that technology, globalization, financial innovation and stronger competition matter. But how much?

Eventually, a great deal. The largest uncertainties about the impact of change are when, not if. Timing is, of course, important, and views on the rate of change in the delivery of financial services vary broadly. But the direction of change is much clearer. What, then, are likely to be some of the ultimate implications of the forces just described as they reshape finance's three major functions: payments, intermediation, and the spreading of risk? How will life change for consumers?

Payments: The Benefits of Digital Money

The workhorse of the payments system, at least as measured by number of transactions, has long been the check, admittedly an old-fashioned device. The average American still writes almost 250 paper checks a year, and checks are used for about two-thirds of all consumer expenditures. But checks are cumbersome and expensive, requiring airplanes and trucks to haul millions of slips of paper around the country every day.

The future of payments in America is clear: paper, whether in the form of currency or checks, is in decline; chips (smart cards) and electrons (on-line payments) are on the rise. This transformation will save money, initially for banks and other payments processors, but also, as long as competition is ensured, for consumers. At bottom, it is simply cheaper, by as much as 50 to 67 percent, to send messages by chip, over telephone lines, or through the air than to print and process billions of pieces of paper and move them around. Moreover, extraordinary and continuing advances in computational power and information resources will only widen the cost gap. For example, between 1987 and 1993 the real cost of processing data in a personal computer dropped by a factor of 100, as did the cost of moving data from point to point. Similar advances are transforming even larger-scale computer systems.

To be sure, the delivery of electronic payments is not free. Customers pay to use their ATM machines, they typically pay for the convenience of having a credit card (even if they do not borrow money on the card), they will pay to use smart cards, and they either now pay or will pay to use on-line payments services. Indeed, the deregulation of deposit interest ceilings, which was made inevitable by the inflation of the 1970s and 1980s, has driven banks to charge for payments and other services that they formerly subsidized with cheap, regulated deposits. Not only are cross-subsidies inefficient (because they encourage excessive demand for the subsidized services and discourage demand for others); they simply cannot survive in a competitive market, as Congress has recently recognized in authorizing the deregulation of local telecommunications services.[1] Moreover, in the banking context in particular, it is important to recognize that consumers benefit as depositors when they can earn higher deposit rates than the old cross-subsidy system allowed and when they can get cash day or night from ATMs that are often located more conveniently than bank branches.

Electronic banking offers other conveniences as well. Credit and debit cards already provide more security than cash, which if lost or stolen is gone forever. Under today's rules, card issuers generally bear liability for lost or stolen cards above a $50 deductible. Smart cards are likely to offer similar protection, whether enforced by regulation or simply by market pressures (which already have induced Visa and MasterCard to extend the $50 liability to their debit cards). A further advantage of smart cards is that their chips can carry more information arrayed more flexibly than can magnetic stripes on credit cards: coupons, shopping records, several credit or debit cards, medical histories, and frequent-flier miles might all be included, as well as information that permits easy and rapid authentication of the user.

Meanwhile, the Internet will make wiring money, today a fairly complicated business engaged in only between banks, as easy as pushing a button. Digital cash also is likely to be downloadable onto stored-value cards or into electronic wallets and then capable of being spent on the street; and unlike today's credit cards and perhaps tomorrow's smart cards, it will be usable person-to-person.

To be sure, there are techno-skeptics who question how fast all these changes may come. They may be right in the short run, but if the extraordinary growth of the Internet in just the past few years is any guide, the long run is not far off. One reason is simply that many consumers like electronic services and snap them up when they can get them. In states that are experimenting with electronic payment of government benefits, digital payment, as against bringing a check to the bank, has proved popular with beneficiaries and businesses alike. Meanwhile, consumers increasingly are using personal finance software packages to conduct their banking business.

A deeper reason for the inevitability of the electronic revolution in payments, however, is the powerful pull that is likely to be exerted by what economists call network externalities. An externality is a cost or benefit of any given economic transaction whose value is not (or not fully) reflected in the prices of the goods traded. That is, someone gets something useful that he has not himself paid for, or suffers a loss for which he is not compensated. The idea of a network externality applies this concept to a situation in which, somewhat self-referentially, a product or service becomes more useful as more people decide to use it. For example, one person's decision to sign up for e-mail has the side benefit

of making e-mail itself a more appealing medium because, as more people join, the system becomes a better way to communicate. Such communications networks may grow only gradually at first but then reach a tipping point: that is, a point where enough people are connected to make the service seem very useful indeed, even indispensable. Then, perhaps quite suddenly, people rush to join.

Far from being exceptional, this mode of growth—slow start-up, followed by an explosive expansion—has been typical in the world of information technology. The examples of telephones, televisions, and videocassette recorders all come readily to mind. The field of finance has been no exception. Neither the credit card nor the debit card is of much use unless consumers know that many merchants will accept it. The more merchants who do so, the more popular the card becomes, and the more popular the card, the more merchants who will sign up.

The same pattern should repeat itself with electronic commerce. The growth of electronic commerce may well parallel that of the Internet, itself a striking demonstration of the power of network externalities. That the number of World Wide Web users is believed to be more than doubling every year is impressive enough, but even more compelling is that the number of Web pages, estimated at between 50 million and 100 million in 1996, grows by a factor of two to *ten* every year, depending on whose estimates you prefer. As the Web's information content explodes, it will attract more users, in turn drawing forth still more information.

Intermediation: Squeezing the Middlemen

The benefits of efficient payment are not to be dismissed. But they are for the most part savings that come from doing more cheaply what is done already. Advances in intermediation—or to be more precise, in disintermediation—offer benefits of a higher order: benefits from reorganizing, sometimes reconceiving, the industry itself. By its nature, information technology makes possible interpersonal contacts on a wider scale than ever before, which means that ordinary consumers will increasingly be able to do for themselves what intermediaries have traditionally done for them. Old-fashioned intermediaries risk becoming like telephone operators in a direct-dial world unless they invent new ways to add value for consumers. So, as the middlemen either fall out of the picture or invent

new services, or both, two things happen: prices drop and consumer choice expands.

Consumers have already seen lower prices in recent decades for some important financial services. In the securities industry, for example, the elimination of fixed brokerage commissions in the mid-1970s has unleashed competition not just between conventional securities firms and discount brokers, but also among the old-line securities brokers themselves. Heightened competition, in turn, has encouraged brokers to pass on to their customers the cost-saving benefits of advances in the processing of trades. Figure 2-3 shows the results: a dramatic decline in commissions.[2] Similarly, the cost of a typical life insurance policy has dropped in real terms over the past several decades, as life insurers have had to compete increasingly with mutual funds as a magnet for consumers' savings.

Perhaps the most widely felt benefits of financial innovation in the past two decades, however, are those realized by anyone who has bought

Figure 2-3. Trends in Brokerage Commission Rates, 1980–95

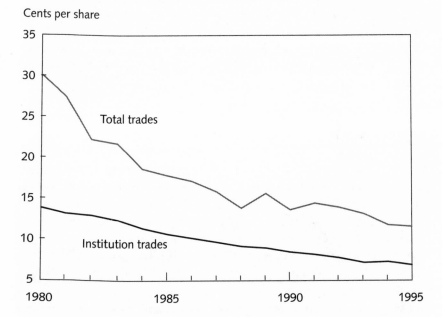

Cents per share

Sources: Greenwich Associates and the Securities and Exchange Commission. "Institutions" are wholesale brokers only.

a home and financed it with a mortgage. The conversion of the individual mortgage into (in effect) a security has broadened the range of investors in mortgages far beyond the savings and loan industry that originally was created to finance home ownership. Today, pension funds, insurance companies, banks, and mutual funds—and not only American ones, but also many financial institutions and investors based abroad—hold mortgage-backed securities in their portfolios. Mortgage borrowers are the beneficiaries of what amounts to a global competition to lend to American home buyers.

The net result, as shown in figure 2-4, is that the spread between interest rates on mortgages and on Treasury securities has narrowed precipitously. To be sure, a significant part of the reduction is due to the credit enhancement provided by such government-sponsored enterprises as Fannie Mae and Freddie Mac. But the deepening of the market for mortgages, made possible by the innovative development of mortgage-

Figure 2-4. Spread of Thirty-Year Mortgage Rates and Thirty-Year Treasury Bonds, 1980–95

Percent

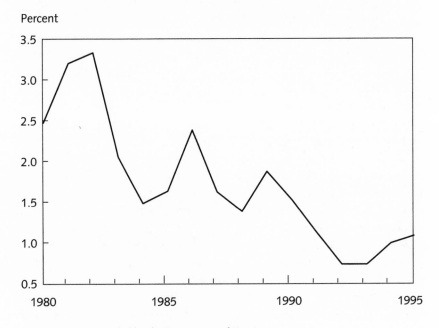

Source: Data compiled by the Department of Treasury.

backed securities themselves, certainly has been important in narrowing the spread, thus reducing the cost of mortgages for millions of Americans.

In fact, the globalization of finance has helped to reduce *all* interest rates by lowering rates on Treasury securities, to which all other rates are loosely tied (with a risk premium above the "risk free" Treasury rate). Thirty years ago, less than 4 percent of the federal government's bonds were held by foreigners. Today, the share is 30 percent and growing. If not for the interest of foreign investors during the past fifteen years, when the U.S. budget deficit soared into previously uncharted territory, interest rates here would have been higher and, correspondingly, investment in new plant and equipment significantly lower.

More broadly, globalization reduces the threat of excessive concentration, which, if unchecked by vigorous competition, can be costly to consumers. In so doing, it improves the prospects for the sort of competition that drives innovation. Some nations have tried to lock out or mitigate the force of foreign competition in finance. Generally, the result of such policies is a sluggish financial sector that trails the cutting edge. America's relatively open financial marketplace helps bring the best services to American consumers while keeping American companies sharp.

Continuing advances in technology, especially the likely growth of electronic commerce conducted over the Internet, should reduce the costs of financial services even further. Financial intermediaries are, after all, just what the term implies: middlemen. While the Internet may not replace them, it will certainly reduce their profit margins by vastly reducing the costs of searching for the best deal. Before much longer, millions of Americans are likely to sit down at home and, with the push of a few buttons, send a software agent off in search of the best rates on certificates of deposit or loans, or the lowest stock commission rates, or the lowest insurance rates, not just here but around the world. And then, having discovered the best choice, consumers will be able to buy on command from a cache of digital cash or by directly debiting their bank accounts on-line. Indeed, for some services, such as long-distance telephone service, personal agents are already here, allowing customers not only to find the cheapest service but to switch to it on-line if they so desire. The continued march of technology may even one day threaten many of the exchanges for financial instruments, which today rely on human cries to match buyers and sellers, but tomorrow may use bits and bytes instead. In such a world of "frictionless" capitalism, as it has been called, all kinds of spreads will be pushed down near their absolute limit, driving inefficient providers and institutions from the marketplace but leaving consumers as clear winners.

The same forces bringing lower prices, meanwhile, should also bring a wider variety of services than consumers have ever known. By bringing financial services not only to their doorsteps but into their homes, the information revolution will make conducting financial business easier and more efficient. Trips to see a banker or broker will become comparative rarities, and sooner than many people may realize.

New providers of financial services will also bring benefits. Financial institutions are, at bottom, information processors, and for years their competitive advantage was their access to financial information and their ability to employ professionals to juggle and analyze it. As software takes over from people, however, and as information grows cheaper to store and transmit, that advantage will continue to erode and new competitors will find it easier to enter the market.

In the recent past, for example, newcomers in the credit business, such as GE Capital and GMAC, were offshoots of manufacturing companies that discovered—learning, in effect, by doing—that they could sell credit as profitably as could the traditional providers. Tomorrow's companies "spinning" in to financial services will be drawn from the sectors holding the keys to the information revolution: software and communications. In 1996 Microsoft and American Express announced an alliance to provide on-line travel services to business customers through both the Internet and in-house corporate computer networks. Intuit, a major player in the personal finance software market, has set up joint ventures with various banks to provide bookkeeping and other financial assistance to the banks' customers. Other alliances, bringing together old-style financial intermediaries with new-style software and network companies, seem to be constantly forming, especially to establish standards to facilitate the use of on-line financial services. Leave aside, for now, the antitrust issues that such linkages might raise; the possibilities for new players to move into financial services, both by themselves and in collaboration with established providers, are many. As companies cross-pollinate, the array of new products and new vehicles for delivery of traditional products will further proliferate.

Moreover, the technologies now reaching maturity offer the promise of the broadest wave of credit democratization to date, in which ordinary

American consumers are likely to benefit from a range of custom-made services offered in greater variety, more conveniently, and more cheaply than ever before. In earlier periods of American history, banks were frequently resented for what was perceived as their power to dictate who could get capital and on what terms. In the future, accounts, portfolios, even investment instruments may soon be custom-made for individuals in ways unheard of today. For example, as personal agents learn their masters' investment choices, they might compile personalized mutual funds from offerings on the Internet: "me" funds. Investors might, by filling out a form on a software "wizard," order corporate bonds with tailor-made maturities and call provisions. An investor's computer might put out a request for a $5,000, eighteen-year-bond with a balloon payment, and various companies' computers might reply with offerings. One might even imagine that at some point individuals and firms may use the electronic highway to obtain an independent credit audit and then issue their own bonds.

Such high-technology, customized financial products are not so far-fetched. Consider, by analogy, the effect of innovation on clothes. Before the industrial revolution, clothes were individually tailored. All but the simplest garments were too expensive for any but the well-to-do to own in quantity or variety. Mass production changed all that, but in the process it required people to conform their expectations to the available sizes and styles. Now some manufacturers of clothing—blue jeans and shoes, for instance—are using new technologies to bring fashion full circle. For not much more money than they spend for off-the-rack apparel, consumers can have their measurements taken and sent straight from a retailer to a factory, where shoes or jeans are quickly manufactured to order. This sort of mass customization, though still in embryo, holds out the prospect of an economy in which the ordinary consumer gets more value for his money than ever before, and there is little reason to believe that the trend will stop with apparel.

To be sure, many Americans will continue to require some face-to-face, person-to-person contact in conducting their financial business. Some will never feel as comfortable buying life insurance by clicking a button on a pulldown menu—and receiving in reply a digital document to be stored on a hard drive—as they do by signing papers in an insurance agent's office and shaking hands. While many investors already place their savings with companies whose representatives they never see or meet in person, they do in any case expect to be able to get a human being on the phone. It is hard to imagine a time when most ordinary consumers, and many business customers as well, will not want to have easy recourse to a human being for advice, help, or complaints. But none of that alters the *direction* of change. Market power is shifting from a relatively staid and stable group of intermediaries offering standardized products at significant markups to a world of consumers who can chart their own course and to a field of new competitors eager to help them.

Risk: Spreading It Thinner

Finally, there will be change for the third major function of finance, spreading risk. Of course, risk is inherent in finance. Indeed, financial institutions exist largely to transfer, diversify, or reduce risk. Financial innovation is, however, rapidly bringing new techniques and new levels of sophistication to the task, largely by exploiting economies of specialization while simultaneously broadening and deepening markets.

To see how this works, consider again the phenomenon of securitization. The transformation of loans into securities has split apart functions—the origination, servicing, and holding of credit—that were previously performed by depository institutions. As a result, specialists in each activity have entered the market. In the mortgage market, for example, mortgage bankers generally do nothing more than originate mortgages and then sell them to investment banks or government-sponsored enterprises, who package them to back their issues of securities representing individual interests in the pool. Other companies specialize in bookkeeping and in servicing loans, collecting mortgage payments from borrowers and routing them to their proper destination. And, as previously noted, now a wide variety of financial institutions, not just banks and thrifts, bear the credit risk by holding the securities backed by the mortgages (and, significantly, they do so in the context of diversified portfolios of assets rather than in portfolios limited by law to a few assets, as was the case with savings and loans). So the marketplace has simultaneously opened up and specialized. In the process, the risk of mortgage defaults has been spread across a far greater population of investors than in the old days when it was heavily concentrated on the books of S&Ls.

In a parallel fashion, financial derivatives have also transformed the market for risk, allowing institutional and even individual investors to hedge risks that they might not want to bear. For example, in a world without options or futures, investors who fear that stock or bond prices may decline would have no choice but to sell their holdings, perhaps incurring a significant tax liability. But with derivatives, investors can hedge against risks of a falling market by selling futures or buying put options. Financial institutions also use derivatives not traded on organized exchanges to hedge against such risks as changes in interest rates or exchange rates. The counterparties to a typical swap agreement—the most conventional form of off-exchange derivative—enter into contracts to redistribute their obligations across varying payment streams: holders of instruments that pay fixed interest rates may want to exchange those payments for ones that vary over time, and vice versa.

More recently, a number of banks have begun to use credit swaps through which banks that believe themselves to be overexposed to a certain type of risk (debt in developing countries in particular) can reduce it by swapping the credit risk (but not the loan itself) with a counterparty willing to assume it. In the few short years since these derivative instruments have been developed, they have grown to cover $50 billion in loans. Some experts believe that the figure could jump to as much as $1 trillion in a few more years.[3]

Derivatives themselves entail various risks; but under normal circumstances risks for any individual derivative contract are no different from those associated with loans and other standard financial instruments. The counterparties may not honor their commitments (credit risk); the market value of the instrument may change because of fluctuations in interest rates, exchange rates, or commodity prices (market risk); and the contracts may fall through because of poor documentation, bankruptcy of one of the parties, or insufficient authority of one of the counterparties (legal risk). Those risks are nothing new in finance, and they are far from unique to derivatives. In fact, at year end 1995, the ten top banks participating in the derivatives market had six times more resources outstanding in loans than in their total exposure to risks from derivatives.

Why then have derivatives become so controversial? One reason is that, because the market has never really been tested in highly abnormal circumstances, it is difficult to know whether derivatives pose truly systemic risks. In addition, as discussed earlier, there is the possibility that the availability of exchange-traded derivatives in particular may make it easier for investors to "dynamically hedge" their positions on the way down, driving down prices in the cash market as well. The sizable leverage that derivatives afford investors may exacerbate this danger. Meanwhile, derivatives contracts that are not traded on organized exchanges tend to be very complex instruments, making their risks difficult to assess even for sophisticated investors.[4]

In any event, a key attribute of many of the new financial instruments is their ability to blur traditional industry boundaries and in the process to convert risk from an insurer's specialty to a marketable commodity. The new asset-backed securities have eroded the case for maintaining a separate thrift industry, since all kinds of institutions and even individuals can now invest in mortgages by buying mortgage-backed securities. One of the most recent and innovative uses of derivatives is to replace or supplement disaster insurance: "catastrophe futures" were pioneered by the Chicago Board of Trade in 1992 and have since been refined. The inventiveness of the marketplace suggests that the pace at which new financial products are introduced will, if anything, pick up in the years ahead. The general level of competition will rise accordingly.

An Industry in Transition

In all of its major functions, then, the financial services industry faces a stream of change over the next decade or two, mostly to the great benefit of the industry's customers. But what of the industry's providers? They, of course, are at the nexus of forces swirling around the digitization and globalization of finance. And for them, change may come less as a stream than as a torrent. The great economist Joseph Schumpeter labeled capitalism a process of "creative destruction." Competition promotes the search for new products and new ways of doing old things. What is comfortable and familiar eventually gets replaced with something new, better, and generally cheaper. But the transition is never easy. Firms and industries that do not adapt to capitalism's constant change die; those that do adapt—or, even better, are successful instigators of change themselves—thrive and grow.

Finance provides many illustrations. For example, the trading rooms of investment banks today, with their sophisticated computers and trading strategies, would be all but unrecognizable to traders of yesteryear. The same is true in insurance and, of course, the mutual fund industry, the latter being a segment of the financial services industry that was virtually unknown before 1960.

Perhaps no part of the financial services industry, however, has undergone a more wrenching transformation than the commercial banking industry, often despite the best efforts of policymakers and regulators to insulate the industry from competition and change. Years ago, banks were able to take the business of borrowing and lending mainly for granted, but those days are long gone. Today banks are merely one of a variety of competitors in the market to deliver credit. They still enjoy a collective monopoly on the handling of demand deposits, that is, deposits that can be withdrawn immediately and against which checks may be written. But this, like the traditional telephone companies' monopoly on copper wires, is a franchise that is arguably no longer worth very much.[5]

In consequence, the traditional business of banking—taking deposits and extending loans—is in relative decline. To be sure, this is a long-term trend, dating as far back as the beginning of this century. Yet it has not been an uninterrupted decline. During the first half of the century the relative shrinkage of banking was very much in evidence, due largely to the growth of pension funds and insurance companies, which were in their infancy at the beginning of the century. The bank share was roughly constant at about 40 percent of assets from 1960 through 1980, but thereafter began shrinking sharply again (figure 2-5). Today, banks' share of all financial intermediary assets is barely 22 percent.

To a considerable extent, the trend illustrated in figure 2-5 is the product of some fundamental economic forces. As economies become more developed, consumers and firms tend to keep a larger share of their wealth outside the banking system and instead use other intermediaries or hold securities directly. In America, this tendency was reinforced in the 1980s when inflation dropped sharply, making real estate much less attractive than stocks and mutual funds as places for people to park their money. The low interest rates of the 1990s have further polished the attractiveness of mutual funds relative to bank deposits. Advances in computer technology have played their part by reducing the cost of attracting and keeping track of the large sums that have poured into the funds. Accordingly, millions of Americans who, two decades ago, would have regarded a stock mutual fund as an exotic investment choice now think nothing of pouring their savings into one

Figure 2-5. Relative Shares of Total Financial Intermediary Assets,
Selected Years, 1945–95

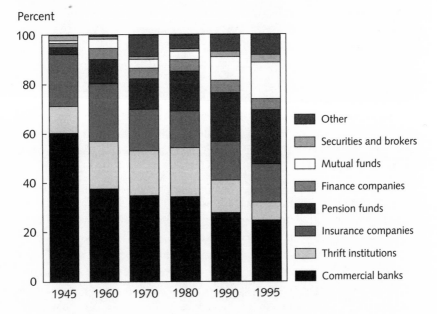

Percent

Source: Federal Reserve Board, Flow of Funds.

(see figure 2-1). Of necessity, banks are responding in kind, becoming
sellers of mutual funds themselves.

Lending, the other half of traditional banking, is also being squeezed.
In part, finance companies, insurers, and securities firms have increased
their share of the lending pie. Nonbank lenders such as GE Capital and
Green Tree Financial have enjoyed spectacular success. As a result, finance companies have been increasing their share of the consumer debt
market.

Meanwhile, many corporate borrowers who once relied on banks for
their funds have turned instead to the markets, issuing short-term commercial paper or longer-term bonds (called "junk bonds" if they are not
highly rated by the credit rating agencies). Between commercial paper
and the growth of nonbank lenders, new competition has eroded banks'
share of the business credit market. Although as recently as 1980 banks
wrote 70 percent of the short-term and medium-term business loans in
America, now their share is barely half.

It may be tempting to conclude from this parade of developments that banks are dying. The truth is that they are thriving, but not by doing what *traditional* banks did. What is under siege today is banking, not banks. Figure 1-5 in chapter 1 provides strong testimony to the resurgence of the banking industry from its near-disastrous experience of the late 1980s. Indeed, in 1996 banks earned record profits in excess of $50 billion.

With competition so much more fierce and banks' market share in decline, how could this be? In part, banks (and thrift institutions, which collectively suffered an even worse fate than banks in the 1980s) gained from the steep drop in short-term interest rates engineered by the Federal Reserve in the beginning of the 1990s: lower rates not only helped lift the economy from recession, they enabled depositories to earn big spreads on their somewhat longer-term loans. More fundamental, however, is that the increasingly stiff competition in their traditional niche has forced banks to transform their business. To earn their keep, they rely less on extending conventional loans and more on charging fees for many services that they once subsidized by drawing on the interest spreads that they earned on their loans. Large sophisticated banks, in particular, have found new ways to assume credit risk and to earn fees in the process: by guaranteeing all or a portion of the loan-backed securities they issue; by providing standby guarantees on the commercial paper issued by corporations (many of whom in the past borrowed from banks directly); and perhaps most important of all, at least for the very largest institutions, by offering and trading various types of derivative instruments.

In combination, all of these off-balance-sheet activities have been accounting for a steadily rising share of the banking industry's income (figure 2-6). That trend ought to give pause to those who would view banks' declining asset base as a symptom of their imminent demise. Similarly, it is a mistake to conclude that America's banking industry has somehow fallen behind its counterparts in Japan and Europe simply because those countries are home to banks much larger in size—as opposed to profitability—than America's biggest. In the more competitive, sophisticated world of finance today, what is happening off the balance sheet can be and often is more important than what is taking place on it.[6]

Dramatic though the recent transformation of banking has already been, even more change is in sight as technology continues to pull apart the various functions now performed by fully integrated banks: product

Figure 2-6. Interest and Noninterest Revenue Shares of Commercial Banks, 1980–95[a]

Percent

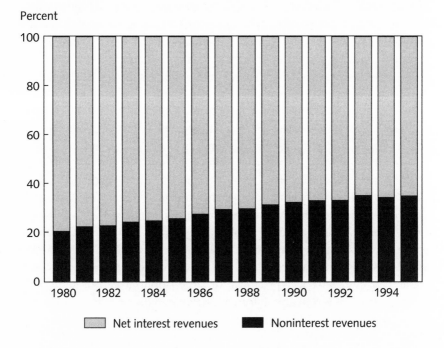

Net interest revenues   Noninterest revenues

Source: FDIC Quarterly Banking Profile Online, 1996.
a. Total revenues is the sum of noninterest and net interest revenues.

origination (deposits, mortgages, and various payments cards such as credit, debit, and stored value); distribution (branches, ATMs, interactive television); and backroom processing (clearing checks and rating credit). To be sure, many institutions may find it cheaper and more advantageous to integrate these functions. But others will find comparative advantage in not performing all of them; indeed, some may perform only product origination, contracting with other businesses to do the rest. Inevitably, as unbundling proceeds, traditional banks will find themselves under increasing pressure. Those that fail to adapt will be the financial dinosaurs of tomorrow.

Banking will not be alone. As we have already observed, all financial intermediaries are threatened by the current and future rise of the ultimate middleman, the Internet. The challenge that all current providers of financial services confront, therefore, is to provide value that users cannot get for themselves. Until recently, financial intermediaries thrived because they enjoyed access to information that no others had. But the Internet and other forms of communication are changing all that. No longer will any particular institution have a lock on any particular kind of information; no longer will bankers, brokers, and underwriters be assured a place in the sun merely by dint of chaperoning a quantum of value from one place to another. The result will be a scramble as banks and other financial services companies struggle to compete with a thousand newcomers, each offering a customized bridge between buyer and seller.

As time goes on, in short, the intermediaries that provide the most value may be those that provide the most information to users of financial services, that is, the intermediaries that organize masses of data to let consumers navigate their way to the customized products they want at the lowest price. Existing banks, brokers, and other providers of financial services whose services are offered on the menu will find their margins shaved to the bone unless they can offer products that are not easily delivered in cyberspace (products for large, sophisticated users, for example) or provide valuable information services themselves.

Coping by Consolidating

As competition intensifies and companies barge into each other's traditional preserves, institutions respond, not unnaturally, by merging and consolidating both within and across traditional industry lines. One major impetus for consolidation is simply that regulation now allows it: regulatory obstacles to geographic consolidation have been lowered. Indeed, since 1980 there have been almost half again as many mergers of banks within multibank holding companies as mergers between firms, a hint that artificial structures designed to circumvent geographic restrictions are being gradually shed. The heightened competition that banks face, too, has impelled them to join forces. As they meet their competitors head-on, banks want to be able to provide a broad range of services in a wide variety of places. Consolidating helps them do so, although it may not guarantee success.[7] And, finally, there is much excess capacity in the financial services industry, especially among depository institutions, and consolidation is a means by which firms can become more efficient.

Whatever the reasons, the result is not in doubt. The number of commercial banks in America held steady at about 14,000 from 1934 through the mid-1980s (figure 2-7). Then it began to drop, to fewer than 10,000 today. Although much of the consolidation was the result of mergers within larger bank holding companies, the number of banking companies also declined, from 12,000 in 1980 to around 8,000 now. It need hardly be added that the savings and loan industry, meanwhile, was facing a painful reorganization: fewer than 40 percent of the 4,000 institutions operating in 1980 are currently in business.

How far and how fast the banking industry's consolidation will proceed, no one can say. Recent economic studies predict further shrinkage in the numbers of banks by the year 2000 of anywhere from 2,000 to almost 6,000 institutions. The implications of the trend, moreover, are debated. Some fear that small businesses will face greater difficulties getting loans

Figure 2-7. Number of Banks in the United States, 1934–97

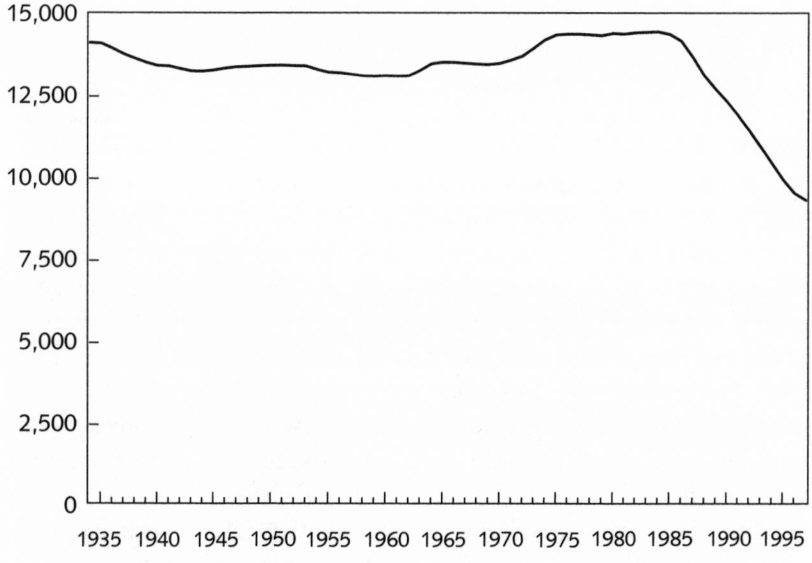

Source: FDIC; 1997 data through June 30.

from fewer, larger financial institutions, especially if mergers reduce competition in local banking markets. But economists at the Office of the Comptroller of the Currency have found that large, out-of-state bank holding companies provide as much if not more small-business lending than in-state bank holding companies and independent banks. Moreover, the traditional geographic limitations on interstate banking tended to depress competition, so their removal could make the industry even more competitive and efficient, thus encouraging lending to small businesses.[8]

Banking is not the only segment of the financial services industry marked by consolidation and merger activity. While in recent years bank mergers have accounted for more than half of the dollar value of all merger and acquisition activity in financial services, several high-profile marriages between banks and securities firms, as well as combinations among non-bank financial companies, have contributed to a continuing reshaping of the financial landscape.

Policy Implications

As chapter 1 argued, too often in the past federal policymakers have erred on the side of promoting stability over change in financial services. That is, too often they have sought to resist rather than welcome innovation, whether by placing direct controls on the financial products that could be offered to the public (interest rate controls, for example), forbidding companies to branch into new regions, or blocking firms' attempts to compete across traditional industry lines. Without doubt, such efforts were well intentioned. They were thought likely to promote a sound financial system, reducing the likelihood of untoward shocks and messy failures. But it ought to be clear from the discussion in this chapter that the sheer magnitude of the forces currently washing over the financial services industry are enormous. They cannot be bottled up, circumvented, or wishfully waved aside. The days when the managers and owners of financial institutions, as well as policymakers, could assume that the world would basically stay the same and that market forces could be made to conform to the dictates of policy are over.

But all of that does not mean policymakers have no role in the financial world of the future. Their tasks—minimizing risk to the economy while looking out for the interests of taxpayers and consumers—continue to be essential. For government to meet those challenges will require not only reforms of the details of the regulatory regime for finance but a reconception of government's role. Various such reforms are discussed in greater detail in the chapters that follow. By way of a road map, however, it may be useful to close this chapter by previewing the main implications for policy of the forces for change that have been thus far been described.

Chapter 3 takes up government's role as promoter of competition, a job with at least three elements. One is to remove impediments to competition that are created or sustained by the government itself. Although many of those impediments were created with the best of intentions and may have been well suited to their times, today neither markets nor consumers are generally well served by restrictions on competition, except in very particular cases. A second element is to help set rules for emerging technologies, notably electronic money. Some rules for electronic money are undoubtedly necessary; the question is how to set them so as to protect consumers adequately without straitjacketing markets, which offer many consumer protections of their own. Finally, competition must be not only allowed and enabled, but also maintained and protected, so that private barriers do not arise in place of public ones. That, however, may be more easily said than done. Just as network externalities may eventually help accelerate the penetration of new technologies and services throughout the economy, they may also make it possible for one or two firms to dominate the industry or activity to which network externalities apply. If that happens, antitrust enforcers must make sure that any such gatekeeper does not use its market power to distort the market and shut out competitors.

Chapter 4 turns to a different sort of challenge: that of systemic risk. Arguably, preventing a financial calamity and the damage it could do both to taxpayers and the broader economy is the most important of government's roles in finance. And it has become evident that the government's approach to that task is due for an overhaul. One reason is that the old approach has grown incoherent. Another is that the rising volume of bank payments, especially those flowing from foreign exchange transactions, is subjecting the payments system to increasing stress. Yet another reason for reform is that, more than ever, regulators need the help of markets. The growing complexity of financial instruments and the big-bank interlinkages impelled by those instruments have complicated financial regulators' jobs. As change continues, they will need to be assisted by well-informed private actors with money at risk. And they will need to be guided by a philosophy that allows failures to happen but that contains failures' impact and gives markets more time to make adjustments. In practice, that means quarantining troubled institutions before their problems spread, providing a steadier stream of information about the health of major institutions, enlisting markets to help set and maintain safety rules, and reducing or eliminating dangerous lags in the payments system.

Finally, chapter 5 takes up the question of access to financial services. The government has, laudably and for the most part successfully, worked to extend access to credit to whole classes of Americans who in earlier generations had been overlooked: middle-income homebuyers, students, and more recently women, lower-income borrowers, and members of minority groups. That job is not finished; but as the financial services industry changes, older broad-gauged tools will need to be supplemented with approaches aimed more specifically at the neediest. A coequal task is to help make sure that the digital revolution does not leave behind inner-city residents who lack access to bank accounts or other forms of reasonably priced payments services, which are essential connections to a modern economy. In an age when computers will assist consumers in searching out the least expensive financial services, a challenge for policymakers will be to help give all Americans a reasonable chance to connect with the possibilities of the information economy.

A Guiding Framework

The problems to be discussed in the next three chapters are of many different kinds and require different kinds of attention. Nonetheless, a few principles shape the framework within which they can best be solved.

First, policy needs to appreciate and keep its sights set on the importance of innovation. The benefits of innovation are probably greater than ever before—and are growing. As competition in the financial industry intensifies and as the costs of gathering and processing information shrink, the capacity of providers to bring new products and services to market expands. By extension, as the potential gains from innovation increase, so do the costs of blocking innovation. Moreover, innovation has long been America's strong suit in a competitive world and can continue to set the U.S. financial services industry apart.

To bear in mind the importance of innovation sounds like an easy thing for policymakers to do, but in truth it often is not. The hazards, mishaps, and abuses that regulations are designed to prevent are usually all too obvious, or else the regulations would never have been imposed in the first place; but the products and services that never reach the market or the new techniques and tools that never reach fruition are by definition invisible. Thus the cost of measures that dampen innovation and entrepreneurial energy, such as the old-style restraints on financial services competition, is hard to see. Yet it is real. Change will bring new hazards and uncertainties, and with those will come pleas for protection and regulation. Often regulation is appropriate, but it should be designed, whenever possible, to maximize the benefits of innovation.

A second guiding principle goes hand in hand with the first: where possible, work with and exploit the power of markets. Resisting, as opposed to channeling and exploiting, market-driven change is likely to be not only counterproductive but futile. There are already so many different sorts of companies providing so many different services that trying to stop particular firms from offering particular products, or requiring that segments of the industry conform to shapes determined by policymakers, will be like squeezing a water balloon: unlikely to improve the shape of things and likely to create a mess. If one sort of company is barred from one sector of the market, other sorts will simply move in to fill the gap. Moreover, the pace of innovation and the growing complexity of the economy both militate against regulators' attempting to look over everybody's shoulder all the time. In many cases, markets can be enlisted in support of policy, to the benefit of both. In the twentieth-century regulatory framework, too often that lesson was overlooked.

Third, again related: attempting to micromanage the economy to achieve broad governmental aims is an increasingly hopeless job. The new world of financial innovations will inevitably be one of rapid experimentation and ferment where many institutions, including some large ones, may rise quickly and fall just as fast. Failures and mistakes, often large ones, must be regarded as givens. The goal of policy must not be to prevent failure in each case, but to create a financial environment in which companies and investors are likeliest to be careful and in which, if they are not careful enough, their troubles can be contained so as not to endanger innocent bystanders.

Finally, a fourth general principle is that where possible the scope of policies should be tailored so as to exceed as little as possible the boundaries of the problems being addressed. Of course, in some cases regulators have little choice but to set broad rules. But as a point of principle, narrower approaches should always be explored: in many instances they will be found to be effective. Thus the next chapter will argue for a selective, case-by-case approach to antitrust matters rather than an attempt to ordain which sorts of companies may and may not merge or form alliances. The fourth chapter will argue that safety-and-soundness regulation should be focused most strongly on the institutions and sectors that are at the heart of systemic risk, notably money center banks and, especially, the payments and settlement system. The fifth chapter will argue for targeted approaches to expanding financial opportunity.

All of these principles will be of use in understanding the ideas discussed in the chapters that follow. And, more important, they will doubtless be of use in framing better ideas that have yet to emerge.

Appendix: A Brief Guide to Derivatives

Because there are so many different types of instruments that are referred to as derivatives, they are often classified in several ways. One distinction is between derivatives that are *forward* contracts, in which a party *obligates* itself to purchase or sell at some fixed date in the future a good or instrument at a fixed price, and *option* contracts, in which the buyer simply obtains the *right* to buy or sell the good or instrument at a fixed price in the future. A *futures* contract is an example of a forward contract. So is a *swap* arrangement, in which the parties may agree to make different sets of payments (one at a fixed rate of interest, the other at a variable interest rate) over a fixed period of time. Both forward contracts and options contracts are considered to be derivatives because their value depends on, or is derived from, the current market value of the good or instrument in question, plus some adjustment reflecting interest, the risk of price fluctuation in the future, and, for a commodity, costs of storage.

Another common distinction is made between derivatives that are traded in organized exchanges, such as those for futures and options, and derivative contracts (such as swaps) that either are traded off the exchanges or over the counter (OTC), or are not traded at all. Organized exchanges typically act as clearinghouses that guarantee payments by the parties to the transaction while requiring traders to provide security down payments up front (like margin) in advance to cover potential losses. For OTC trades, by contrast, the counterparties are at risk of nonpayment by the other party, and typically no up-front payments are made.[9]

Trading in derivatives on organized exchanges has grown dramatically. In 1972 there were fewer than 20 million futures contracts on the American markets; by 1994 the number had risen to well over 400 million, a twentyfold increase. Off-exchange derivatives have also mushroomed in volume. At the end of 1996 the total outstanding "notional" amount of derivatives held in all U.S. commercial banks reached $20 trillion, more than double the amount four years earlier. Eight banks accounted for 94 percent of the total volume. Roughly two-thirds of the total involved interest rate contracts, with virtually all of the balance involving foreign exchange contracts.

The notional figures do not accurately indicate the risks to which counterparties to derivatives contracts are exposed, however, because they refer to a benchmark (such as the principal amount of a loan) against which the exchange of cash actually due (such as interest payments) is calculated. A much more revealing indicator of risk instead is the cost of *replacing* derivatives contracts, which determines their market value. By this measure, the ten largest banks that dominate derivatives activity actually had at risk at year-end 1995 approximately $130 billion, according to calculations using the banks' own models.

Both *end-users* and *dealers* participate in derivatives transactions. End-users typically use derivatives contracts, especially futures and options, to hedge against certain financial risks; some end-users are speculators using the contracts as a relatively inexpensive way to bet on price movements. Most financial institutions and many commercial firms are end-users of derivatives. Dealers, in contrast, earn income by serving as the counterparty for derivatives, those who might write options contracts, for example. Dealers tend to be large financial institutions.

Derivatives reduce the costs of entering and leaving the market. This is, of course, good for investors who want to hedge their positions. Whether it is good for the safety of the market as a whole is not clear. By making it easier to leave the market as well as enter it, the availability of derivatives may facilitate so-called dynamic hedging strategies that call for selling into a down market. In this way, selling in the derivatives market can feed a downward spiral in cash markets.

Moreover, unlike the investor who buys an underlying security and must pay for its entire value, the purchaser of a futures contract can put up in cash or liquid Treasury securities a small fraction of the value of the contract, technically known as a *performance bond*. This takes advantage of leverage in an almost literal sense: that is, it enables the purchaser to reap very big payoffs or suffer very large losses if the face value of his contract changes by even a relatively small amount. Leverage also makes it cheaper for speculators to gamble on price movements, and therein lies another potential for risk. Two simple examples of futures and options contracts illustrate the point.

Suppose, for example, the investor can buy a futures contract on the S&P 500 index whose face value is $350,000 by putting up only $17,500, or 5 percent of the contract's face value. If the S&P futures index goes up by 5 percent, raising the face value of the contract to $367,500, then the investor has made $17,500, a gain of fully 100 percent on his capital. The same effect works in reverse, however. A 5 percent drop in the face value of the contract, or $17,500, would completely wipe out the investor's position, and the clearinghouse would require him to post additional margin of about $17,000 to retain the position.

Options afford a similar degree of leverage, but without as much downside risk because the most that the purchaser of an option can lose is its purchase price. Consider, for example, the purchaser of a *call option*, which gives the right to the owner to buy a stock at $10 a share. If the market price of the option rises to $12, the option is said to be "in the money" by $2 a share. If the purchaser of the option paid only $1 for it, he or she has made 100 percent on the money from just a 20 percent change in the price of the stock. (The relative percentage payoffs or losses from the option become even more advantageous or disadvantageous as the percentage change in the price of the stock grows larger.) The risk in the options market is borne by those who write the options. They pocket the purchase price if the option later proves worthless, but can run up potentially large obligations if the options are later exercised.

There have been a number of celebrated instances in recent years— the $1.4 billion loss by the British bank Barings in particular—in which financial institutions have suffered major losses associated with derivatives. A common factor in most of these cases is that management failed to monitor and control rogue traders who put their institutions at risk. A central challenge for regulators in the future is to ensure that managers exert tighter controls over their trading operations.

3

· ·

Energizing Competition

THE QUESTION of whether to admit new competition into finance has been settled—not by Congress or by regulatory officials, but by markets. Even if politicians and regulators were prepared to try very hard, they would find that building a seawall against the rising tide of competition in finance is an impossible job, one that at best might divert or temporarily stave off change, but that in the end could not stop it. The first two chapters of this report have tried to make clear why this is so. First, the old regulatory paradigm that viewed competition as the enemy of stability is now in tatters, largely (but not entirely) refashioned by regulators and financial providers alike. Second, new technology and new financial instruments and techniques have made nonsense of the idea that the financial services market can be segmented into several different kinds of providers, with walls built between them. Securitization, globalization, digitization, and the rise of such new competitors as mutual funds have meant that financial services of all sorts are now provided by companies of many kinds and in many places.

For policymakers, the question is not *whether* to allow new competition in financial services, but at what pace and under what conditions to permit it. In making the world safe for competition—and in making competition safe for the world—the detailed decisions are many and intricate, but most can be subsumed under a few basic questions. First, what impediments should be removed to allow robust and healthy competition? Second, what should government do to protect the interests of taxpayers—who ultimately stand behind the deposit insurance system—as old barriers come down and depositories embark on potentially hazardous new ventures? Third, what rules of the road, if any, should the government set for the newest vehicle on the financial highway, electronic money? Fourth, what should government do to help make sure that markets stay competitive and that abuses and excessive concentration are minimized? Finally, in a more open, competitive world, what needs to be done to protect financial markets and the economy from instability and shock?

This last question, arguably the most important, will be the subject of the next chapter. About the others there is more to say than can be fully explored in the short space at hand in this report. But the following discussion may at least help clarify the issues, each of which is taken up in turn.

Removing Impediments to Competition

Few if any other countries in the world have committed themselves as vigorously to the ethic of competition as has America. Yet for most of this country's history that ethic never took hold as firmly in finance as in other areas of federal policy. As chapter 1 showed, generations of policymakers tended to take a dim view of freewheeling competition in finance, regarding it both as a threat to the stability and safety of the financial system and as an invitation to dangerous concentrations of power. The reasons for this suspicion of open competition were many: the nation's agrarian background, with its Jacksonian distrust of Wall Street and of people who make money with money; the heritage of trust-busting, from the days when the great financiers seemed to have fingers in every pie and designs on every market; the fear that unfettered banks and securities firms would put short-term profits ahead of sound judgment, taking unwise risks; and the realization that financial instability, especially bank failures, can damage the broader economy in ways that turmoil in other industries usually does not.

Whatever the causes, of the outcome there can be little doubt: the government itself has often stood in the way of open competition in finance—not just accidentally, but as a deliberate matter of policy, as chapter 1 detailed. "We regulators and other government policymakers have too often been part of the problem, discouraging—not encouraging—innovation," Eugene Ludwig, the Comptroller of the Currency, said in 1996. "Banks have been so restricted by laws and regulations in the products and services they could offer for so long that I believe the innovative spirit of banking had been stifled." Although today banks and other depositories are well down the road toward providing more innovative and wide-ranging product lines, until the 1980s one bank was nearly identical to the next. They were like restaurants that served only two or three dishes or automakers that produced only two or three styles of car. And the major reason was that the government's controls on their products actively discouraged inventiveness in finance.

In fairness, government was not the only reason for finance's relatively limited offerings. Technology also played an important part. In the past, computational power was mostly limited to what each banker or insurance agent knew about his customers. Each provider might know his own clients well, but he would have had a hard time, in the days of eyeshades and adding machines, performing a sophisticated spreadsheet analysis of portfolio-wide credit risk. Moreover, in the days of paper records and carbon copies, exchanging information was complicated and expensive, and slicing it into many different sorts of marketable quanta—bits of knowledge of value to others—was nearly impossible. So, naturally, service providers specialized and segmented. Each offered a few core products, built around a few broad categories of knowledge, not because of any law of nature, but because no one could talk to enough other people at once or crunch enough numbers fast enough to make anything but standardized deals. Having made its deals, each provider then held them on its own books, because there was no way to bundle and sell them. Technology has changed all that. Lenders sell their loans to investors they will never see or know, and those investors, in turn, neither know nor care whether the loans standing behind any particular asset-backed security were originally written by a commercial bank, a finance company, a mortgage bank, or some other provider.

In today's world, even if it made sense to bar competition between financial service providers of differing notional type, doing so is no longer possible—not, at least, in any rational way. And it does not make sense, least of all from the consumers' standpoint. In the main, fully competitive markets, far from allowing the strong to wipe out the weak and dominate the market (as policymakers earlier in this century tended to fear), instead typically bring better service and more choices. Just ask the millions of investors who have benefited from the lower commissions since the fixed commission system was abandoned in the mid-1970s.

Actually, investors are still being denied the full benefits of competition in securities markets, thanks to outmoded institutions. In this digital age when seemingly everything is being reduced to zeros and ones, it seems anomalous, to say the least, for American securities markets to continue trading in minimum increments of one-eighth of a dollar, a historical relic dating back to the divided Spanish dollar (the piece of eight) of the 1700s. The archaic rules against trading in finer increments than 12.5 cents almost certainly harm marketplace participants by making prices sticky, offering sellers less than they might otherwise reap and costing buyers more than they otherwise need pay.[1] Moreover, the current system confuses investors. "Even those of us who work in this industry every day have to go through many mental gymnastics to determine the profit on a stock sold for 27⅞ that was bought at 19¼," former Securities and Exchange Commissioner Steven Wallman has said.

It is more than welcome news therefore that the New York Stock Exchange announced in June 1997 that it was intending to honorably retire the fractional trading system by the year 2000 and replace it with decimalization, as Commissioner Wallman initially suggested, as SEC Chairman Arthur Levitt later endorsed, and as would have been mandated for all stock exchanges in legislation proposed by Representatives Michael Oxley and Edward Markey (a step that now seems unnecessary). The NYSE's move came on the heels of a move by NASDAQ to have all stocks on its system traded in sixteenths, which the NYSE itself will do for some interim period before switching to the decimal system.[2]

The larger constraints on competition, however, come from government policy itself, notably the market-segmenting restrictions. The old product-line barriers sequestering banks from other institutions have now become so porous as to hinder open competition without serving any clear public policy purpose at all. They have become, largely, rules that are there because they are still there. No wonder, then, that regulators have found ways to pull one brick after another from the wall—without, however, fully tearing it down.

As the country prepares to enter a new century, the time is right symbolically as well as substantively to make a clean break. A number of studies have found that there are sizable inefficiencies in the financial services industry, which added competition could help wring out by unleashing managerial and technological expertise gained in each of the separate sectors and using it in the others. For example, a preliminary analysis by economists at the Federal Reserve Board has estimated that costs of banking services could be reduced as much as 20 percent if all inefficiencies among banks were removed. Even larger inefficiencies— exceeding 50 percent—have been estimated for the life insurance industry. And a wealth of evidence indicates that deregulation and the accompanying innovations it has spawned have led to major cost reductions in other industries—airlines, railroads, and trucking. According to the Bureau of Economic Analysis, in 1995 American households spent nearly $300 billion on brokerage, insurance, and banking services. Business spending on financial services was of comparable magnitude. Accordingly, even if the added competition from breaking down existing barriers between segments of the financial services industry reduced costs as little as 1 percent—and there are good reasons to suppose that this estimate is highly conservative—the potential gains to all users would be in excess of $5 billion a year.

For more than fifteen years, Congress has debated proposals for removing the remaining legal barriers that prevent full-scale competition between the various providers of financial services: the Glass-Steagall Act's barriers to commercial bank participation in investment banking, the restrictions on owners and affiliates of banks, and the artificial distinctions between banks and thrifts. So far the debates have been to little avail.[3] True, as discussed in chapter 1, regulators and the states have stepped into the breach and taken matters, gradually to be sure, into their own hands. For example, after looking on as stalemate continued in Congress over the previous four years, the Comptroller of the Currency issued new regulations in late 1996 establishing procedural rules for entertaining applications by national banks, through separately capitalized subsidiaries, to engage in various financial activities that might be deemed to be part of the "business of banking" or "incidental to banking." In addition, in December 1996 the Federal Reserve further liberalized the securities underwriting authority of bank affiliates, a decision that has since unleashed a spate of purchases of securities firms by major banks (at this writing, more than forty bank holding companies have created or acquired securities firms).

Nonetheless, incremental deregulation within the bounds of existing law is not an adequate substitute for broader legislative action—action that ensures a level playing field for bank and nonbank competitors alike and thus maximum benefits for consumers. Regulators may find cause to hold up mergers or new ventures in particular cases, and they may rightly insist that firms and investors take adequate precautions when venturing into volatile markets. But when presented with a company or industry that wants to enter a formerly protected or sequestered market or that wants to put a new product before the public, policymakers' first instinct should be to let consumers, rather than federal policy, choose winners and losers.

Protecting Taxpayers

The fact remains, however, that finance is different from other industries. Government cannot simply wave its hands and take a walk. The activities, especially the more risky undertakings, of banks directly involve the government for at least two compelling reasons: because the failure of a rash of banks poses "systemic risks" to the wider economy in ways that failures of nonfinancial institutions do not and because the deposit insurance that has been introduced to reduce systemic risk (and provide a safe haven for small investors) ultimately is backed by the taxpaying public. Accordingly, the government has two key interests, both of which may impinge on banks' freedom to compete at will with other institutions. First, government needs to make sure that banks' behavior does not put taxpayers unduly at risk. Second, government also needs to make sure that the presence of taxpayers' indemnification does not lead banks to put themselves unduly at risk.

The architects of twentieth-century financial policy, and their successors in the postwar years, were hardly blind to those concerns. They understood clearly that federally insuring bank deposits could lead to a variety of dangerous temptations. Banks might put taxpayers' money at risk by sinking it in sweetheart deals with sister companies, or the failure of a bank's affiliate might bring down the bank itself, forcing an expensive taxpayer bailout. Or, indeed, the very existence of deposit insurance might attenuate market discipline—so much so that depositories would be free to invest wildly while insured depositors benignly looked on (which is exactly what happened in the thrift crisis).

The old approach to this complex of problems, however, was only half right. Sensibly, it imposed capital standards (unfortunately, poorly enforced during the 1980s) and bank supervision to help make sure that insured depositories walked the straight and narrow. But, not so sensibly, it also sought to separate banks from the rest of the market, thus (it was presumed) reducing the likelihood that their fiduciary judgment might be clouded by empire-building ambitions.

As this report has been at pains to argue, the attempt to wall off banks is doomed. Yet it remains undeniably the case that taxpayer-insured funds are special and pose a variety of unique risks. If banks are to be allowed to affiliate as they please and to venture into all sorts of commercial businesses, those risks need to be addressed.

The problem of sweetheart deals is not hard to cope with, at least in principle. The foremost concern is that institutions that benefit from deposit insurance will have incentives to take foolish risks at the behest of their nonbank relatives, thereby compromising the safety of the insured depositories themselves. A bank might, for example, make unwarranted loans on preferential terms to its affiliates or subsidiaries or to their customers. Such loans would be a backdoor way of propping up the subsidiary—and, of course, the bank itself might break if the subsidiary that it was supporting collapsed. However, the sweetheart deal problem has already been solved, for the most part, through restrictions under existing law on the granting of loans to affiliates; and those restrictions can as effectively apply in the more liberalized environment of tomorrow as in the relatively constrained environment of yesteryear.[4]

Another way a company that mixed banking with other businesses might be lured toward risky behavior is if an affiliate or subsidiary got into financial trouble. In that case, the bank might be pressed to come to its sister company's aid—either voluntarily, out of a desire to protect its own or its parent company's reputation or because a court might disregard the technical, legal firewall between the bank and the nonbank. If the bank had to dip too deeply into its pockets to bail out its relative, then its safety might be compromised. Such a bailout, true, could not take the form of a loan to the affiliate, because of the restrictions just noted. If allowed to do so, however, the bank could give aid in the form of a capital infusion to its ailing partner. Or the bank holding company might provide such an infusion, drawing on its bank subsidiary as a source of funds (in the form of a dividend).

Yet another worry is that deposit insurance amounts to a subsidy for banks and thrifts, because it attracts customers who want the unique security of a government safety net, and that this subsidy could be used to support the nonbanking activities of a depository's affiliates or subsidiaries. Recent reforms, however, have greatly reduced the extent to which deposit insurance is an implicit subsidy. Stricter capital requirements, prompt corrective action, requirements that bank holding companies guarantee capital restoration plans imposed on banks, and the introduction of risk-related deposit insurance premiums—actions discussed in chapter 1 and in more detail in the next chapter—have largely wrung the subsidy value out of deposit insurance. Moreover, banks pay a price for deposit insurance in the form not just of insurance premiums but also of fees they pay bank supervisors and the measures they must take to comply with regulatory safeguards. While some small net subsidy may still remain—on account of the recent elimination of deposit insurance premiums for the safest banks—its presence is too insignificant to justify the continued restrictions on competition, which unnecessarily raise costs for consumers and impair innovation.[5]

In fact, many banks or their holding companies are already engaged to some extent, under existing law in some states and pursuant to regulation at the federal level, in a variety of businesses not traditionally associated with banking, including selling insurance, real estate, stocks, and mutual funds. And, so far, no safety-related problems to speak of have arisen from those activities. Instead, when banks or thrifts have gotten into financial peril, it has been because they have blundered in using their *traditional lending powers*. Indeed, the savings and loan crisis established that merely preventing cross-ownership may do little or nothing to improve lenders' judgment. Effectively, hundreds of thrifts became speculators in real estate in the 1980s, driven far more by financial considerations than by ownership arrangements. Separateness is no guarantee of soundness.

Nonetheless, policymakers would be mistaken to ignore the possibility that some or conceivably many banks or their holding companies, when given more power to compete in more kinds of businesses, may take advantage of the liberalized environment to assume more risks and leave taxpayers holding the bag. How, then, can policy minimize risk while maximizing competition?

The approach taken by two previous presidential administrations has been to allow only holding companies, rather than banks themselves (or their subsidiaries), to engage in a broad menu of financial activities while also requiring that banks belonging to these holding companies be well capitalized. The idea was that if the banks were sturdy, their parent companies could safely broaden into new businesses. Although this approach was not accepted by Congress, it did have the advantage of building on existing bank-holding-company law. Moreover, by limiting the exercise of broader nonbank powers to holding companies whose banks were well capitalized, it addressed the concern that insured banks might use their broadened powers to expose taxpayers to heightened risk.

Requiring banks to conduct their nonbanking operations through affiliates rather than subsidiaries, however, is unduly costly, since it requires banks to set up holding companies, which entails an unnecessary additional layer of corporate management and expenses (as well as the inconvenience and expense of dealing with two regulators rather than one). The holding-company approach also rests on the false premise that a bank—or for that matter, the deposit insurance system—is somehow more insulated from a nonbanking activity if that activity is conducted in an *affiliate* of the bank (owned by a holding company) rather than in a *subsidiary* of the bank. One reason this premise is unfounded is that the restrictions on banks' supplying capital or loans to their nonbank siblings can be applied with equal force whether the nonbank is an affiliate or a subsidiary. Another consideration is that, just as a bank belonging to a holding company must meet its capital requirement regardless of the nature and extent of its affiliate's operations, so banks also can and should be required to raise *additional* capital to carry out the nonbanking operations of their subsidiaries.[6] In fact, the Comptroller's recent ruling allowing national banks to carry out an array of activities in subsidiaries included such a requirement. Finally, if policymakers are concerned about any small subsidy from the federal safety net "leaking out" to nonbank activities, this leakage is equally possible whether those activities are located as subsidiaries of the bank (and thus financially supported from bank funds) or as affiliates (which are funded by holding companies that, in turn, depend for their financial health on dividends bequeathed to them by their bank subsidiaries).

Beyond those considerations, the Treasury Department has urged Congress to include in any financial modernization package a provision making clear that creditors of the nonbanking entity, whether it is a subsidiary or affiliate of a bank, cannot "pierce the corporate veil" so as to charge obligations of the subsidiary or affiliate against federally insured banks. This additional measure, coupled with each of the foregoing protections plus the continuation of an effective system of prompt corrective action, would ensure that banks cannot be weakened—voluntarily or involuntarily—if their nonbank operations run into trouble. With all of these protections in place, banks should be allowed to choose whether to locate their nonbank activities in subsidiaries or affiliates.

To be sure, it is possible to imagine even more foolproof methods of walling off a bank (and any deposit insurance subsidy that it may receive) from any nonbanking activities. One that has been suggested would condition the exercise of nonbanking activities (beyond those that holding companies or banks may conduct under existing law) on a requirement that the bank back all its deposits (or, in a less restrictive form, all its insured deposits) with safe, liquid assets, such as Treasury bonds and highly rated commercial paper and municipal bonds. A suitable transition period could be allowed for institutions to comply with the asset restrictions. With the introduction and effective implementation of the prompt corrective action feature of FDICIA, however, it is not clear how much additional protection such a "narrow" or "collateralized deposit" banking requirement actually would provide to the banking system or whether it would be worth the disruption it would cause to current relationships between banks and their borrowers.

Finally, a question remains as to how much freedom banking organizations should have in their nonbanking operations: whether they should be restricted to "finance" as such or be completely unrestricted. Critics of mixing banking and finance with commerce express concerns over the undue concentration of economic and political power that "super banking-commercial giants" may come to enjoy. They also argue, with some justification, that banks are likely to find fewer opportunities for synergies in undertaking commercial, as opposed to strictly financial, activities. Finally, they charge that banks allied with commercial businesses would face conflicts of interest and either bias their lending toward affiliates or away from competitors of affiliates.

Those who take the opposite side of the argument observe that the logic suggesting that safeguards can effectively wall off banks from the financial misfortunes of their affiliated nonbanking operations applies with equal force to both financial and commercial activities. Meanwhile, they note that as long as lending markets are competitive, then no customer can be disadvantaged by a bank that biases its lending one way or another because of the availability of alternatives (which, in turn, would dissuade banks from engaging in such bias in the first place). In addition, proponents of dropping current barriers to mixing banking and commerce point to the difficulties of distinguishing between "finance" and "commerce." Is an information provider that enables its customers to use information of all types "financial" or "commercial?" Efforts to draw bright lines, it is argued, are likely to be just as doomed as past efforts to define the terms "closely related to banking" or "incidental to banking," which have been steadily expanded over time to meet the changing facts in the marketplace. Finally, supporters of dropping all restrictions on what kinds of enterprises can own a bank point to current "unitary" thrift holding companies—firms owning a single thrift—which a number of commercial companies (and increasingly, nonbank financial enterprises) have used to enter the depository business, thus far without encountering or generating the dangers voiced by critics of mixing banking and commerce.

In short, the "banking-commerce" issue is a vexing one that Congress will have to wrestle with as it completes work on financial modernization legislation.[7]

Setting Rules of the E-Road

Competition only functions, of course, in the context of rules, which may be set by social traditions, private markets, government policies, or, in practice, all of the above. Markets would crumble into chaos without clear and detailed rules securing property and without binding mechanisms to settle disputes. One of the beauties of markets is their ability to *evolve* rules as people discover how to trade for the maximum advantage of all concerned. Yet government plays an essential role. It enforces contracts and punishes fraud through the judicial system; it defines fundamental marketplace concepts, such as intellectual property (patents, trademarks); and it sets ground rules in applying those concepts (how long patent rights are retained, what happens to unclaimed assets at death, and so on). In those ways and others, the government defines the rules of the road for markets, allowing private traffic to get from here to there in a safe, stable environment. Moreover, in finance in particular, the government seeks to protect consumers in a few basic ways: by requiring honest disclosure in transactions, for example, and by limiting the losses of consumers when credit cards are stolen or when banks fail.

In most of those functions, the government's basic role is well established and intricately worked out. Property and tort rules have their roots in the ancient common law; rules against counterfeiting and intellectual theft go back to the earliest years of the republic. But now economists, financiers, and policymakers find themselves in an odd position: the development of electronic money is forcing them to ask again, as their ancestors did centuries ago, basic questions about what money is, who should provide it, and on what terms.

Take, for example, a stored value card, or "smart card." Say it contains a computer chip carrying up to $100 of electronic money, to be debited by a merchant at the point of sale. What, precisely, is this card? It looks a lot like cash. People use it in small, or smallish, denominations to make daily purchases. They carry it in their pockets and use it in vending machines. When they exhaust it, they must replenish it, as they would a purse. If it functions as hoped, it will be widely accepted for transactions of all sorts, settled (at least from the consumer's point of view) on the spot, and usable without delays as payment authorizations clear. So, if it walks the walk and talks the talk, surely it must be cash? If so, perhaps the rule should be "finders keepers, losers weepers," as with ordinary currency. Perhaps, for that matter, the government should issue smart cards, as it does cash.

But the case is not so clear. Debit cards, which people use in place of checks at the cash register, are plainly not cash: they draw from bank accounts, which are federally insured. The difference between a debit card and a smart card is that when a customer uses a debit card, the merchant must electronically communicate with the issuer and confirm the withdrawal, simply because the account information is held, physically, at a distant bank. The smart card merely moves the account information from a huge computer far away to a tiny computer inside the card itself. Perhaps, then, the smart card is just a handier sort of debit card. In that case it is not like cash, but like a portable bank account. On that reasoning, some observers argue that smart cards should be issued only by banks.

What about digital money, which might, for example, take the form of bits on people's hard drives? Is that cash? A deposit account? Something else? Who, if anybody, stands behind it if it is lost to a hard disk crash or stolen by a hacker? The questions abound. And, unfortunately, there are no easy answers. Nor can there be: the new media of exchange defy old categories and so challenge standard regulatory conventions. In trying to set rules of the road for smart cards and digitized money, the government faces an especially delicate problem. On the one hand, the advent of these new and potentially useful monetary vehicles could be slowed if some rules of the road are not set early. Indeed, if sufficient protections to consumers are not provided against abuses, then if and when problems emerge, the danger arises that policymakers may overreact and thus thwart the technology. But, on the other hand, until the instruments themselves appear and settle into regular patterns, it is impossible to know just what is to be regulated, let alone how to regulate. And if the government lays down too many rules too early, it may distort or misdirect the development of the very instruments whose usefulness it seeks to refine. So, even in principle, it is impossible to know with any precision how many rules, or what sort of rules, the government should try to set.

There is, quite simply, no clear path out of this swampy terrain. It is possible, however, to map out some general strategies, both for how to think about the issue of electronic money and for how to handle it. For convenience, a welter of complex issues will here be summarized under four heads. Who will be permitted to issue electronic money, just banks or other institutions also? What accounts and balances will be covered by deposit insurance? How should consumers' concerns about their privacy be balanced against law enforcement officials' interest in detecting and punishing criminal activity? And should the government, faced with the loss of income from issuing conventional money, itself issue stored value cards?

Who should issue electronic money? A central issue for the financial services industry, as well as for the officials who must set ground rules for competition, is who can "coin" digitized money, whether it is stored virtually or on plastic. The companies now in the vanguard of e-money's development, such as DigiCash and CyberCash, are not banks and could easily choose companies other than banks as their partners. Similarly, although checking accounts today can be offered only by banks, smart cards, in principle, could be offered by nearly any company with a good reputation among consumers. As for purely virtual money, that may be no more than data stored on home PCs and validated with codes provided by companies whose specialties are software and cryptography. Instead of moving from bank to bank, payments could move from computer to computer, potentially bypassing depositories. Who, then, should be allowed to compete?

The countries of the European Union and Canada have thus far kept nonbank competitors out of the payments business to protect its soundness and to protect against counterfeiting (although Canadian regulators have been considering ways to relax the prohibition). The appeal of such a policy is that it keeps payments in the hands of familiar providers, known and trusted for safety. Unfortunately, that source of reassurance is the downside of the policy as well. This report has stressed the importance of policies that foster rather than block innovation—and, where electronic innovation is concerned, banks are hardly shining exemplars. Nonbank companies have so far led innovation in the digital realm. In fact, only in response to the competitive threat posed by these upstarts have many of the nation's largest banks begun to embrace the digital age. Some banks have formed joint ventures, both with each other and with certain Internet providers, to develop the technology and standards to let consumers bank on-line. Regulators are not, nor should they be, blocking the path of such innovations; both the Comptroller of the Currency and the Federal Reserve Board have issued regulations or clarifications that have eased such joint ventures. But regulators should also bear in mind that some of these ventures would not be happening but for the competitive jolt provided by nonbank competition or the threat of it.

On balance, the wisest course at so early a stage probably is to err on the side of innovation: let nonbank providers show what they can do before deciding what not to let them do. The result may be a plethora of companies providing smart cards and digital money—companies ranging from old standbys, such as banks, to telephone companies, airlines, Internet providers, and even trade groups and entertainment companies (who may issue promotional smart cards). No doubt there will be some degree of confusion. The alternative, however, is to restrict the development of electronic money to the companies with least incentive to push it forward (banks, which already issue both checks and debit cards, are competing against themselves by offering electronic money).

However, companies that do enter the e-money business should be prepared to show both regulators and consumers that they know what they are doing. Thus, at a minimum, the government should focus on developing guidelines for disclosure, so that holders of smart cards or on-line e-money accounts know just what they are getting, and markets know whether e-accounts are adequately capitalized.

Should e-money be covered by deposit insurance? Most consumers using e-money are likely to gravitate to large companies with trusted names, and those companies, protective of their reputations, will in general have every incentive to invest their customers' funds wisely. Nevertheless, allowing companies other than banks into the payments business carries potential risks. Customers who use the Internet to place their funds with uninsured institutions cannot turn to the federal government to get their money back if it disappears. If enough people sink enough money into such institutions, and if one or more of them fail, the result might be a general run on issuers of virtual money—just the sort of situation that federal deposit insurance was designed to prevent. Similarly, people might rush to spend down their smart card balances if they hear that one or more prominent issuers have failed. If issuers were backing their smart cards with illiquid assets, they might find themselves short of the cash they need to pay the merchants with whom the cardholders have done business. For this reason, nonbank issuers of e-money, or at least of smart cards, may find it in their own interest to adopt a "narrow bank"–type requirement that would limit the investments backing their e-cash to safe, liquid assets.

An alternative way to prevent e-money runs, some might suggest, is to restrict issuance of e-money to insured, supervised banks. But before taking this step, it may be well to bear in mind some distinctions. During the Depression, people launched runs on banks because their whole life savings were at risk, not just the odd bit of pocket change. Even if people did stage a run on smart cards, the average balances on the cards are not likely to be large, and many cards are likely to be issued by banks. So the total sums issued by nonbanks should be quite small in relation to the overall money supply. A run on smart cards is therefore unlikely to cause a general financial panic or indeed any other systemwide crisis. More likely, it would merely blot the reputations of a few institutions. And the main point of deposit insurance is not to protect depositors against any loss, large or small; it is to protect the *financial system as a whole* from stampedes caused by fear of losses. Since the failure of even many smart card providers is unlikely to do much more than irritate the particular customers concerned, the government can probably take a relatively relaxed attitude, letting consumers look after themselves and learn by experience—with the help, of course, of appropriate disclosure requirements. Besides, consumers take a risk—up to any liability limit established by either smart cards' various issuers or by future regulation—of losing the money that they may hold on their smart cards if they lose the card itself.[8] So consumers presumably will understand that the sums they hold on smart cards are, to some extent, at-risk funds.

The possible growth of e-money accounts held in uninsured (perhaps "virtual") institutions, domestic or offshore, is more difficult to assess. On the one hand, institutions that issue such accounts would not be burdened by the costs of supervision and regulation that insured depositories must bear and for that reason should be able to offer higher interest rates than insured banks. On the other hand, precisely because e-money accounts held at nonbanks would not be insured, consumers might be wary of them. Whether uninsured e-accounts prove attractive or not, existing law already restricts access to the Federal Reserve's payments facilities to insured banks, which means there is no danger that the failure of an uninsured issuer of e-money could "infect" the payments system. However, if the sums held in uninsured accounts became large, then trouble in the "parallel uninsured banking" system could have systemic consequences as account holders rushed to withdraw their funds, generating broader liquidity problems.

Still, virtual money may pose fewer new problems than a cursory glance suggests, at least where federal insurance is concerned. There is no reason virtual banks cannot be federally insured. In fact, a number of banks have begun to offer insured virtual accounts. Of course, some consumers will be tempted to invest their savings in uninsured institutions advertising on the Internet or elsewhere. But millions of people already invest billions of dollars in uninsured accounts, such as mutual funds, and they do so sensibly and responsibly. Consumers need to understand clearly which virtual accounts are federally insured and which are not, and the government will have a role to play in making sure that accounts are clearly and accurately labeled. But provided that consumers have the information they need, they should be allowed to take chances with their virtual cash. If the government allowed only federally insured and supervised depositories to issue or hold on-line or virtual e-money, it would slow or stunt the evolution of e-money itself, much as, in the 1970s and 1980s, the government could have stymied or distorted the growth of mutual funds had it required that various types of such funds be federally insured.

The government, therefore, should probably not act as guarantor of digital money. But then who, if anybody, should? Such questions are important, not only to consumers, but to the marketplace itself. Credit cards were not broadly embraced by the public until Congress enacted rules to cope with billing disputes and to limit consumers' liability for unauthorized charges. "It is these protections that allow us all to walk around with numerous credit cards in our wallets, with substantial credit limits, without significant fear for their loss," notes Robert Pitofsky, the chairman of the Federal Trade Commission. In deciding what rules of the road to set for e-money, and who should set them, financial service providers and policymakers will need to parse more than a few complicated issues. For instance, if a big issuer of smart cards fails, should it be merchants' responsibility to identify and reject that issuer's cards? (In accepting a card issued by an insolvent company, merchants would be able to download "cash" from the card's memory chip, but they would then be unable to collect their money from the issuer.) If merchants, especially smaller ones, fail to identify bad cards and mistakenly accept them for payment, with whom does the liability rest—themselves, the issuer, or the customer who (literally) passed the buck? Or should merchants and card issuers agree, as a courtesy to customers, to honor all smart cards and spread any losses among themselves? And what about counterfeits?

Such thorny questions have been little discussed in a private context since the nineteenth-century era of "bank money." Until Congress created the national banking system and authorized national banks to issue paper currency backed by Treasury securities in the early 1860s (to help finance the Civil War), America's currency consisted primarily of 7,000 different kinds of notes issued by 1,600 state banks. Most people, in those days, were careful about accepting bank money, and most banks were careful about issuing it. Banks competed on reputation, touting the high capital ratios backing their notes; elaborate aftermarkets evolved in which suspect currencies traded at below-par rates reflecting the security and reputation of the issuing banks.

The pre–Civil War period of "free banking" remains controversial among scholars. Some decry the period as being marked by volatility and wildcat banks. Others, such as Federal Reserve Board Chairman Alan Greenspan, are more sanguine. As Greenspan told a Treasury Department conference on e-money in September 1996, "losses to banknote holders and bank failures were not out of line with other comparable periods in U.S. banking history."

At this point, however, the scale of e-money in comparison with the overall economy nowhere approaches that of privately issued banknotes during the 1800s. The prudent course for policymakers, it would therefore appear, should be to go slow and give markets the first crack at developing standards and conventions for smart cards and electronic cash. It is probably better for the government to set too few rules of the digital roadways, at least in the beginning, than to set the wrong rules, because laws restrict the scope of experimentation and, once enacted, are hard to change.

How should the government balance consumers' privacy interests against the needs of law enforcement agencies? Of all the issues surrounding electronic money, this one may well be the most vexing, because it involves not only financial issues, which are difficult enough in themselves, but law enforcement problems as well. Police agencies that track drug deals, fencing operations, smuggling, and organized crime must be able to trace transactions. And consumers who want to secure their money against loss must, in effect, write their name on it—by using instruments, like checks, that are not bearer negotiable and that leave a paper trail. In principle, electronic money can be similarly tagged with a digitized "signature," so that only its rightful owner can use it. But doing so could allow both government and, to the extent the law permitted it, private businesses to trace people's commercial dealings down to the penny.

These issues are not new. Credit cards and bank checks leave paper trails, along which, in principle, people's commercial dealings can be retraced in minute detail. Current laws—the 1970 Bank Secrecy Act and the 1978 Right to Financial Privacy Act, for example—spell out rules for transactional confidentiality while also establishing procedures under which federal authorities can breach that confidentiality with a court's permission. The new challenge with e-money is that it may, with the help of secure encoding and other technologies, be capable of handling large transactions anonymously.

Today's criminals generally prefer to use cash, precisely because it is so hard to trace. But cash is not altogether anonymous, since it must usually be spent person-to-person. And it is cumbersome: since 1969 the Treasury has printed no bills in denominations larger than $100, which means that large-value cash transactions are hard to carry off inconspicuously. Banks and merchants, moreover, must report to the government all cash transactions over $10,000. In principle, e-money faces none of those obstacles. By definition, it is not physically cumbersome. Also by definition, the denominations can as easily be large as small. And, in principle, cryptography could guarantee a level of secrecy that no judge's warrant could breach.

One answer would be to require traceable tags for electronic transactions, but that risks stripping them of precisely the anonymity that many consumers, as well as criminals, may desire. In donating money to charities or downloading videos over the Internet, consumers may understandably be loath to have all their preferences recorded by businesses, which may then bombard them with solicitations or compile and sell their profiles to marketing companies.

Weighing privacy interests against the needs of law enforcement is, strictly speaking, not a finance issue and so is largely beyond the compass of the present report. But if electronic money is to live up to its potential, policymakers will need to make decisions about these trade-offs, preferably sooner rather than later.

Should the government issue smart cards? In America, the federal government has a monopoly on issuing coins and paper money. No one, of course, proposes a federal monopoly on the issuance of electronic money: no surer way could be imagined to stem the tide of innovation in digital commerce. (The federal government can and will, however, encourage the adoption of electronic transactions by switching to them itself, as chapter 5 will discuss.) But why should government not at least be a competitor in the provision of, say, smart cards? A "USmart card," or what have you, would certainly provide consumers with full security as to its issuer's soundness. And, from the government's point of view, it offers fiscal dividends, by helping the government retain its earnings from seigniorage.

Seigniorage refers to governmental profits earned by printing and coining money. When the federal government issues paper currency, it backs that currency with U.S. government securities, which pay interest that is ultimately recycled to the U.S. Treasury. In 1994, according to the Congressional Budget Office, the government's income from seigniorage ran to more than $20 billion. The CBO estimates that if electronic payments replaced 10 percent of the coin and currency in denominations of $10 and under, the government would lose an estimated $370 million a year.

The government could avoid some of this loss by issuing general-purpose stored value cards itself, collecting interest on the money people pay for the cards.[9] Federal stored value cards could thus be profitable as well as secure, and they might make nice commemoratives, to boot. Yet, where new high-tech products are concerned, the government is no inno-vator; and being forced to compete with Washington might all too easily steer private issuers shy of the market. Especially when the market is in its infancy, government's primary interest is in opening the door to innova-tion, albeit at some (fairly modest) cost to the Treasury. Even in making smart cards (or debit cards) available to recipients of federal benefits that are paid electronically (as most benefits soon will be), the government should strive to work through private sector institutions. Otherwise the government risks becoming an obstacle to the very technological change it seeks to encourage.

That lesson is more broadly applicable: in general, unless and until pressing problems arise, the wisest course is to let the market find its own way in the arena of high-tech payments. The government should strive to set rules only where there is a clear need for it to do so, erring, when in doubt, on the side of caution. No doubt some e-money issuers will make mistakes, and some consumers will be disappointed or burned. But only through trial and error, and sheer multiplicity of ventures, will companies figure out what sort of innovation is genuinely useful and what kind of security and convenience they must offer to win consumers' allegiance. As businesses of many kinds—banks, merchants, software companies, Internet providers, and alliances of every stripe—all struggle for pride of place in the emerging market for electronic payment services, consumers can expect to be the winners.

Preserving Competition

This report proposes to reconcile two mutually inconsistent strands in the fabric of American financial policy. One strand is a deep suspicion of concentration and fear of the anticompetitive abuses to which concentra-tion might lead. The other strand is a deep suspicion of competition and fear of the marketplace instability to which, it has been supposed, compe-tition might all too easily lead. Caught between these two apparently conflicting goals, policy has faced a dilemma: how to make markets com-petitive enough to prevent concentration, but not so competitive as to overheat and rupture. Policymakers' answer for a long time was to slice up the financial services market, allowing competition only in narrowly defined zones and between carefully limited products.

That answer proved to be no answer at all. By limiting interstate banking, the policy *increased* the likelihood that local markets would be dominated by a few major providers. By constraining the products that financial companies could bring to the market, the policy produced laziness and poor service. It did not produce a more sound financial system; indeed it probably weakened banks relative to their less regulated competitors. And, of course, in the end it largely collapsed, leaving mounds of rubble to clutter the field. The rubble should now be cleared away.

But once that is done, the problems of market power and concentration remain. What is to be done about them? The fact that the tools fashioned by earlier generations may have addressed those problems misguidedly, or that the tools no longer serve their purpose, does not mean that the problems themselves are nonexistent. As policy has recognized for many years, there are times when markets need to be protected from themselves or, more accurately, protected from accumulations of market power that allow particular players to tilt the whole field. So it seems fitting to conclude this chapter with a discussion of the concerns that led to so many policy entanglements in the first place. For clarity's sake, that discussion is perhaps best divided into several questions. First, is there a general problem of excessive concentration in finance? Second, can standard antitrust tools handle any concentration problems that may arise? And, third, looking ahead, what about the potential market power of gatekeeper companies that control access to software or networks?

Concentration Today

To what extent are financial markets today overconcentrated or in imminent danger of becoming so? Here, for a change, the answer is easy: hardly at all.

In saying so, it is important to note a distinction between concentration and overconcentration. As documented in the last chapter, consolidation, especially in the banking and thrift industries, is well under way and looks likely to continue. In fact, many students of the industry believe that further consolidation is essential to the depository industry's long-term health, as the industry scrambles to regroup in the face of new competition from providers of many kinds.

On this score, the recent past probably provides a reasonably good guide to the future. As figure 3-1 shows, the banking and thrift industries at the *national level* are, in fact, growing more concentrated. The largest institutions, in particular, have collectively recorded the largest gains in market share during 1984-94; indeed, within the 200 largest banking organizations, the bottom 150 have collectively lost some market share, to the advantage of the top 50. As the country continues its march toward nationwide interstate banking, the emergence of a number of large, nationwide institutions is inevitable and is likely to reinforce the concentration trends already under way.

But there are several reasons not to view this increase in *national* concentration with alarm. To begin with, the trend toward consolidation at the national level does not necessarily mean that competition *in the relevant markets where institutions compete* will be any less vigorous or that users of financial services will be any worse off. For many banking services, notably loans to smaller businesses, banking is still very much a local affair. Although consumers are swamped with credit card offers from every side, small business borrowers may have fewer choices for credit: local banks and finance companies, which usually lend only on heavier collateral and at higher rates than do banks. From these businesses' point of view, what matters is not the level of lender concentration nationally, but the level in the geographic area in which they can realistically and practically obtain such alternative sources of credit.

To be sure, in many smaller markets, local concentration remains quite high and thus warrants concern, especially where banks in those markets seek to merge. At the same time, however, according to recent data published by the Federal Reserve, average concentration levels in more localized credit markets generally have increased only a little over the past decade. Moreover, if recent merger patterns continue, as they probably will, most bank consolidations will involve mergers between banks from different locations. Those cross-border mergers entail little or no loss of competition in each of the local markets involved, and can improve efficiency in all those markets by reducing overhead costs.

More broadly, the financial marketplace is rapidly becoming too big and too diverse for any few providers to dominate. And as new instruments arrive on the scene, domination will become still harder. For example, in time, much small business lending is likely to be securitized, allowing small businesses to borrow in the national capital markets—and, for that matter, in the global capital markets. As Internet banking takes

Figure 3-1. Shares of Deposits by 200 Largest Federally Insured Banks
and Thrifts, 1984, 1994

Percent of deposits

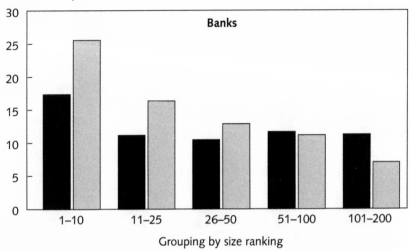

Grouping by size ranking

Percent of deposits

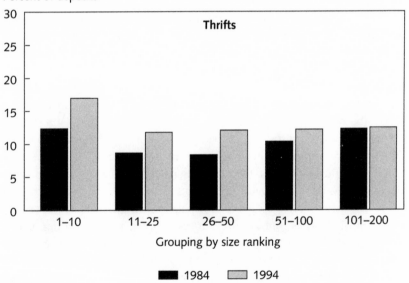

Grouping by size ranking

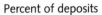 1984   1994

Source: *Federal Reserve Bulletin* (January 1996).

hold, users of financial services will be able to find the cheapest provider anywhere in the country (or the world) with a click of a mouse. The old thinking assumed that when concentration increased, competition decreased. But technology and globalization have changed the equation. Even as concentration increases among particular kinds of financial providers, the categories themselves become less meaningful as markets become more freewheeling and competition grows.

In any case, although figure 3-1 shows nationwide concentration among depositories to be increasing, it also shows remarkably little concentration among banks. In few industries, for example, can one find that the top ten firms control no more than a quarter of the market, yet that was the case among banks nationwide in 1994. Even if concentration among the top ten should double or triple, banking would not be among America's most concentrated industries and certainly would remain far below the concentration levels now typical of many local markets. And, as a further reassurance, the 1994 law that finally removed restrictions on interstate banking also limits bank concentration so that no institution can, by merger, gain a nationwide deposit share in excess of 10 percent or a statewide share in excess of 30 percent (with the recent spate of large bank mergers, a few banks seem to be approaching the 10 percent national limit).

Despite the recent wave of consolidation in finance, the United States remains, by international standards, remarkably heavily banked. Indeed, as shown in figure 3-2, as of 1994 this country had more than 55,000 bank branches, five times as many banks per person as in the United Kingdom, ten times as many as in Germany, and thirty-five times as many as in Japan. In no other large industrial economy is the banking concentration ratio—the concentration of banking assets held by the three largest companies—as low as in the United States. The story is similar in the insurance industry. Although the number of insurers in the United States has fallen since the mid-1980s, the United States still boasts more than other developed countries, as figure 3-3 shows.

Early in this century federal policymakers worried not just about mergers within industries, but about mergers *between* them, creating, it was feared, long-armed octopuses capable of using cross-subsidies and horizontal integration to drive competitors out of business. And, indeed, as the barriers that now sequester banks from other parts of the commercial world are removed, consolidation might proceed across traditional industry boundaries. Banks, or their holding companies, will increasingly own

Figure 3-2. Number of Commercial Bank Branches in Selected OECD Countries, 1985–94

Number

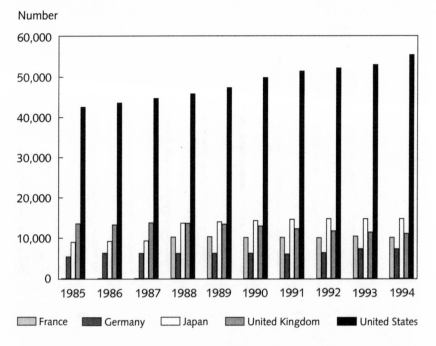

Source: OECD, *Bank Profitability* (1985–94). Data unavailable for France before 1988.

other kinds of enterprises, and nonbanks will own banks. What effect is this trend toward cross-industry consolidation likely to have on competition in finance?

Many observers believe probably not much. To the degree that the mergers involve parties now in different parts of the industry, they will be "product extension" or "conglomerate" mergers, the kinds that have typically presented the fewest antitrust problems. Such mergers do not lessen overall competition in each market unless they eliminate the possible entry of the firm most likely to have entered on its own and there are few other potential entrants, conditions that are rarely found. Much more often, cross-industry mergers give consumers the convenience of one-stop shopping and increase competition by getting more kinds of companies involved in more parts of the market.

Figure 3-3. Insurance Companies in Selected OECD Countries, 1985–94

Number

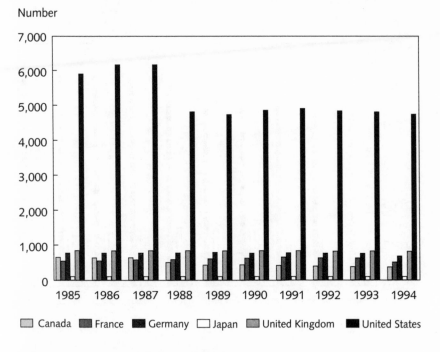

Source: OECD, *Insurance Statistics Yearbook.*

Of course, as the lines between different parts of the financial services industry continue to blur—that is, as securities firms and insurers come to look more like lenders and as mutual funds come to look more like banks (at least on the deposit side)—mergers between banks and nonbank financial service providers will, to some extent, involve combinations between competitors. Even so, there is room for optimism about the competitive effects. The continued melding of financial service activities, taken by itself, will expand competition in each formerly distinct phase of the industry, since more providers will be involved in each phase: extending loans, providing a home for savings, and so on. Consolidation may attenuate this heightening of competition somewhat, but it is very unlikely that, in the end, consumers will have fewer choices in finance than they do today.

Today's Antitrust Tools and Protecting Competition in Financial Services

In light of the preceding discussion, one can say that for the most part the tools do protect competition. On balance, there is little reason to be particularly frightened about concentration in finance, any more than in any other industry. That is not to say that worrisome antitrust problems may not arise in particular situations. But regulators have tools to deal with them. The current antitrust laws, such as the Bank Merger Act and Section 7 of the Clayton Act, already empower the Justice Department and the banking regulators to stop mergers that are likely to dampen competition. The antitrust enforcement agencies have issued guidelines over the years to demarcate the conditions that might warrant an antitrust challenge, and those guidelines have become well accepted among legal practitioners.[10] The only real question is whether the current wave of consolidation in financial services will trigger more frequent, or more aggressive, antitrust interventions as the standard guidelines are applied. Whatever the answer, there seems to be no special call for new antitrust measures pertaining to financial services generally.

Gatekeepers and Keyholders

A special case, however, deserves careful thought and extra regulatory vigilance. The rise of the Internet should make it easier than ever to borrow and lend, to sell and invest. But everyone who wants to do so will need to pass through a gateway to an electronic network. And everyone will need software—an operating system, a browser, an encryption system, and so on. To be of the greatest use to the greatest number of people, many of these systems will need to be standardized: otherwise it will be hard for people to "talk" and trade with each other. Standards, in markets, are usually proprietary. And here arises what may emerge as tomorrow's antitrust challenge in finance: how to deal with providers—typically nonfinancial ones—who hold the keys to the digital kingdom.

Gatekeepers and keyholders pose some difficult antitrust problems, difficult even in principle. On the one hand, the winner-take-all tendency of network markets means that domination by one provider is always a possibility. On the other hand, the nature of those markets also means that they may function best when a few leaders set the rules and others follow. "In traditional production industries," notes the Congressional Budget Office in its 1996 report on electronic money, "individual firms provide products or services, and antitrust law ensures that firms remain independent and are not involved in collusion. Network industries, in contrast, require interconnection among companies. In fact, the broader the network is, the more valuable it is to consumers."

Will the gatekeepers abuse their position, whether by adopting pricing or other business strategies that shut out potential rivals or by using their deep pockets and ubiquitous reach to launch bids for other markets? If they do, then it is safe to say that antitrust enforcement officials will take appropriate action. After all, it is well established that the Sherman Act prohibits firms from using their power in one market to impede competition in another. Government must not be in the position of removing artificial barriers to competition in the financial world of the future only to find that private actors have successfully erected barriers of their own.

At the same time, policymakers and enforcement officials should not take steps simply to constrain the growth or market share of firms or alliances that assume a gatekeeper function. The very same alliances that raise potential antitrust concerns are often also the ones that create marketplace efficiencies by setting standards and laying down system infrastructure. If policy tries to break up companies that control access to networks, it may destroy any incentive to build networks in the first place. One answer is to require dominant network operators to give access to their competitors. But that may merely encourage companies to hang back and wait for a free ride, letting others make risky investments in new networks or standards.

In earlier decades, policymakers tended to assume that industries relying on common infrastructure or network economies—telephone or power companies, for instance—needed regulation. But recent economic thinking has cast some doubt on that assumption. For one thing, if regulation operates on the premise that one provider must dominate, it risks making that premise come true, enforcing a monopoly where competition might have flourished. Telephony has proved more susceptible to competition than regulators once assumed; yet for years public utility laws shut out competition by creating a regulated monopoly structure.

Moreover, the mere presence of a dominant provider, even a powerful one, does not necessarily imply price gouging or other abuses. If a monopoly fears that new competitors will arise or knows that alternative technologies are waiting in the wings, it will often behave as though it faced competition. Traditional antitrust thinking tended to underestimate the prevalence of substitution; if a dominant provider abuses its position, it may merely encourage inventive consumers and businesses to develop alternatives. And in the world of the Internet and other high-tech communications, new alternatives are emerging all the time.

Finally, markets are fast-changing places, and high-technology markets change fastest of all. Regulators who rush to assume that today's gatekeeper or keyholder is a threat to competition might discover, if they only wait a while, that the threat soon passes. If a single software or network company dominates a particular market, that may be a reflection of temporary technological or competitive conditions in that market, not of insidious goings-on.

None of those are reasons to be blithely unconcerned about the emergence of powerful gatekeepers and keyholders. They are merely reasons to be careful, and to be wary of overly broad or impulsive regulatory behavior. In the heyday of the twentieth-century paradigm, it seemed to make sense to cordon off whole markets to protect them from particular abuses. If that framework were applied today, software companies might be flatly prohibited from selling Internet access or operating on-line catalog or banking services. Today's regulators need to stand that mentality on its head. In the world as it is emerging, there is no alternative to thoughtful, case-by-case application of sensible judgment in antitrust: judgment that strives to be as free as possible of prejudice about the "natural" shape of markets and that tailors its interventions as narrowly as possible. At a time when creativity is the key to economic success, the goal of antitrust policy must be merely to check the most threatening excesses, not to strike fear into the hearts of all who would form groundbreaking mergers or innovative alliances.

Is Competition Dangerous?

There remains one further question for those who would tout competition in financial services as the wave of the future. The architects of yesterday's framework for financial policy were, of course, driven by more than just their worries about concentrations of money and power. They also feared for the viability of the financial system itself. The pillars of Wall Street had come crashing down around them, and freewheeling competition seemed to have been a major cause.

It would be reassuring to know that all such fears are misguided—as, indeed, some economists believe. But many people believe otherwise. Even traders who have been in the business for decades often worry that nobody fully understands what might happen if something went badly awry in a marketplace whose fathomless complexity and lightning speed would beggar the imagination of any New Dealer. True enough, the old model—failure prevention—was deeply flawed, and competition and innovation are all to the good. But what if competitive, innovative markets crash and threaten to take the economy with them? That is the subject to which we turn next.

4

● ●

Containing Risk

RISK IS THE ESSENCE of finance; and it is the essence, too, of government's regulation of finance. The first chapter of this report argued that government's core responsibilities in finance are three: protecting consumers, protecting taxpayers, and reducing systemic risk. Of those, many might consider the last the most important. More than a few countries, America among them, have learned the high cost of a financial catastrophe. For most of the Americans who experienced it, the greatest trauma in living memory remains the financial crash of 1929 and the long depression that followed. This report's criticisms of what we call the "twentieth-century" policies that followed are in no way meant to deny the reality of the problem those initiatives were intended to fight. Surely government can have no higher priority in finance than to do what it can to prevent anything like the financial collapse of the 1930s from happening again.

Coping with risk in a competitive environment, however, is not an easy job, either for private actors or for the government. To be an investor, a borrower, a fund manager, or a financial executive is to face an endless procession of choices about how much risk to bear and how much security to hold onto in case everything goes wrong at once. The government's financial policymakers must make analogous calculations, but at a higher level of aggregation. It is the safety of the financial *system*, rather than any particular bit of it, that must concern them above all. So the question is how to let individuals and companies make financial decisions that suit their needs, while still making sure that the system as a whole operates with an ample margin of safety if the worst happens.

This is no academic problem. Few either in the markets or among financial regulators will forget the shudder of dread on October 19, 1987, when for a brief time many wondered if the nightmare might happen again.

117

In the period following the 1929 crash, monetary authorities acted perversely, tightening the money supply to support the currency rather than easing money to support the market. The result was to aggravate—some scholars even argue to create—the economic downturn of the 1930s. In 1987, by contrast, the Federal Reserve reacted wisely, announcing its readiness to lend to banks to prevent a panic in the securities markets and temporarily flooding the market with money ("liquidity," in the jargon), steps that kept the financial crash from causing an economic crash as well.

But what if things had gone differently? And what if they had happened in the light-speed, globalized, and increasingly competitive environment described in the preceding chapters? What about all the complex and often mystifying new financial instruments, such as derivatives, which some observers argue could produce or aggravate a downward spiral in a bear market? How might new instruments, new technologies, and linked markets interact in crisis?

This chapter tries to understand how today's rapidly innovating markets may intersect with the government's responsibility to look after the safety and soundness of the financial system. It begins by outlining sources of what economists have called "systemic risk" in the financial system. It then offers a framework for mitigating this risk without at the same time either saddling taxpayers with new liabilities or stifling competition and innovation. It attempts, in short, to sketch a framework for coping with an ancient problem (financial risk) in a new era.

Sources of Systemic Risk

Systemic crisis is something quite different from ordinary financial loss or marketplace turbulence. It must strike suddenly enough, and affect enough people and companies simultaneously, to compromise the performance of the market as a whole, rather than just costing some people some money. How fast and extensive must a crisis be to qualify as systemic? Academics debate that question at length. For purposes of the present report, however, the following working definition should suffice: *Systemic risk refers to the possibility of a sudden, usually unexpected, event that disrupts the financial markets, and thus the efficient channeling of resources, quickly enough and on a large enough scale to cause a significant loss to the real economy.*[1]

Bringing the whole financial system to the verge of dysfunction requires a special sort of shock. If a systemic breakdown happens, its cause is likely to be a *cascade,* a *contagion,* an asset implosion, or, most likely, some combination of the three. Those phenomena are worth exploring before considering solutions.

Cascades

Financial institutions, and banks in particular, conduct business not only with their customers but with each other. Small banks typically hold deposit balances at larger banks. Systemic risk theoretically can crop up if one or more of the largest links in the chain—a large bank or securities firm—fails, triggering in domino-like fashion the failure of other firms that are owed money by the failed institution.

For instance, the risk of a cascade of losses was a major reason why in 1984 the government extended the federal safety net to cover *all* depositors, including uninsured ones, of the failed Continental Illinois Bank. Many smaller banks had uninsured accounts at Continental in excess of their shareholders' equity and thus would have been forced into insolvency had they been forced to write off all their deposits at Continental. In reality, this fear was misplaced: although uninsured depositors' exposure to Continental was large, their actual losses were not. In fact, none of them lost more than a small fraction of their deposits. And so the cascade of failures that regulators feared was never a real problem, at least not on that occasion. In any event, one provision in the Federal Deposit Insurance Corporation Improvement Act of 1991 (FDICIA) substantially reduces the threat in the future that the failure of a large bank could produce liquidity problems for smaller banks that may have funds on deposit with the larger institution: the FDIC is now explicitly authorized to give uninsured depositors their funds based on its average recovery experience (which in recent years has been about 90 percent, implying that uninsured depositors are at risk for only about 10 percent of their funds). Nevertheless, the Continental Illinois episode illustrates at least how, *in principle,* interlinkages can be the mechanism by which the failure of one especially large institution can trigger insolvencies, or at the very least cause significant losses, among the others.[2]

A relatively new source of interlinkages among the very largest banks and securities firms has been the explosive growth in the volume of off-exchange or over-the-counter derivatives contracts. As chapter 2 noted, dealing in financial derivatives is heavily concentrated among the largest banks, insurance companies, and securities firms. Optimists take comfort from this concentration, pointing out that each of the participants in the derivatives markets has strong incentives to be careful in its dealings with the others. But the margin of safety is not clear. For it is also possible that the concentration of derivatives activity in the largest institutions may in fact increase, rather than reduce, systemic risk because the inability of one of the counterparties to honor its obligations would be focused within a small circle of institutions. Although this risk is mitigated by various buffer devices, including collateral requirements and "netting arrange-ments" between counterparties (which balance out contracts that counterparties may have with each other and thereby reduce overall net credit exposure), it is not clear whether particular netting arrangements will be enforceable in all jurisdictions.[3] Besides, derivatives contracts of-ten contain early termination clauses that the counterparties may be able to invoke in a crisis. And so the default of a major player in the market could expose that player's counterparties to heavy losses. Perhaps more important, default by a large institution could trigger any number of other dealers to withdraw from the market entirely to wait for the dust to settle, in the meantime drying up liquidity in the market.

Nevertheless, it is important to bear in mind that derivatives contracts represent just one form, albeit a new and sometimes unusually complex form, of the interlinkages that weave the fabric of modern financial mar-kets. And interlinkages need not be disastrous. The failure of any very large party, for whatever reason, inevitably causes headaches for its credi-tors. But creditors (and counterparties) generally try to stay conscious of those risks and diversify to manage them. Moreover, the arithmetic of dispersion across a large financial universe makes it difficult for even large failures to cripple the whole system. Say Bank A fails. Bank B, which has invested 15 percent (say) of its assets in A, certainly has a problem. But at one further remove, Bank C has (say) 15 percent of its assets in Bank B and none in Bank A, which means that, at most, only 2.25 percent of its own assets are at risk from A's failure (the true figure almost certainly being less, since even uninsured depositors typically get some of their money back if their bank fails). At still one more remove, Bank D is only trivially affected. Of course, the example is much oversimplified. A number of institutions may be in Bank B's position; and if those banks fail, they may become new sources of disruption. So the arithmetic of dispersion does not mean that cascades cannot happen. It does mean, however, that in a very large marketplace, where few institutions are large enough to absorb more than a small fraction of the economy's assets, shock waves tend to diffuse quickly as they radiate outward from their source. Particular institutions may indeed be subject to shocks, but, like jelly beans in a jar, they are not very good at *transmitting* shocks more than short distances. To endanger the functioning of the financial system, a triggering event would need to be huge, much larger in impact, for instance, than the Continental Illinois failure turned out to be.

There is, however, one portion of the financial sector that can potentially serve as an efficient shock transmitter, one capable, in principle, of spreading a local crisis throughout the system in a matter of hours. This is the set of mechanisms for clearing and settling transfers among banks and securities firms each day.

Just as a computer cannot run without an operating system—a program that tells the hardware what to do with the software and vice versa, and that lets the user tell the computer what to do—the financial markets have their own operating systems without which they, too, would be useless. No such operating system is required when buyers pay with cash; the clearing and settlement is then done instantaneously and in person. But payments made by check or electronically require a system of bookkeeping to ensure that money and securities are credited and deducted from the proper accounts every day, so that the parties in every transaction leave the market with the payment or financial instruments for which they bargained. The fortunes of thousands of banks and securities firms are linked to each other through the settlement system, and the volume of funds flowing through this system is staggering—several trillion dollars every day. If the system fails, commerce can literally come to a halt. That is why the smooth functioning of clearing and settlement is the most essential financial task in the economy and why ensuring that it is carried out each and every day must always be a central objective of financial policy.

The United States has two principal bookkeeping systems for clearing and settling transfers between banks, and many more clearing systems for stocks, bonds, options, and futures. Most are linked, in one fashion or another, to the Federal Reserve, which essentially keeps score of who owes how much at the end of each business day by crediting or debiting the clearing accounts that banks maintain with it. The appendix to this chapter describes in greater detail these little known but critical financial operations. Several points are worth emphasizing here, however.

FEDWIRE VS. CHIPS. The most important clearing and settlement systems are the two for banks, and the two are, in several crucial respects, quite different from one another. Fedwire, operated by the Federal Reserve for large-dollar transfers among the roughly 9,000 banks that belong to the system, entails no systemic risk because all transfers are settled instantaneously (in "real time") and are guaranteed by the Fed (which thus stands to pick up the tab in case things go wrong). The other large clearing system, the Clearing House Interbank Payments System (CHIPS), is privately operated. CHIPS acts only on behalf of its members—approximately 100 of the world's largest banks, including the biggest American banks—and not as a guarantor in its own right. Furthermore, CHIPS settles only at the end of each day and then only on a "net" basis, keeping track of all the transactions posted on the system throughout each day and at day's end sending instructions to the Federal Reserve to add or deduct the net amounts due to or owed by each participating bank.

While netting vastly reduces the number of accounting instructions and is therefore more efficient, it also entails a risk of possible cascades. Since CHIPS waits until the end of each day to settle accounts, it is possible that during the course of the day one or more of the members may fail and be unable to meet its obligations. As the appendix explains in greater detail, if several of these failed institutions were very large, their demise could cause a chain reaction that ultimately could force CHIPS to erase all of the many transactions posted on it during the course of the day. At least for a time, many participants could be unsure of their financial positions, and confusion could reign. The result could be a generalized loss of confidence in the system, temporarily freezing up or otherwise impairing the commercial and financial exchanges on which the economy depends.

This is not a merely theoretical concern. In 1974 CHIPS suffered dislocations when Bankhaus Herstatt was closed by West German banking authorities on account of foreign exchange and other losses eventually totaling more than $450 million. Though Herstatt had already been paid the deutsche marks that it was owed in its transactions, its doors were closed before the settlement system in New York had opened, and hence before it could pay out the dollars that it owed in return. Banks in America and elsewhere around the world thus suddenly discovered themselves to have sold millions of deutsche marks for, in effect, an empty suitcase. This caused a crisis of confidence in the international interbank market and funding difficulties for Japanese and Italian banks, while triggering a run by large depositors on smaller West German banks. Moreover, trading in the dollar–deutsche mark foreign exchange markets temporarily collapsed. Although the West German authorities responsible for Herstatt ultimately settled claims with the bank's counterparties, the Herstatt scare was traumatic enough to induce the central banks of the G-10 industrialized countries to establish a standing committee on banking regulations and supervisory practices. It also led to the formation of the Basle Committee of banking supervisors from twelve leading industrialized countries in 1975 (which has since set common capital standards for banks in those countries).

Concerned about a repetition of such an event, but perhaps on a much larger scale, the Federal Reserve—as the obvious source of backstop liquidity in case of a CHIPS failure—has quietly encouraged CHIPS in recent years to reduce the risk of collapse. CHIPS has responded by adopting measures that have made it invulnerable to the simultaneous failure of the two largest banks on the system. But even more safety can be engineered into the clearing and settlement system by moving to more rapid settlement, a subject explored later in this chapter and in the appendix.

FOREIGN EXCHANGE VS. DERIVATIVES. The goal of shockproofing settlement systems has always been important, but it becomes steadily more so as financial markets grow and globalize. The volume of transfers on the system continues to outpace the growth of the economy; and, at least as important, not only are transactions growing in size, they are also giving markets, and regulators, less time to react. In earlier years of this century, trading in the stock market could be safely regarded as a discrete event, opening in the morning and closing in the afternoon. In between, people slept. But, of course, the markets in Tokyo are in full throttle while Americans are sound asleep, and globalization effectively means that events across the world can quickly be transmitted abroad. Yet settlement remains much slower, only once a day and at different times in different markets.

For all the concern about possible interlinkages among banks due to derivatives, CHIPS is considerably more exposed to risks arising from the heavy volume of foreign exchange transactions on the system, running at about $600 billion each day. Many U.S. banks now routinely settle foreign exchange trades worth well in excess of $1 billion to a single counterparty every day; indeed, some institutions' exposure in foreign exchange trans-actions can exceed their capital during the course of *each day*. Moreover, foreign exchange transactions take longer to complete and to settle than those involving only domestic institutions, because they are settled at different times in different countries. In fact, often three or more days may elapse between the time a U.S. bank initially is exposed to a foreign exchange risk (by sending a certain amount of foreign currency to an-other institution) and the time it is no longer at risk (when it has received dollars in exchange from its counterparty).

For its part, the Federal Reserve is addressing foreign exchange risk by moving the opening time of Fedwire each day back to 12:30 a.m. (eastern time) from 8:30 a.m., so that the system can receive and process transactions while both European and Asian markets are also open. This will do much to reduce "Herstatt risk" (payment lags due to the different hours of operation of settlement networks in different time zones) on Fedwire, and, because CHIPS competes with Fedwire, CHIPS has been induced to adopt the same hours of operation. But earlier opening times will not reduce the exposure of CHIPS's members unless CHIPS also settles its accounts more frequently throughout the day rather than on a net basis only at the end of each day.

To be sure, since Fedwire and CHIPS are substitutes, it is quite likely that if CHIPS ever failed (had to endure an "unwind"), its members would quickly move to Fedwire to complete their transactions. Yet this would not necessarily eliminate systemic fallout from a collapse of CHIPS. Many banks could have been running up large intraday debits on Fedwire dur-ing the day of the CHIPS failure, counting on receiving net payments over CHIPS to settle their accounts on Fedwire by the end of the day—pay-ments that would never arrive. As a result, the banks caught short could be forced to liquidate securities or loans to meet their reserve require-ments. If many banks found themselves in this position, a systemic prob-lem could be very real.

CLEARING OF SECURITIES AND DERIVATIVES. A disruption in the clearing and settlement of securities and exchange-traded derivatives also could have systemic consequences. Unlike CHIPS, all private clearinghouses for trades in financial instruments act as the central counterparty (assuming the position of buyer or seller, as the case may be) or guarantee payments of all unsettled transactions on the system (as Fedwire does). The clearinghouses reduce their risks, however, by limiting the net obligations of their participants, while requiring members to share losses if any participants default (features also common to CHIPS). All clearinghouses require members to post collateral, with some requiring continuous adjustment and instantaneous collateral. As a further protection, some clearinghouses, as well as their members, also maintain standby credit arrangements with banks. In a crisis, however, even those arrangements could provide less comfort than may be desired, as will be discussed shortly in connection with the events surrounding the October 1987 stock market correction.

Contagion

The financial equivalent of shouting "fire" in a crowded theater is contagion. A deposit run on one troubled bank, for example, becomes contagious when depositors at other banks run as well, deciding it is better to be safe than sorry. If monetary authorities fail to provide sufficient liquidity (as happened in the 1930s), then runs on many banks at the same time can lead in turn to the downfall of many more banks, in turn damaging the economy as lending grinds to a halt. Unlike cascades, which are characterized by interlinkages between banks and other financial institutions, contagious deposit runs can bring down banks whether or not they have claims on each other.

Contagion arises because of a lack of accurate and timely information. Depositors run because, having seen one prominent institution fail, they cannot easily know whether their own is completely safe. The contagious bank runs of the 1930s prompted the introduction of deposit insurance, which has handily achieved its objective: no deposit run has ever been mounted by insured depositors, nor is any likely.

UNINSURED DEPOSITORS. Potential runs by *uninsured* depositors are another matter. It was to prevent such runs that policymakers extended the federal safety net to cover all depositors of a number of large banks (beginning with the failure of Franklin National in the 1970s and repeated with Continental Illinois and other large institutions in the 1980s). But such blanket guarantees may tempt big banks to take excessive risks. So, in FDICIA, Congress made it more difficult (but not impossible) for the government to extend protection beyond the $100,000 per account insurance ceiling.[4] That firmer limit on the federal safety net, along with FDICIA's stricter capital standards and its requirements for prompt action when banks get in trouble, should help make large bank failures less likely in the future. But because the risk of large-scale failures has not been eliminated (nor can it be), it is important to consider other ways to prevent contagions before they begin, an issue taken up later in this chapter.

COMMERCIAL PAPER. Contagion need not be limited to bank depositors. As corporations have discovered that they can borrow directly from the market rather than through banks, the commercial paper market—that is, the market in unsecured, short-term debt instruments—has grown by leaps and bounds. Defaults in this market were once rare, but in more recent years a number of issuers have failed, although none has ever approached the size of a Continental Illinois or a Bank of New England failure. What would happen if a very large issuer of commercial paper, especially one active in financial markets, were to default? Would such an event trigger the equivalent of a run by holders of commercial paper throughout the market, so that other corporations that depend on rolling over their paper when it comes due would be unable to do so? Perhaps even more important, would investors in money market mutual funds, which are large investors in commercial paper, mount a run because of fear that the commercial paper losses would force some funds to "break the buck" and not honor redemptions at the $1 per share par value at which the funds' shares are issued?

Those who worry about such outcomes point to the only real commercial paper scare this country has had: the 1970 Penn Central railroad bankruptcy and the subsequent default on its commercial paper. Although the Federal Reserve Board turned down the company's request for credit (because, among other reasons, the Fed had concluded that the firm was insolvent and thus incapable of repaying any loan), the Board nevertheless was worried enough about the potential systemic consequences of Penn Central's default to urge a number of large money-center banks to lend to any corporations that found themselves unable to roll over their paper, which in fact several banks later did. Experts continue to debate whether the Fed's actions during the Penn Central episode were truly necessary, but clearly, at the time the Fed was not keen to find out.

Fortunately, today and in the future the market, unassisted by the Federal Reserve, should ordinarily be able to withstand the default of a commercial paper issuer, even one much larger than Penn Central. One reason is that the commercial paper market is far deeper and more advanced than in 1970, with many more issuers and investors; today's commercial paper market comprises over $700 billion in total outstanding debt, compared with less than $40 billion then. With greater size has come much more liquidity and sophistication on the part of both buyers and sellers, who have become accustomed to assessing the financial health of issuers and distinguishing the strong from the weak. Accordingly, market participants are much less likely to practice the financial equivalent of guilt by association, which was so feared when Penn Central failed. The reaction of municipal bond investors in the 1980s to the default by the Washington Public Power Supply System is a good example. While the bond market experienced some short-term tremors, investors staged no massive run from other bonds. Similarly, the failure in 1990 of Drexel, Burnham, Lambert and the default by Olympia and York Development in 1992 did not damage the overall commercial paper market.

Even if the failure of a large issuer of commercial paper caused other issuers to have trouble rolling over their obligations, banks probably would be able to fill the void, albeit perhaps at higher cost to the borrowers involved. In fact, virtually all firms today issuing commercial paper have the backing of a bank guarantee or commitments by banks to come to the issuer's aid should it become unable to meet its commercial paper obligations (although in a true crisis, there is always the possibility that some banks would seek ways to avoid fulfilling those commitments).

As a last resort, the Federal Reserve should be able to prevent the failure of even a large issuer of commercial paper from having systemic effects; and it can do so without either lending to the issuer directly or pressuring banks to lend to companies having trouble rolling over their paper. This useful trick can be accomplished by temporarily opening the monetary spigots: by taking action that would have the market effect of reducing Treasury bill rates, the Fed can lure investors back to the relatively higher rates offered on commercial paper, stemming any possible run in that market.[5]

Meanwhile, the Securities and Exchange Commission has already taken action to minimize the impact on money market mutual funds from volatility in the commercial paper market. In February 1991 the commission amended its rules governing the diversification and asset quality investments of money market funds so that none may now hold more than 5 percent of its assets in the commercial paper of any single issuer, regardless of the issuer's credit rating. In addition, a money market fund may not put more than 5 percent of its assets into commercial paper (of all issuers combined) that has less than the highest credit rating (with investments in a single issuer of less-than-top credit limited to no more than 1 percent of fund assets).

MUTUAL FUNDS. Just as corporations have rushed to bypass banks and plug straight into the capital markets, so have millions of individual investors. Indeed, half of the net growth in the liquid assets of American households in the 1990s has been poured into mutual funds. According to one recent estimate, the end of 1996, stock funds in particular held 21 percent of all outstanding equity (valued at market), up from 7 percent in 1987 (although much of the increase in the assets held in mutual funds represents funds switched from the holding of shares of individual companies).

Like commercial paper, mutual funds are not guaranteed by the government (although some hold assets that are government backed). As stock prices have continued to climb, more people have worried that, should the market suddenly reverse course, investors in mutual funds, many with relatively little experience with this type of investment and no experience with a bear market, might dump their shares, reinforcing any initial price decline and sending the stock market into a free fall.

In fact, the market has been tested in just this fashion several times during the past two years: in July 1996 when the Dow Jones Industrial Average (DJIA) plunged almost 7 percent in a single week; in March and April 1997 when the Dow dropped about 10 percent; in August 1997 when the Dow and the rest of the market gyrated wildly over several weeks, but modestly in downward direction; and in late October 1997 when the Dow fell by more than 7 percent in a single day following turmoil in Asian stock markets. In all cases, there was evidence of some selling by mutual fund investors, but in each case the abrupt slide in stock prices abated quickly (although at this writing, it is premature to know what will happen to stock prices in the weeks and months following the late October price plunge). In the first two episodes in particular, stock prices resumed their upward climb, just as they did after the October 1987 correction, and without the need for Federal Reserve intervention.

No doubt, complacency about investor behavior would be a mistake. For one thing, the recent price drops occurred during a robust economic expansion; there is no assurance of an equally happy ending in a harsher economic environment. Moreover, pension investors may not be quite as willing to stand pat in a crisis as some observers have supposed. It is true that a substantial fraction of the increase in equity fund assets has come from people investing through self-managed retirement accounts—IRAs, Keoghs, and 401(k) plans—and that pension investors can be logically supposed to invest their funds for the long haul and thus to be unlikely to flee in a downturn.[6] In fact, however, even long-term investors can and will move funds out of their equity mutual funds if they fear further price declines, as some did in each of the recent price declines. In a future stock price plunge, selling by even supposedly long-term investors could be much more extensive.

Still, even after such fears are taken into account, three other factors provide some comfort. First, equity funds typically maintain a cash reserve ranging anywhere from 3 percent to 10 percent of assets. Unlike money market mutual funds, which can invest no more than 10 percent of their assets in illiquid instruments, equity funds are not required to hold a liquidity reserve against any sudden rush for redemptions; that they do so anyway gives them a cushion against investor flight. Second, since the 1987 crash the larger funds, in particular, have arranged for backup lines of credit with banks, in case cash is needed in a hurry, although according to recent reports some funds have *replaced* cash with bank credit lines (which may not be fully available in a true crisis). Third, an important distinction exists between mutual funds and fractional reserve depositories, such as banks. With the exception of money market funds, whose shares are redeemable at par, bond and equity mutual funds repay their investors only at prevailing market prices at the time of redemption.[7] Thus mutual fund investors have less reason to run than do uninsured depositors in a bank. Mutual fund investors can always get out at prevailing prices. Although in a falling market there is some profit in being the first out the door, the incentive is nothing like that to be the first to bail out of a troubled bank: uninsured depositors (technically, those with deposits in excess of $100,000) run the risk of finding the bank's doors closed and their accounts frozen until the financial mess can be sorted out.

Granted, these three factors are not foolproof protection against a mutual fund contagion (and, of course, no perfect protection will ever exist). But they do considerably reduce risk.[8]

COUNTRY DEBT. One other, quite different, category of contagion is worth mentioning. The crisis in the Mexican economy several years ago and the financial difficulties in Southeast Asia in the summer and fall of 1997 show that depository institutions or the commercial paper market are not alone in being susceptible to the risk of contagion. The same can happen with countries beset by temporary severe liquidity problems analogous to those experienced by cash-short, but solvent, banks.

The government of Mexico ran into just such difficulties in 1994 when it found itself without sufficient dollar reserves to service its *tesebonos*—that is, its short-term, dollar-indexed debt. Had the U.S. government not orchestrated an international program of lending to satisfy Mexico's temporary need for liquidity, frightened investors might well have pulled their funds not only out of Mexico but also out of other countries in Latin America and eastern Europe. Indeed, mutual funds specializing in emerging markets in eastern Europe declined significantly in value because of the so-called "tequila effect" of Mexico's economic troubles, and turned around only after the rescue package was put in place. Two years later, the Mexican economy has made good progress, repaying its loans to the United States ahead of schedule.

The Mexican crisis shows that the international community can play an important role as lender of last resort for fundamentally solvent countries. And it shows, too, the importance of disseminating timely, accurate information about countries' economic health, always important, but more so than ever in an increasingly global capital market. The United States, other G-7 countries, and the International Monetary Fund have recognized as much by requiring Mexico and other IMF borrowers to make more transparent and timely the disclosure of their currency reserves and other key financial indicators. The importance and limitations of information disclosure are discussed again later in this chapter.

Asset Implosions

Beyond cascades and contagions, of course, a further important source of systemic risk is a sudden and sustained drop in asset values. The three most worrisome financial events of the 1980s were of this type: the October 1987 stock price plunge, the savings and loan crisis, and the developing country debt crisis, when loans to commercial developers and to Third World countries went sour. What are the prospects for future asset collapses?

ANOTHER STOCK MARKET CRASH. One way a deep plunge in equity values can cause broad problems is simply by unnerving people, sapping consumer and business confidence and thus triggering a decline in aggregate spending and therefore a downturn in the economy as a whole. But, beyond that, a stock market crash can be characterized by both contagion and cascade. An element of contagion is almost always present when stock prices drop suddenly: many investors may simultaneously panic, driving prices down regardless of objectively determined fundamental values. And cascades can worsen any initial price decline. For example, the selling induced by the very low margins before the Great Depression can be viewed as an example of a cascade. And arguably it was largely the Fed's timely intervention that prevented another stock-sparked cascade in 1987.

That year, as in 1929, margins played a role. The 23 percent drop in the Dow Jones Industrial Average on October 19, 1987, was ostensibly triggered by a dispute between America and West Germany over interest rates, along with the introduction the preceding week of a bill in Congress to tax corporate takeovers. Only the two-day drop of nearly 24 percent in October 1929 approached the severity of the 1987 price decline. After the events of October 1987, securities brokers were obliged to extend what were, for them, massive amounts of credit to customers who needed to meet margin calls (requirements that customers put up more collateral against the stock they had purchased). Yet given the huge drop in stock prices, many of the banks on which the brokers depended for financing were understandably quite nervous about extending additional credit to the broker borrowers. Meanwhile, the principal options clearinghouse in Chicago was hesitant to remit funds to investors who had sold options until it was confident that the corresponding buyers (or their brokers) would be sending payment. The miasma of uncertainty threatened to bring trading in the options markets to a halt. Had that happened, investor confidence in the clearinghouses for other financial instruments could have been impaired, producing a further downward spiral in the prices of many instruments or even shutting down the markets altogether.[9]

The Federal Reserve saved the day with several measures. It announced readiness to provide liquidity, while reportedly encouraging key money center banks to lend to securities firms (just as it had encouraged some of those same banks to lend to Continental Illinois three years before). Also, the Fed pumped money into the financial system by purchasing Treasury bills, driving down interest rates and thereby making stocks more attractive. The Fed's several-pronged assault succeeded: the stock market quickly turned around after its October 1987 free fall. A year later, stocks had fully recovered the ground they had lost in that fateful month. To many economists' amazement, the stock price scare had little if any apparent effect on the wider economy, which continued to grow at a healthy pace during the quarter of the price drop. In that respect, the crisis could not have been more different from the 1929 crash. But might a downdraft in stock prices be more damaging next time?

Many who fear so point to the dramatic recent proliferation of exchange-traded derivatives. In principle, options and futures could significantly aggravate a downturn in stock prices, once one began for whatever reason. And as figure 4-1 shows, the trading volume of options and futures has indeed exploded since 1987, when the market last suffered a severe drop. By itself, however, this trend does not necessarily mean that the markets have become less safe. Financial derivatives allow financial institutions—banks, insurance companies, and pension funds—as well as nonfinancial companies and even individual investors to hedge or insure themselves against marketplace fluctuations of all sorts less expensively and, for that matter, less dangerously than if their only choice in a downturn is to dump securities. Indeed, there was little evidence that derivatives played an aggravating role in the most recent plunge in stock prices experienced in late October of 1997. Yet derivatives markets could, during some future downturn, behave more like a trampoline than a safety net, mainly because of the substantial leverage that these instruments afford investors.

Indeed, precisely because buying an option or selling a future is so much cheaper than buying or selling the underlying stock, the widespread availability of options and futures makes it easier for speculators to jump on any downward bandwagon and push prices down faster and further. Even so-called hedged investors can produce similar effects if

Figure 4-1. Volume of Trade of Futures, Options, and Stocks, 1985–96

1985 = 100

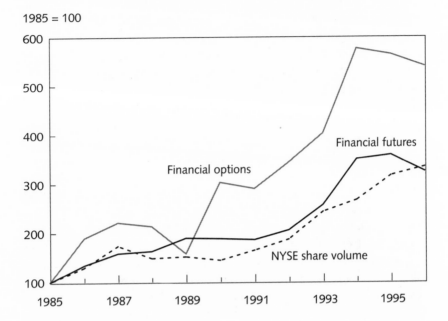

they use "dynamic" hedging or "momentum investing" strategies, techniques developed recently whereby futures are sold or put options are
bought as securities prices fall. These strategies are now touted, much as
automatic selling programs (portfolio insurance) were during the 1980s,
as insuring investors against loss after any initial price decline. But just as
formal portfolio insurance programs were discredited in 1987, dynamic
hedging or momentum investing strategies used today could fail to protect the investors using them if many market participants bolt for the door
at the same time and if selling pressure in the derivatives market gener-
ates a downward spiral in the cash market.

Fortunately, several developments since October 1987 have helped
insulate the market against a repeat performance. Perhaps most significant, in 1987 the physical and computer infrastructure of the New York
Stock Exchange was unable to keep up with the 600 million shares traded
that day, causing confusion about where prices stood at any moment. The

result was to produce further selling pressure from panicked investors who did not know the value of what they held and wanted to escape before they could find out. Today the major exchanges' computer infrastructure is much better equipped to cope with the large increase in volume that could accompany any sudden market collapse. The NYSE is now capable of handling 3 billion shares traded on a single day, up from an average of fewer than 200 million traded daily in 1987; indeed on the day after the stock price plunge in late October 1997, the NYSE successfully handled almost 1.2 billion shares, or more than double the peak daily amount traded in October 1987.

Trading volume on NASDAQ was even higher that day—1.4 billion shares.[10] Faster completion of trades and more rapid reporting of prices should do much to prevent the uncertainty about prices that in 1987 induced panic selling on all fronts.

More, as a direct response to the events of October 1987, the New York Stock Exchange introduced various "circuit breakers," trading halts that kick in automatically if prices change very sharply. The most important breaker, a one-half hour halt in trading if the Dow Jones Industrial Average moves more than 350 points in either direction, was invoked for the first time in late October 1997.[11] Given the level of the Dow, this circuit breaker kicked in after only about a 5 percent move in stock prices, compared with the 12 percent price change that would have triggered the original post-October 1987 breaker.[12] At this writing, debate continues on whether this particular breaker aggravated or dampened the stock price plunge on October 27, 1997. The New York Stock Exchange seemingly has settled the debate by proposing much larger, percentage-based triggers.

Will circuit breakers and higher-volume handling capacity, combined with the abandonment of formal portfolio insurance, be enough to protect the markets from a reprise of the events of October 1987? No one really knows. Even if circuit breakers or similar devices did manage to stem a large price decline, there continue to be risks that the initial fall in prices could bring down a clearinghouse, as already discussed. After a big slide in prices, for example, those who had written put options would be exposed to significant losses; if they could not pay, the relevant options clearinghouse might withhold payments to the holders of the options, who in turn may be counting on those payments to meet their own commitments. Similarly, a large drop in futures prices would wipe out the performance bond, which would be used to cover the loss on the contract. If the losses on the contract exceed the bond, a clearinghouse has various protections: it can look to the clearing member's assets and its security deposits; if those resources prove inadequate, the clearinghouse can draw on the Exchange's surplus funds and the capital of other clearing member firms.[13] What is unclear is whether these backstops would prove adequate if the markets were to suffer a truly major shock.

It is important to keep in mind that, even if there were no financial derivatives to speak of, the stock market could still drop dramatically if investors all ran for the door at the same time, as they did in 1929, and as has happened in Japan, where stock prices have fallen by more than half since the late 1980s. Nonetheless, given the enormous growth in derivatives in recent years and the ease with which they have allowed investors to speculate on downward movements in the market, the appropriate level of margin requirements for exchange-traded derivatives is a subject that deserves further study.

A DECLINE IN ASSET VALUES. Apart from a stock market crash, what about another episode of constricted lending, like the one in the 1980s in the United States when loans for developing countries and commercial real estate went sour, or the one in Japan, when the bubble economy of the 1980s burst, leaving banks severely stressed? Or, to take another example from the past, what if interest rates were again to spike into double-digit territory, causing the market value of all loans with longer maturities to drop sharply in value? In cases like these, the economy can suffer harm not so much from the lending losses themselves as from the corrective action—enforcing capital requirements that inevitably curtail lending—that regulators eventually must take to prevent further financial damage and losses to taxpayers. Many economists believe that the recovery from the 1990–91 recession was, once begun, slowed by the reluctance of many banks to lend as they struggled to rebuild their balance sheets and meet stricter capital standards.

Scholars debate whether large-scale lending losses suffered by depository institutions really qualify as "systemic events." Skeptics point out that such troubles, far from appearing suddenly, typically are drawn-out affairs more like business cycle downturns than financial shocks. Others retort that, in any case, widespread lending losses can hurt the whole economy, not only by inhibiting investment and spending, but also by draining the pockets of taxpayers, who stand behind the deposit insurance funds.

This academic debate, however, need not be resolved for all to agree that, whatever label one pins on a broad drop in asset values, policymakers should want to avoid the phenomenon. Clearly, one key to doing that is to discourage depository institutions—indeed all financial institutions—from concentrating their assets by type and geographic region. If depositories are broadly diversified in their investments, few will be exposed to failure simultaneously if any particular class of loans becomes troubled. And regulators will not then be confronted with the Hobson's choice of closing them all at the same time, thereby threatening confidence in the financial system, or forbearing and thereby encouraging lenders to take greater risks.

In the case of thrifts, some progress has already been recorded. Congress has reduced the extent to which thrifts must invest in mortgages, and since the early 1980s thrifts have been allowed to invest in variable-rate mortgages. Meanwhile, by authorizing both banks and thrifts to expand nationwide, Congress has promoted needed diversification in the geographic composition of loans. But more needs to be done. As chapter 3 suggested, the time has come to remove the remaining distinctions between thrifts and banks and to let all depositories choose their own mix of loans, thus serving the interests of competition and safety at once.

The Case against Quiescence

The perception of danger, and the willingness to take risks, varies greatly from one person to the next, as any parent or driver knows. Looking into the future, some readers will be more troubled than others by the areas of vulnerability sketched above. All, however, might profitably bear in mind that assessing the riskiness of the financial system as a whole involves vast uncertainties. Much might go wrong, but that is hardly to say that much *will* go wrong. The new world of digitized, globalized, fast-adapting finance may turn out to be a safer place for investors and for the economy, or it may not.

Undoubtedly, medium-size crises somewhere down the road are easy, if painful, to envision: the failure of a money center bank or a large nonfinancial company, for example. But the next step—a general marketplace disaster happening with little or no warning and feeding into the larger economy—is harder to imagine. Such a general breakdown requires, in most cases, that several things go wrong at once and that the shocks be quickly transmitted throughout the financial system. Of course, sometimes several things do go wrong at once. Interwoven derivatives contracts or a blow to the settlement system, to name only two examples, might indeed make a crisis rapidly infectious. On the other hand, a great deal went wrong in the mid-1980s: tumbling real estate values and farm prices, the savings and loan debacle, Third World debt defaults and re-scheduling, and the stock market decline itself. All those problems came on top of one another. Yet the financial system weathered the storm.

Perhaps all that can be said with certainty is that the next system-shaking crisis—if there is one—is likely to look different from any that has gone before. This leaves policymakers in the uncomfortable position of a person who must drive through a thick fog, able to see clearly only in his rearview mirror. Or, perhaps more aptly, it puts them in the position of a bridge engineer who knows little about the stability of the ground under the water.

What, then, is a sensible attitude? One approach simply dismisses the possibility of systemic crash as too unlikely to worry about. The supposi-tion is that any crisis large enough to bring the financial system to its knees will be too big and too surprising to plan for. The sensible thing to do is muddle through when the time comes. If all else fails, the Fed will always be there to act as the rescuer of last resort, just as it did in 1987. At a minimum, it can inject liquidity into the financial system to ensure that all solvent enterprises get the funds they need. Besides, by temporarily pumping up the money supply, the Federal Reserve can lower short-term interest rates and thereby increase the relative attractiveness of equities, commercial paper, or any other financial instrument whose market shows signs of imminent collapse. If generalized liquidity is not up to the job, the Fed also can intervene directly, by lending to troubled enterprises or clearinghouses. This is a tool the Fed has never used and a precedent that it is hardly eager to set, but it is in the closet just the same. Short of using it, the Fed can urge the banks that it supervises to lend to troubled sectors, just as it is widely reported to have done in October 1987.

All that is true, as far as it goes. But it does not go far enough. The country would be mistaken to build policy on the notion that the Fed can always rescue the financial system if need be, even if the Fed can and should do so when all else fails. For one thing, any implicit or explicit understanding that the Federal Reserve will lend to individual institutions, especially nonbanks that have never received credit from the Fed directly, would send the wrong signals to all other similarly situated firms, encouraging them to act less prudently than they would if they did not expect a bailout. This is no idle concern. The consequences of imprudence can be very real: an unduly broad financial safety net allowed, indeed encouraged, excessive risk taking in the 1980s, when banks and thrifts collectively poured hundreds of billions of dollars into unwise investments.

Under certain circumstances, moreover, the Fed may face macroeconomic constraints in attempting to flood the market with liquidity as a way of coping with a crisis. Although lower interest rates on Treasury bills can help jump-start demand for alternative financial instruments, such as stocks, they can also significantly reduce investors' demand for dollar-denominated assets. As interest rates for T-bills fall, and under the right (actually, wrong) conditions, investors (domestic and foreign) might run from the dollar, sending it into a decline or even a free fall. Knowing that a plummeting dollar would worsen inflation, investors might also then demand higher interest rates on *long-term* bonds, an outcome that could more than offset any positive effects on stock prices from the lower interest rates on bonds with short maturities. The upshot is that under certain conditions, and especially if a crisis arises against the backdrop of a high or rising rate of inflation, the fear of the chain of events just described could tie the Fed's hands—or the events themselves could enfeeble monetary policy's power to stop an incipient financial crisis from snowballing.

Another constraint the monetary authorities may face is knowing that temporarily pumping up the money supply to prevent the financial and economic systems from collapse can make it more difficult later to fight inflation and avoid recession. It is also conceivable that adding more money to an economy that is already deeply depressed at a time when interest rates are already very low may not do much good. Although it is true that the monetary authorities were misguided in allowing the money supply to shrink during the Great Depression, many economists also believe that, even had the Fed followed an expansionary course, recovery still would have been slow. Interest rates were already so low, confidence was so badly eroded, and production capacity so far in excess of demand, that monetary policy would have been pushing on a string in its attempt to stimulate investment and consumption. Japanese economic policymakers have faced just such an impasse in the 1990s as they have tried, with only limited success, to use monetary policy (and near-zero interest rates) to nudge their economy toward recovery.

Finally, it is important to recognize that the Federal Reserve is not a computer that reacts automatically to any set of events. Rather, it is an institution composed of people who must make hard decisions, often quickly, with highly imperfect information—and potentially in the middle of the night, since any crisis originating abroad is likely to arise when Americans are in bed. And however much the people at the Federal Reserve have learned from that institution's errors during the Depression, as well as from its more recent successes in averting financial crises, human judgment is always prone to lapses.

The central challenge for financial policymakers, then, is to develop shock-absorbing mechanisms that neither rely entirely on the Federal Reserve to ride to the rescue nor are themselves undercut by a fundamental flaw, in principle or as implemented. Moreover, such mechanisms need to be encompassing enough to absorb shocks from any of a variety of quite unpredictable sources, yet flexible enough to do so without dampening innovation or prejudging change. Plainly the twentieth-century policy framework is no longer the answer. What might work better?

Containing Risk

By way of introduction, an analogy may be helpful. If finance were a road system, the first great regulatory regime, the one preceding the Great Depression, would have been a system with few stop signs, traffic lights, or lane markings: a system that was adequate when traffic was light, but unstable when many drivers streamed onto the highways at once. An attitude of laissez-faire, tempered by restrictions to prevent undue concentrations of economic power, characterized the regime. Although policymakers got around to creating national traffic cops—the Comptroller of the Currency and the Federal Reserve—they did not evince great fear that the road system itself might tumble into chaos.

With the Depression and the financial and economic turmoil that defined it, both the extent and the direction of government's involvement took a decisive turn. At that time and during several subsequent decades, Washington knit together a patchwork of legislative measures—deposit insurance, deposit interest rate controls, segmentation of banks from other enterprises, continued prohibitions of interstate banking, and regulation of securities firms and markets, plus ad hoc extensions of the federal safety net—all aimed at improving systemic soundness. Together those measures defined a general approach that, so to speak, assumed a mishap anywhere could bring disaster everywhere and that therefore set out to prevent any failures. Figuratively speaking, the post-Depression financial "road system" set a 35 mile-per-hour speed limit, separated cars into types, put each type in its own lane, and promised a free tow and repairs to anyone who got dangerously stranded.

What happens, however, when new sorts of vehicles are appearing at ever shorter intervals? When new technologies and faster cars make low speed limits not only harder to enforce, but inimical to innovation? When free towing seems to encourage reckless driving? Considering this problem, a thoughtful traffic engineer might note that accidents will inevitably happen, even after reasonable safety precautions have been put in place. Similarly, some intersections will suffer gridlock at rush hour, even after roads have been made as wide and as well marked as sensibly possible. Anyway, predicting either the cause or the location of the next accident is growing hopeless as new vehicles and routes proliferate. So this engineer might increasingly turn to another sort of strategy, one that works no matter where or how the next accident happens, one that looks for ways to ensure that an accident at any one intersection will not paralyze the others.

In short, the aim would be to *isolate and contain mishaps,* localizing, and so minimizing, the systemwide effects of crashes. Emphasis would shift toward early quarantine of problem cases, rather than last minute rescues; toward the use of timely information, rather than just flat mandates, as a safety system; toward buffers and shock absorbers designed by market participants and enforced by the marketplace as well as by the government, rather than one-size-fits-all standards enforced only by regulators; and, finally, toward real-time-settlement mechanisms (or their functional equivalents) that insert control rods, so to speak, in the path of chain reactions.

Before getting down to specifics, a few caveats. First, some of the policies discussed here are already being phased in, and others are in regulators' and academics' "in" boxes. What we do here is to pick out what may at first appear to be disconnected strands in financial regulation and show how they are parts of an emergent design: a successor to the financial paradigms of the nineteenth and twentieth centuries. Second, the distinction between prevention and containment is often blurry, even in principle. Nonetheless, the conceptual distinction is important, not because it can sort all policy instruments into one of two neat categories (it cannot), but because it helps outline a broad strategy for future policy and regulation.

Finally, this study does not propose finely detailed policy remedies or a legislative checklist for specific, near-term problems. Rather, we give examples of the sorts of measures that together can build the skeleton of a containment framework suitable as a transition toward the governing structure for finance in the early part of the twenty-first century—in other words, a philosophical sketch into which particulars can, over time, be fitted.

Early Quarantine

A good place to start is with a reform already in place: one that, though often viewed as a patch on the old system, is at least as properly regarded as one of the first important pieces of the new one. The 1991 Federal Deposit Insurance Corporation Improvement Act has been much alluded to already, but deserves revisiting in the present context. The act requires federal regulators to take "prompt corrective action" to catch weakly capitalized banks before they fall into insolvency and cause a loss to the deposit insurance fund. For example, regulators can order troubled banks to cease paying dividends, to raise more capital, and to curtail growth. Regulators can also take over very weakly capitalized depositories and sell them to other parties. The theory underpinning FDICIA departs from the Depression-era model, which sought to prevent failure at all costs. Instead, FDICIA allows, but seeks to minimize the likelihood of, failure by disciplining institutions well before they reach insolvency.

In doing so, FDICIA well serves the goal of containing financial shocks. For one of the most important sources of contagion, and therefore of systemic risk, is the fear that if one institution has gone bad, many others might be bad as well: that is, a general loss of confidence. A further worry is that if the government waits to act, an insolvency will mount in size and cause a bigger shock to the system. Finally, if it waits to act, the government may lose the opportunity to shut down a bleeding depository while doing so is still relatively inexpensive; but once the problem becomes very expensive, the high cost of resolving it may itself tempt the government to duck the problem, as the savings and loan experience so memorably showed.

FDICIA provides the mechanism for, in effect, a reliable early quarantine. That is, it takes ailing institutions in hand before the damage has gone deep. This step considerably reduces the element of surprise, which is itself a prime cause of panic. If regulators take staged action, markets have ample time to react and take account of the uncertainties generated at each turn. The stepwise quarantine process also allows investors who are connected with a troubled institution to make adjustments and stabilize their positions, so that the institution's failure, should it happen, sparks no combustive reaction. Knowing that regulators are likely to reveal and isolate problem institutions early, investors are less likely to panic for fear that the situation is much worse than it looks. In short, the 1991 reform set in place a powerful tool for shock containment. With FDICIA, traffic is diverted around blocked intersections before it causes pileups.

So far, prompt corrective action has worked largely as envisioned. Bank failures are down sharply, capital levels are up substantially, and the losses to the deposit insurance fund during the past several years have been minimal. Nevertheless, the prompt corrective action regime has yet to be tested by recession or a wave of lending problems. To be sure, the new regime itself, coupled with the new hurdles erected in FDICIA against protecting uninsured depositors, should help make a repetition of such lending problems less likely, by encouraging banks to be more prudent. But lending problems have not been outlawed. And large banks in particular are increasingly engaged in complex financial transactions that pose new challenges for regulatory supervision. So other steps will be needed as well.

Early Detection

As every listener to drive-time radio knows, one of the best ways to keep traffic moving is simply to make sure that everybody knows where the trouble spots are. FDICIA's prompt corrective action is itself, of course, a warning alarm, but it is still a comparatively late one. In the future, technology can do better: the day may be coming when the financial equivalent of a heart monitor can be placed on banks (as well as other financial institutions), alerting regulators and the market instantaneously to the financial condition of institutions and their vulnerability to market swings. Given the rapid pace of advances in information technology, that day is not as far off as may be thought. In Britain, the Securities and Futures Authority is already at work designing an automated monitoring system (Business Envelope Alert Monitoring), in which a computer program would examine several hundred thousand securities transactions each day (virtually all the important ones), collate them with other information on firms' health and activities, and kick out reports of odd behavior patterns. The Commodity Futures Trading Commission here engages in a similar set of activities. Certainly now is not too soon for financial policymakers more broadly to begin thinking about how to harness information technology to make finance safer.

Prompt corrective action, for instance, can be only as effective as the information on which it must rely. In the fast-moving environment of finance, however, late information almost by definition is inaccurate. Financial institutions that may appear to be well capitalized at the end of one quarter can look very different just one quarter—or less—later. This is true even if banks are required to report their financial condition based on the market values of their assets and liabilities, as is now required of securities firms, rather than on the basis of their historic costs. Indeed, given the widespread availability of derivatives, a bank can change its risk exposure within hours, if not minutes. So there is a compelling case for enabling regulators to check more often on the financial health of the institutions they supervise. Financial problems, after all, are often like tumors: not all of them require the scalpel, but the sooner they are spotted, the better the options are likely to be.

There is no reason, in principle, why regulators should not some day be able to monitor the market values and risk exposure of banks so closely as to give them the ability to consider (though not necessarily take) corrective action virtually instantaneously. Moreover, financial institutions also should be able to disclose continuously their exposures to individual counterparties and the concentration of their lending risks, by geographic region, industry sector, and type of loan. Regulators could then warn banks quickly about avoiding excessive concentrations. The safety and soundness of regulation of securities firms by the SEC and of insurance companies by state regulatory commissions could be conducted in the same way.

There are limits, of course, to how effective an instantaneous supervisory system can be in reducing systemic risk. For one thing, the system should not drown companies in new reporting requirements; nor should it let regulators look over financiers' shoulders and drive from the back seat. Care must be taken to make sure that the heart monitor becomes neither a pacemaker nor an electrode-studded monstrosity. Moreover, some firms, especially troubled ones, will varnish or distort the data they release, a problem that instantaneous real-time monitoring will not solve. More broadly, the heart monitor model does little to prevent contagion from other markets—a crisis sparked by a stock market correction or a run on commercial paper, for instance.

Still, the potential gains from early warning are real, and the concept is worth developing. It might reduce losses suffered by deposit insurance (in the case of banks) or by guaranty funds (in the case of insurers); and, for banks and securities firms, it could reduce the risks of a cascade through the clearing and settlement networks.

The informational strategy might be still more powerful—some would argue, in fact, too powerful—if it brought to bear the disciplinary pressure of markets as well as regulators. Imagine information on banks' health being fed continuously not just to regulators, but through them to the marketplace as well. Markets tend to be less forgiving than regulators, who may be more willing to give a troubled institution time to work through its problems. In contrast, creditors and uninsured depositors can have much less patience and less tolerance for risk, a fact that underscores both the advantages and the drawbacks of relying more heavily on market discipline. Precisely because market reactions can be harsh and quick, institutions are likely to be more careful about taking excessive risks if they fear rapid punishment from depositors or creditors than if they are disciplined only by regulation and supervision. In the world of the future that we have been describing, the constant flow of accurate financial information should greatly reduce the risk of contagion, since, after all, the absence of timely and accurate information is precisely what causes contagion in the first place. In the real world, though, information often emerges in lumps and is not continuously audited for accuracy, so losses suffered by uninsured depositors at one bank might still trigger flight by uninsured depositors at others. That is why—to get ahead of the story a little—many believe that a strong case can be made to rely especially on the market discipline provided by investors in uninsured subordinated debt, who are more stable creditors than are uninsured depositors.

Though today's world is distant from the ideal of perfect information, information nevertheless gets better all the time, and as it does so, disclosure becomes a more powerful weapon against financial calamities of many sorts. Those who doubt that a lack of timely information about economic and market conditions is itself a major source of systemic risk might recall the 1995 Mexican peso crisis, in which the failure to issue timely economic data created a backwash of bad news, which, when it finally hit the markets, caused a sudden rush for the exits. Indeed, having learned that lesson, the International Monetary Fund has set about encouraging countries to publish economic data more frequently and according to agreed-upon standards—and, more to the point, is also posting on the World Wide Web up-to-the-minute lists of the countries that meet those standards, along with details of the data each country provides. As the IMF recognizes, the more that investors know at any given moment, the less likely they are to stand for too long on the wrong side of the boat.

This is not to say that more information is a perfect answer to preventing financial crises. Investors recently ignored warnings well in advance of Thailand's currency difficulties that the country's banking system was in trouble, and when they did react, they did so all at once. Still, better information, timely disclosed, is a necessary (albeit not sufficient) condition for disciplining countries and firms against following imprudent policies.

Market-Tailored Buffers

In the real world, policymakers use both regulation and market discipline to contain systemic risk. But the mix has varied markedly across different segments of finance. In banking, regulation and supervision are relied on more heavily than is market discipline. In the rest of the financial services industry—securities, mutual funds, and so on—the reverse is true: disclosure and markets are the main means of discipline, with regulation used more in a backup role. That difference is not without reason: only the depository sector is federally insured. But one of the biggest questions for financial policy in the years ahead is whether the current mix of regulation and markets is the right one, whether policy should tilt further in one direction or the other.

Here again, the rapid pace of change in the industry is forcing policymakers' hands. The onrush of innovation and the growing complexity of the financial marketplace—trends documented in chapter 2— argue for moving in the market direction.[14] Banking regulators in the United States and other industrialized countries made an important breakthrough in the late 1980s in establishing a common set of capital standards for banks, thereby bolstering bank capital ratios around the world. But the regulators' continuing struggle to refine those standards in the face of continuing changes in the way banks do business provides powerful evidence of the inherent limits of top-down, one-size-fits-all capital rules.

True, regulators have been trying mightily to catch up to market developments, taking the initial capital standards that assigned (admittedly arbitrary) risk weights to different types of loans and then adding components to reflect the risk posed by interest rate movements to which banks expose themselves. But regulators have faced their greatest challenge so far in attempting to devise capital rules for trading activities, whose risks can be and are measured in a variety of quite disparate ways. Rather than arbitrarily mandating the use of any single measurement technique, regulators began this year to allow the large banks that engage heavily in these activities to use *their own models* for estimating risk (the European Commission and the Bank for International Settlements have done likewise for European banks). Then those estimates would be used to set requirements for additional capital. The policy implicitly, and correctly, recognizes that big banks are different from small ones because their failure may spark a general crisis. But, even more important, by deferring to the risk measurement techniques used by banks themselves, the policy acknowledges that banks are very different *from each other* and that the growing complexity of large bank operations increasingly favors market-driven rather than mandated strategies for ensuring safety and soundness.

There is room for moving much further in this direction. To resort again to analogy, imagine that a way were discovered to tailor auto safety rules to particular cars and, for that matter, to the habits of each particular driver. And imagine further that those rules could be enforced not just by police officers but by the other cars on the road. In finance, it may be possible—within limits, of course—to use such an approach, at least as a supplement to more traditional strategies. In 1995 the Federal Reserve Board proposed an innovative way of ensuring that the large banks active in securities trading and in the derivatives market have enough capital to back their trading activities. Under what the Fed has called a policy of "precommitment," banks would periodically specify the maximum losses that they believe they might accumulate from certain of their trading activities.[15] If losses exceeded the specified amount, the bank would pay penalties (which would be made public). Precommitment thus would go beyond relying on banks to use their own models to estimate risk exposures and then applying a capital requirement determined by a mandated percentage of those exposures. Under precommitment, banks estimate both the market risks to which they are exposed *and* the additional capital they believe those risks warrant. The Fed is now testing the approach in a pilot study organized by the New York Clearing House.

The precommitment idea is not foolproof. The government may be reluctant to impose penalties at precisely the time when institutions face severe losses; in fact, the Fed's proposal explicitly contains a systemic risk exception, much like FDICIA's exception to the rule that uninsured depositors are not to be protected against loss. Yet the precommitment approach has several advantages. First, it lets institutions themselves tailor their capital requirements, while giving them an incentive to do so carefully. In effect, precommitment compels banks to put their money where their models are. Second, by releasing data on banks' chosen precommitment levels, it gives the markets information about the amount of risk that an institution is expecting to incur. Thus it engages markets' scrutiny. Most important, it is a good example of the kind of thinking that can advance policy beyond inflexible, uniform requirements, and that will become increasingly important as mercurial markets make uniform rules less workable. The Federal Reserve Board should be commended for proposing the precommitment concept.

If letting banks set their own capital requirements for difficult-to-measure market risks (subject to penalties if they prove wrong) is such a good idea, why not apply the precommitment notion to *all* the risks banks face; that is, why not permit banks to set their overall capital standard themselves, rather than relying on fixed standards? Eventually, such a policy may indeed be appropriate, though not until it has been tried for market risks alone and then only for those large banks that are heavily engaged in securities trading and derivatives activities. Policymakers need experience with the more limited version of precommitment before extending it.[16]

In the meantime, another way to engage markets as safety regulators is worthy of serious consideration: requiring banks belonging to large banking organizations—say, those with assets exceeding $10 billion—to back a limited portion of their assets with uninsured, subordinated debt (unsecured debt that is "subordinate" to the claims of depositors).[17] Subordinated debtors act like the proverbial canary in the mineshaft. Unlike uninsured depositors, investors in subordinated debt cannot "run" at the last minute, but instead must wait until their debt instruments mature. For just that reason, investors in subordinated debt are much more stable sources of market discipline than are uninsured depositors: they can sell their instruments to other investors at reduced prices, but they cannot pull their money out of the bank.

To be sure, banks are already allowed to count subordinated debt toward meeting part of their risk-based capital requirements, and, indeed, a number of larger banking organizations that have access to the capital markets have issued such instruments.[18] But as long as the issuance of those instruments remains voluntary, large banks can avoid having to subject the expansion of their activities to a regular market test. If instead big banks could expand only by selling additional subordinated debt in the marketplace every quarter (rather than backing expansion with additional reported earnings that add to shareholders' equity and that can be manipulated by clever accounting), they would have much stronger incentives than they do now to avoid imprudent risk taking.[19] Equally important, regulators could not as easily resort to the kind of "forbearance" that in the 1980s encouraged the expansion—and unwarranted risk taking—of many large banks whose loan portfolios had market values well below the values that regulators were letting the banks carry on their books. If a bank could sell its debt only at premium interest rates, that would send a strong danger signal to both the market and regulators.

Of course, the discipline of subordinated debtholders can only be as effective as the information made available to them. When the Bank of New England failed in early 1991, it became clear that the bank had not reported its problems promptly to investors. Even managers inside the company (some of whom bought stock in the bank as late as the year before its failure) were unaware of regulators' grave concerns about the bank's commercial real estate loans. Such episodes underscore the importance of requiring banks to disclose promptly any regulatory warnings and sanctions against them, as well as the continuing need for bank supervision and capital regulation even as a greater role for market discipline is introduced. Moreover, given the increasing reliance of large financial institutions (not just banks, but also securities and insurance firms) on derivatives transactions, financial regulators will need to pay special attention to collecting and publicizing data on the extent to which these institutions are exposed to individual counterparties.[20]

A subordinated debt requirement would itself prod market participants toward better disclosure. Because subordinated debtholders have much to lose from risky bank behavior (their investments are not insured) and only limited room to gain (the interest rate on their bonds is fixed), they would form an important constituency for timely information. They might press banks to use market values rather than historical costs in reckoning their financial health and push them to report in much greater detail the concentrations of their risks by counterparty, region, and industry, as well as by type of loan.[21] Armed with a clearer picture of banks' health, investors would be in a stronger position to discourage depositories from straying into trouble. And if trouble occurred, regulators would have better information with which to handle it—and to decide how to keep problems from spreading. So in the end, market-tailored buffers indirectly strengthen the other elements of containment.

Faster Settlement

By now the reader is likely to have noticed that many of the measures discussed so far have to do with *time*: reducing lags or dead spots between the time trouble emerges and the time markets (and regulators) learn of it and thus can take countervailing steps. The accumulation of uncertainty over time is a major, if not *the* major, element of systemic risk. And the core of a containment strategy is to engage corrective action, both from markets and regulators, before a local accident causes a general gridlock. One way to do that is to shorten, and ultimately eliminate, the payment lags that expose the financial system to the risk of interruption or collapse.

Consider CHIPS, the large-bank clearing system that is most vulnerable to risk. As noted, CHIPS has developed the means to withstand the failure, not just of the single largest bank on this system, but of the *two* largest institutions simultaneously. But even more risk could be taken out of the system if CHIPS moved toward what the financial community calls *real-time gross settlement* (RTGS), a system whereby each transaction is cleared and settled immediately, rather than being toted up and settled at the end of the day. The failure of any one institution would cancel only the transactions actually in progress rather than all those accumulated during the course of an entire trading day—so there would be no need in an emergency to unwind all transactions of all banks on the system, and thus much less chance of a gridlock in payments.

In fact, CHIPS is considering measures that move very closely toward RTGS without requiring clearing members always to hold the potentially large (and costly) positive intraday balances that a pure version of RTGS would formally entail.[22] The new settlement system would settle accounts on multiple transactions continuously throughout the day as funds in each member's clearing account become available to complete the transactions. The new system appears promising and CHIPS is encouraged to implement it as promptly as possible because the current daily net settlement arrangement effectively offers member banks free intraday credit and therefore exposes the financial system as a whole to risk for which no one pays.

Indeed, several years ago, the Federal Reserve recognized that it was granting banks free "float" by letting them borrow intraday on the strength of the Fed's guarantee of settlement finality; now the Fed charges banks for the privilege (although not at a true market rate). Once CHIPS is settling much more frequently, then as a matter of parity, it would be appropriate for the Fed to reconsider its need to guarantee payments on Fedwire. In addition, even without waiting for CHIPS to further minimize its risk, the Fed should consider operating a real market in intraday funds rather than arbitrarily price such credit as it does now at only 15 basis points (a level far below the current rate on overnight "fed funds").[23]

The clearing of securities transactions should be expedited, too. Systems for clearing securities trades in the United States have moved in recent years from settling securities transactions (delivering them at the time of payment) in five days (T+5) to three days (T+3). We now clear trades much more rapidly than elsewhere in the world. Nonetheless, as a long-run objective, we should move to settling every 24 hours (T+1), initially for larger transactions and eventually even for smaller investors.

In fact, T+1 is already the standard for futures and options; securities settlement should be no different. The SEC should work with the industry and its counterparts in other countries to accomplish this objective.

To all but a few devotees, the payments system looks like a bafflingly arcane tangle of financial plumbing. But the value of attending to it is worth emphasizing. With real-time settlement, it will still be possible for a big bank failure or other financial problem to roil the markets and damage innocent bystanders. But it will be much less likely that a chain reaction in the payments system would spread the shock far and wide. In contrast to the failure-prevention paradigm, which tried to stick financial dominoes upright in glue, the containment paradigm seeks to move the dominoes farther apart, so that the fall of one need not bring down all the rest. And when the system as a whole is less vulnerable to the failure of one of its parts, regulators need not rush to treat every failure as a systemic threat. So regulators' promises not to rescue the foolish are more likely to be believed, which means that financial institutions are more likely to be careful. Thus a system that is safer for failure may also be one in which failure is less likely to happen.

Whither International Cooperation?

The globalization of finance has led regulators in the United States to work increasingly with their counterparts in other countries to exchange information, coordinate regulation and supervision, and at least in the case of bank capital standards, actually to harmonize rules. In principle, there are several reasons why such efforts are in the interest of each nation that participates in them.

One reason is that financial problems in one country can spill over into others, and thus entail externalities that have traditionally justified some sort of government intervention. When the externality affects different countries, each may be better off if it at least coordinates its policies with the others. This is a principal rationale for U.S. participation in setting the Basle capital standards, as well as for U.S. leadership in encouraging such international institutions as the World Bank and the IMF to strengthen supervision and capital standards of banks in developing countries where banking problems have been even more pronounced than they were in America in the 1980s.

The desire to prevent financial externalities, however, justifies only the setting of *minimum* safety standards or at the least cooperation in enforcing national standards. The Basle capital standards were also intended to *harmonize* rules for banks to ensure that banks in less restrictive regimes would be unable to take advantage of greater leverage and thus a lower cost of capital, to the competitive detriment of banks headquartered in other countries. While this goal has not been completely attained—primarily because important differences between countries in tax rules and accounting standards remain—the playing field for banks is measurably more level across countries than it was before the Basle standards were set.

In some cases, countries need not actively work to harmonize rules; the market itself can do so wherever regulated activities can easily move across national boundaries in response to relatively small differences in regulatory regimes. In such cases, individual nations cannot impose regulatory regimes that are significantly stricter than those in other nations without seeing the activities in question flee to those other jurisdictions. A good case in point is margin requirements on stock index futures, which are traded not just in the United States but in London and Asian markets. These requirements are set by the individual exchanges, although they are supervised by the Commodity Futures Trading Commission (to which the Federal Reserve Board has delegated responsibility in this area). Given the ease with which traders (and their brokers) can and do move to markets in different countries, U.S. exchanges contend that they are heavily constrained in their ability to set margins that are significantly higher than those in other markets where U.S. investors also feel secure (a fact of which any study of margin requirements should take account). Similarly, Japanese policymakers are feeling pressed to open up their financial markets to greater competition in the face of traders' movements to other Asian financial centers, such as Singapore and Hong Kong.

To what extent, therefore, should U.S. policymakers seek to coordinate with other countries in implementing any of the suggestions already made for strengthening protections against systemic risk? Some actions, such as movement toward real-time settlement for CHIPS, do not require international coordination. Others, such as implementing a precommitment approach to requiring capital for trading purposes or requiring large banks to issue subordinated debt, could be placed on the international negotiating agenda, because they modify existing capital standards. However, the United States should not wait until other nations agree to these measures.

It would be a mistake to let any desire for a level playing field stand in the way of improving the resiliency of the U.S. financial system, especially because countries already differ in the way they implement the current Basle capital standards.

The international nature of markets and the rapid movement of capital and contracts between them nevertheless make a compelling case for attempting to harmonize disclosure and accounting rules. In a global capital market, investors looking out across various markets need to be able to understand what is on offer. Yet accounting standards across countries differ widely, so that financial results that look strong under one country's rules may turn up in the red in another's. The result may be to flummox investors and regulators alike.

To be sure, disparate accounting standards have advantages as well as disadvantages. They allow experimentation and prevent the international adoption of a single standard that fails to meet local market expectations or that is downright mediocre (or worse). There is much to be said, however, for international coordination to establish a common set of accounting guidelines to make possible ready comparison across borders. The International Accounting Standards Committee continues to work on such a set of guidelines, which can then *supplement* rather than supplant various national ones, just as, in many parts of the world, English serves as a supplementary common tongue. The result would be win-win for all. U.S. securities exchanges could trade the shares of any foreign company that abides by the international standards. Similarly, the shares of U.S. companies abiding by the international standards would be more easily traded in foreign markets. In the process, markets would become even more efficient in allocating capital, here and around the world.

Working Together

It is worth reemphasizing that the various proposals offered in this chapter are meant to be exemplary rather than conclusive: a starting point, not an ending place. In due course, other and better ideas will emerge. More important, however, than any few of the particulars is the way they can combine to make a coherent whole. The approach suggested here tries, above all, to make the main elements of the regulatory structure reinforce rather than attack each other, and to make regulation work with robustly competitive markets, rather than against them. Thus continuous disclosure and market-tailored buffers engage market discipline; more rapid settlement and early quarantine allow the government to let market discipline take its course without disrupting the market itself; and market discipline, as opposed to market segmentation, allows for more competition, more innovation, and more safety, all at once.

Admittedly, none of the foregoing suggestions for mitigating systemic risk is perfect, and by no means would they eliminate worrisome risks or obviate regulatory trade-offs. What they can do, however, is improve on the old model. By engaging firms and markets in setting appropriate cushions against risk and by pinpointing and isolating problems before they can echo through the system to cause a general crisis, the containment framework can make shocks less disruptive, whatever their source. And that should help make less likely the sort of meltdown that would force the Federal Reserve to open its monetary fire hose.

To emphasize containment over failure prevention is not to abandon all concern about failure. Government continues to have a duty to make sure that financial institutions, especially federally insured ones, take reasonable precautions, just as cities need to enforce fire codes. Nor is it to suggest a radical change of policy—at least not if radicalism implies replacing all old policies with new ones. To the contrary: in finance, there probably is no such thing as a good radical policy. Having set rules, government should not change them casually. Capital standards, regulatory supervision, deposit insurance, and a number of other elements of the familiar regulatory regime will remain as important as ever. What should change is the mix of policies and, perhaps even more important, their goal and organizing philosophy. Where the nineteenth-century regulatory model shrugged at financial shocks and the twentieth-century model spent considerable effort to prevent them, the containment philosophy would seek to isolate and absorb them. If the adjustment to the new philosophy is made correctly, which is to say gradually but steadily, ordinary Americans should never notice the difference. Those who know finance, however, will sleep easier.

Appendix: Clearing and Settlement Systems

Probably the least widely understood, but almost certainly the most critical, links in the financial system are the various mechanisms for clearing and settling the transfers of funds and securities. Since all transactions eventually go through banks, the Federal Reserve ultimately plays a crucial role in all clearing and settlement activities by keeping track of the balances in banks' "reserve accounts," while the banks and securities firms serve as bookkeepers for their customers.

The Fed does all this through various mechanisms: it processes checks and certain automatic payments, such as direct-deposit instructions, in its automated clearinghouse (ACH);[24] operates Fedwire (a clearing mechanism for large-dollar transfers); keeps track (through a "book entry" bookkeeping system) of the ownership of securities issued by the U.S. government and by various federal or federally sponsored agencies; and supports various private sector clearinghouses, which handle large-dollar transfers between major banks and trades of all sorts of financial instruments (bonds, equities, options, and futures).[25] To keep these various systems running each day without fail requires that their operators and policymakers meet two sorts of challenges.

One challenge is technological: ensuring that the networks have backup mechanisms in case the primary computer systems fail; preventing errors in computer software from sending money to the wrong places or crashing the system; and taking all reasonable steps to prevent hackers or cyber-thieves from wrongfully diverting funds. This is not an insignificant assignment. In November 1985 a software glitch caused the Bank of New York to run an overdraft in its reserve account at the New York Fed of almost $30 billion (fortunately, the error was corrected the following day). While policymakers cannot be expected to oversee or understand the technical details of the hardware and software required to keep the clearing and settlements functioning, they can and must ensure that appropriate resources and management are devoted to the task.[26]

The upgrading of the technology for handling trades on the New York Stock Exchange provides a good illustration. At the time of the 1987 stock market correction, the New York exchange was not equipped to handle the roughly 600 million shares that investors wanted to trade that day. Accordingly, trade prices were reported late, creating uncertainty that induced many investors to sell out of fear. At the prodding of the Securities and Exchange Commission, the NYSE and the other stock exchanges have since upgraded their computer software and hardware so that they are capable of handling much larger trading volumes. In addition, the SEC encourages the exchanges to maintain appropriate backup systems.

Clearing and settlement systems also depend on a much more intangible factor, which constitutes the second challenge. Participants will belong to a settlement network only if they have *confidence* that the other members of the network will always have sufficient funds to honor their obligations, or, if some institution defaults, that the network itself will make good on the obligations of its members. If for any reason confidence should evaporate—for example, because one or more of the largest members of the network fail and become unable to honor their obligations—the participants may run from the system, refusing to send payments to the other members. In a highly complex economy like America's, which requires banks to make payments constantly to other banks here and around the world, the breakdown of clearing and settlement of payments between banks could be catastrophic. If, after all, banks will not deal with each other, then they cannot process payments for their customers, who are the individuals and businesses in the economy. Potentially less catastrophic but nevertheless worrisome is settlement outside the banking sector: if participants in the systems that settle securities, options, or futures trades lose confidence in those systems, trading in these markets can come to a standstill. The resulting uncertainty in the prices of securities could cause significant harm to the real economy, by preventing even the soundest of corporations from issuing securities to finance their activities, while inducing consumers to cut back on their spending for fear that their financial instruments may no longer be readily convertible into cash.

As explained in the body of the chapter, a payments nightmare arising from a loss of confidence is impossible with Fedwire, because the Federal Reserve itself, as operator of Fedwire, guarantees all payments between participants. Thus if Bank A sends payment to Bank B over Fedwire, Bank B knows that it will receive credit *immediately* from the Fed whether or not Bank A holds enough money in its reserve account to cover the payment at the end of the day. In the rarefied language peculiar to this activity, the Federal Reserve provides "gross settlement" (settling each transaction as it comes) on a "real-time basis" (immediately upon receipt of instructions) and thus guarantees "finality" (so that each transfer is irrevocable and unconditional once the Fed processes the payments instructions).

In guaranteeing payment, however, the Fed risks picking up the tab if a bank fails and cannot meet its obligations during the course of a day.

The Fed could eliminate its clearing risks by requiring all banks to maintain positive reserve balances throughout the day. But because the Fed does not pay interest on reserve balances, any such requirement would be costly to banks, which now can deploy those funds—even temporarily—in profitable endeavors.[27] Instead, the Fed extends credit during the course of the day to banks that run net negative positions on their reserve accounts. During the 1980s and early 1990s, banks took increasing advantage of this free intraday credit, more than doubling the daily peak daylight overdrafts outstanding from 1985 ($81 billion) to 1993 ($188 billion). In April 1994, the Fed began charging fees for overdrafts, while enforcing tight credit limits (or caps), and the average amount of intraday credit has since fallen off by more than 40 percent.

CHIPS is the other large-dollar clearing and settlement system for banks. Unlike Fedwire it is privately operated by the New York Clearinghouse, whose members include 11 large banks in New York City. Roughly another 90 banks from the United States and around the world also belong to CHIPS, which processes an even larger dollar volume of transactions than Fedwire ($1.2 trillion versus nearly $900 billion, as of 1995).[28]

For several reasons, CHIPS is susceptible to forms of systemic risk to which Fedwire is immune. One is that, whereas Fedwire is used primarily for domestic transactions (between U.S. banks), dollar payments processed by CHIPS are primarily related to foreign exchange transactions involving foreign banks. This difference makes CHIPS susceptible to monetary and financial crises abroad—as the 1974 Herstatt episode dramatically illustrated—in a way that Fedwire is not.[29] Moreover, in contrast to Fedwire, which provides instantaneous settlement and guarantees the payments itself, CHIPS does not guarantee payments and does not settle until the end of each day, when it adds up net debits and credits for each participating bank and transmits bookkeeping instructions to the Fed.

Although netting is more efficient than gross settlement, it is also riskier, because one or more members may fail and be unable to meet its obligations. In that event, CHIPS performs a "recast": it erases the transactions of the failed bank from its bookkeeping and settles accounts among the remaining members. If, after reshuffling the figures, settlement is not possible—for example, if some otherwise solvent banks were counting on large payments from the failed institution and could not meet their obligations without receiving those payments—CHIPS may then have to unwind *all* of the transactions posted that day, or in effect start all over as if the whole business day had never happened. A total unwind, which has never happened, is the nightmare systemic risk scenario for CHIPS: not only might banks refuse to deal with each other (thereby freezing payments by their customers), but the foreign exchange market, which is essential to international trade and investment, could also effectively be forced to shut down.

At the Fed's urging, CHIPS has taken several measures in recent years to reduce the risks to which it is exposed. It has tightened membership standards; imposed "net debit" caps (analogous to the Fed's credit limits) on any members' net negative positions during the day; established explicit rules for sharing any losses if bank members fail; and, what is perhaps most important, established a reserve, filled with securities contributed by the members, which could be used as collateral in case CHIPS needs to seek a loan in the market (or, in the worst case, from the Fed) to keep operating. In combination, those measures have insulated CHIPS against the failure of the two largest banks, or the simultaneous failure of the twenty-five smallest on the system. Moreover, as explained in the text, CHIPS is now considering the introduction of a new method of settling payments throughout the day that is a close substitute for real-time gross settlement and insulates the system even further against a possible worst-case breakdown.

The two methods of clearing—gross and net—for bank payments have their counterparts in the clearing and settlement of trades on securities and derivatives exchanges, with corresponding implications for systemic risk. A "delivery versus payment" (or DVP) system, under which financial instruments are delivered to buyers *simultaneously* when sellers receive their funds, is analogous to a real-time gross settlement system for bank payments. The Fed maintains "book entry" DVP systems for the securities issued by the federal government and by federally sponsored organizations (such as Fannie Mae and Freddie Mac); ownership of those securities is recorded on the Fed's computer at the same time as payments are recorded in banks' clearing accounts. In contrast, there are multiple private clearinghouses for trades of securities, options, and futures, as well as related depositories for clearing funds, many of which settle their accounts on a *net* basis with banks or, more typically, with the Federal Reserve.[30] This means that, throughout each day, the clearinghouse keeps a running tab showing which members owe and are owed payment for trades; at the end of the day, the net debtors pay the depository, while the depository credits the accounts of those who are owed money. Securities transfers are settled only when *all* the participants who are in a net debit position have made their payments.

Clearinghouses that do not operate on a DVP basis run risks similar to those entailed by CHIPS, and for the same reason: between trade and actual settlement lies a delay during which supposedly finished transactions could potentially unravel. In fact, the delays for equities and most corporate and municipal bonds are longer than for bank payments—three days (down from five days several years ago). In contrast, customer positions on futures exchanges are settled at least every twenty-four hours and in some cases more frequently.[31] Because participants in these clearing arrangements often rely on credit extended by banks to meet their payment obligations, problems in securities or derivatives clearing can infect the banking system.

The multiplicity of securities clearing systems contributes to systemic risk because parties may be overextended on more than one exchange without either knowing about the other. In the Market Reform Act of 1990, Congress directed the SEC, the Fed, and the CFTC to "facilitate the establishment of linked or coordinated facilities" for securities clearing. While some have advocated unifying the various clearing systems into a single system to carry out this suggestion, various legal obstacles stand in the way. Instead, the clearinghouses have taken a variety of incremental steps, similar to those recently adopted by CHIPS, including sharing information, harmonizing settlement times, and, in selected cases, concluding "cross-margining" arrangements (whereby gains and losses on related positions held with different clearing organizations are netted for purposes of determining margins) and "cross-lien" agreements (that permit one clearing organization to recover losses from a defaulting participant by claiming its collateral deposited with another clearing organization).

Finally, an issue related to clearing and settlement, but nevertheless distinct from it in important ways, is the possibility of a crisis sparked by technological failure or fraud, not necessarily in the clearing and settlement network itself (although that remains a possibility), but within or affecting individual banks. All technologies, of course, are susceptible to failure, including some very old ones. Banking records maintained on paper, for instance, are flammable (and, unlike computerized data, are cumbersome to duplicate and store at multiple sites). And, as the multibillion-dollar computer glitch at the Bank of New York in the 1980s suggested, even computer error is hardly a new problem. Advances in error correction techniques and improvements in data management have made computer technology more reliable than it was a generation ago. Still, as the world of finance digitizes, the potential costs of a major technological disruption grow, though the ease of creating and running backup systems grows as well. The difficulties of solving the "year 2000" problem present another critical set of challenges that all financial institutions must overcome. It will continue to be the job of regulators and the monetary authorities to ensure that the physical and informational infrastructure that underpins the country's financial structure remains adequate to the task and is appropriately backstopped in case primary systems fail.

What might eventually prove a more pervasive problem—although rarely, if ever, a source of systemic shock—is fraud. In the past few years, several major financial firms have been plunged into jeopardy or outright insolvency by the fraudulent or incompetent dealings of their employees. Most notoriously, in February 1995 Barings, a prestigious British bank, collapsed following the discovery that a poorly supervised trader had accumulated and hidden losses of $1.4 billion. Banks are not immune from such problems. In 1996 Japan's Sumitomo Trading Company suffered losses when a rogue trader bet and lost more than $2 billion of the corporation's money, over the course of a decade, in the copper market.

In neither case did institutional failure threaten to spark systemic failure. Still, some observers point out that as the world of electronic commerce grows, so will the returns to developing the means for high-tech fraud or sabotage. It is not hard to imagine crime syndicates developing exotic schemes to break into electronic banks, or whiz-kid counterfeiters having a field day with electronic money. Whether new technology will make such criminals easier or harder to catch remains to be seen and depends heavily on the outcome of a cat-and-mouse game between e-cops and e-crooks that is yet to be played out. It is encouraging that the officials within the Federal Reserve System have launched an effort to assist banks in fighting cybercrime. That effort will require continued attention in the years ahead.

5

· ·

Expanding Financial Opportunity

THE BLESSINGS of democracy and capitalism are many, but if they had to be expressed in two words, those words might well be freedom and opportunity. Alone among all the world's political systems, democracy strives to give all people, however grand or modest their means or their standing, a voice in great decisions and the opportunity to make the most of their lives. And alone among the world's economic systems, capitalism depends upon, rather than represses, the will of individuals to frame careers, build businesses, and express their choices by exchanging freely with one another. Americans are rightly proud of the extent to which the ethic of opportunity has taken root here, drawing countless immigrants from numberless shores to pursue dreams denied them at home.

In politics, opportunity means the franchise to vote. In economics, it means something much more complex. Reasonable people will disagree on the minimal conditions in which economic opportunity can be said to thrive. Many, however, will at least agree on this: economic opportunity cannot thrive where access is denied or choice suppressed. In general, of course, markets are good at spreading access and choice. Their particular genius, indeed, is in finding new ways to bring new products to new customers—so much so that few can escape the icons and jingles of the marketplace, even if they try. But there may be times when markets either fail or are stunted, whether by governments or by private action. And in such cases, an essential function of government is to seek remedies, if they are to be had.

This report has argued that government has three missions in regulating finance: reducing systemic risk, reducing risk to taxpayers, and protecting vulnerable consumers. The previous chapters have concerned themselves with competition and risk and have argued for an approach that both gives providers more freedom to serve their customers and takes steps to make sure that mishaps, when they occur, will not disrupt the financial system. But the story does not end there. Government's job in finance is to help all members of society to have access to financial services at market clearing prices, without facing discrimination by gender, race, religion, or national origin. To be cut off from financial services, or denied them at market clearing rates, is to face economic isolation and be shunted aside.

That fact has, of course, always been true. But concern about it arguably heightens as the digital age overtakes finance. When many or most payments are made electronically (as virtually all regular federal payments soon will be) and much financial commerce is conducted on-line (as it eventually will be), what will become of the person who lacks access to a computer or who does not know how to use one? The digitization of finance makes possible the expansion of services in all sorts of ways, but it also may leave at least some people stranded in an increasingly archaic economy bound by the confines of cash and local boundaries. More remains to be done, too, in bringing fair access to credit to all classes of Americans. To those potential problems, the report finally turns: "finally," not because the vulnerable are least important, but because it is fitting to end a discussion of an ever more vibrant financial world by paying due attention to the problems of those who may be left behind.

The Democratization of Credit

In general, Americans are hardly cut off from finance. To the contrary: nowhere in the world are consumers better served by financial providers. And that, of course, is a tribute to the power and effectiveness of financial markets. Yet government, too, has played its role. Public policy's concern with access to financial services dates back many decades. And it is an arena in which government has unquestionably accomplished much.

Of all the elements of financial policy pursued this century, arguably the most impressively successful has been the extension of extraordinary opportunities for credit to ordinary people. Americans take for granted the sea of credit that washes through their lives today, but in fact until comparatively recently bank credit, as opposed to loans from family, friends, or patrons and bosses, was available only to a few. "If the credit terms of 1776 still applied in today's Washington," Eugene Ludwig, the Comptroller of the Currency, has said, "only a handful of people would qualify for a bank loan."

To help broaden the market for mortgage credit, the government created a number of institutions, as detailed in chapter 1: the Federal Home Loan Bank System, the FHA, Fannie Mae, Freddie Mac, and Ginnie Mae. In combination, these institutions have helped create a whole new financial product: the mortgage-backed security, representing a pool of loans. Instead of being illiquid bank assets, mortgages are now fully liquid securities. The result was to revolutionize the mortgage industry by, in effect, letting it tap directly into the country's and world's capital markets and, in the process, providing thrift institutions with enough comfort to write mortgages for thirty years instead of just five (a process that was under way before the secondary market was developed but that was accelerated by the creation of that market). Today, the availability of long-term mortgage credit is taken for granted, though many are still alive who could, if they stopped to think about it, remember when a thirty-year home loan was a rarity.

The extension of long-term mortgages to tens of millions of Americans is, in itself, only a part of the story of the expansion of credit opportunities. As recently as 1954, only 41 banks offered credit cards, and fewer than half a million people used them. Three decades later, 42 million American families held at least one charge card, and 3,000 institutions offered them. Today, credit cards are nearly ubiquitous, offered by more than 6,000 institutions (banks and nonbanks) and used by roughly two-thirds of American households. In its day, the auto loan was a comparable innovation. In the early Depression era, few banks would lend for purchase of a car; but between 1930 and 1940, auto loans written by commercial banks grew from $30 million to more than twenty times that amount. Today, auto loans are made not only by banks, but also—in fact primarily—by the finance arms of the auto companies themselves.

Finally, before World War II banks did not lend money to families or their children to finance college or postgraduate education. The risk of doing so was perceived to be great; where, after all, was the collateral? As in the case of mortgage lending, the federal government played a pivotal role, initially through the GI Bill in 1944, which provided grants to veterans to attend college. Subsidies and guarantees on college loans have since been extended to all students from middle-income families. In combination, those measures have taken all the risk out of bank lending for higher education (by transferring it to the government). As a result, Americans today take as a given that their university expenses, which were once swallowed whole, can be spread over a working career, extending the benefits of higher education much beyond an elite to the broad middle class.

The Government's Role in Access

Even as the reach of credit has expanded, however, another kind of concern has grown: whether certain classes or groups might nonetheless be either excluded or disadvantaged in the financial markets. And that concern, too, is an outgrowth of a long tradition in policy. For more than two centuries, government has been used to bring the basic prerogatives of civic life to an ever broader circle of people: expanding voting rights beyond just the propertied classes, and then further extending the vote to African Americans and (finally) women; promoting the civil rights revolution, which extended to African Americans and other minorities due process and access to schools, jobs, and restaurants and hotels; and then assuring fair access to housing. All of these measures have helped millions of Americans to break the glass ceiling in public and private life.

Access to credit was a relative latecomer in this tale. Gradually, as other kinds of participation were extended, it became clear that many members of minorities or disadvantaged groups needed full and fair access to credit to enjoy real economic opportunity. On this score, postwar American practices left much to be desired, and the federal government often was no friend of the poor, minorities, or central cities. Both the public and the private sectors actively abetted the migration of middle class whites from central cities to suburbs. Real estate companies used racial criteria in appraising property values, and in many cases discouraged neighborhood integration; and government agencies gave explicit approval to the use of racial and ethnic composition in classifying neighborhoods for credit risk. In 1938 a Federal Housing Administration manual declared that "if a neighborhood is to retain stability, it is necessary that properties shall continue to be occupied by the same social and racial classes." The underwriting policies of the FHA, as the economist Jeffrey Lacker notes, "strongly favored newly constructed homes in all-white suburbs," and indeed the FHA "recommended racially restrictive deed covenants on properties it insured until the Supreme Court ruled them unenforceable in 1948."

Such discriminatory practices were made illegal in the years following World War II under the Equal Credit Opportunity Act, the Fair Housing Act, and other civil rights statutes. However, discrimination may persist despite even the most vigorous enforcement of laws against it. Few would assert that all problems of systemic bias have disappeared in America. And what is more important, even in the absence of overt discrimination there are reasons for government to play an active role in ensuring opportunity in credit and financial markets.

One reason is simply that the federal government's responsibilities in finance have a social as well as purely economic or financial dimension, as, indeed, do the government's responsibilities in most spheres. Blighted cities and desolate poverty are obviously of great concern to those affected by them, but they also have wide and often ugly ramifications for the larger society. The collapse of an inner city can lead to crime, homelessness, public sector neglect, and a general climate of decay, all of which inevitably spill over into neighboring suburbs—and which debase the civic environment of the country as a whole, to say nothing of the environment of the people trapped in squalid conditions. Even if markets functioned perfectly in providing credit and financial services to inner cities and minorities, the government has undertaken to ameliorate extremes of deprivation and to help open opportunities to all Americans, particularly the disadvantaged, on many dimensions, and finance is no exception. It is not the job of private lenders to consider the broader benefits that flow from extending opportunity widely; but that is, of course, a central consideration for government. This is not to say that government should impose unfair or excessive requirements—whether in the form of taxation, regulation, or mandates—on private actors. It is to say that the government cannot and should not walk away from correcting market failures in its deliberations on financial policy.

In fact, many observers have pointed to reasons why a governmental nudge on the behalf of opportunity may be particularly appropriate in credit markets, which may not, so to speak, necessarily give credit where credit is due. All allegations of market failure are contentious in economics, and the issue of credit is no exception. However, many economists have pointed out that poorer neighborhoods may suffer from a shortfall of credit because of a collective-action problem. In a derelict neighborhood, renovating any particular property may seem, to a rational lender, a poor credit risk: the run-down or dangerous condition of the neighborhood as a whole would depress the value of the improved property. The same is true for property owners: redeveloping a single property is not so attractive if the property is bordered by an abandoned tenement on one side and a crack house on the other. If many borrowers and lenders simultaneously decided to redevelop the neighborhood as a whole, then all might profit; but no one or two of them can easily start the ball rolling without assuming considerable risk of failure. So a neighborhood may decline even though its redevelopment could, in the end, prove profitable.

One solution to this problem is for one or more large developers to buy large tracts of inner-city property to develop an entire neighborhood and so capture the full value of the general improvement in the local environment. But that is much harder to do in center-city areas than on greenfield sites in the suburbs. Moreover, a variety of inner-city problems may militate against the involvement of deep-pocketed outsiders—as opposed to local community groups and entrepreneurs—in such neighborhoods. Unquestionably, problems of crime and infrastructure should be met head on by local, state, and federal governments. And in seeking to expand opportunity, the government should take care not to distort markets or encourage unsound investment. But if the federal government can help make investment and entrepreneurship in low-income or inner-city areas a more attractive proposition, it may help remedy the reluctance of particular private actors to step forward individually. In effect, it may make lending in such areas more profitable by creating a positive-sum dynamic in which each lender gains from the efforts of all the others.

To make these points is not, it bears repeating, to assert an unlimited role for government intervention in housing or credit markets. Government works best when it bears down lightly and picks its shots with care. Nonetheless, the history of discrimination, the government's broad interest in alleviating social ills where that can be done effectively and efficiently, and the likelihood of at least some degree of market failure in low-income credit markets all combine to give the government a role in expanding opportunity in the market for financial services.

Indeed, financial opportunity figures to become more important than ever in the digital age now upon us. Increasingly, digital media—from automated tellers to home computers and, before long, personal financial "agents" spidering across the Internet in search of financial bargains—are becoming the window into commercial opportunities of every sort: credit, investment, saving, shopping. Electronic payment will become increasingly prevalent, not only over the Internet but at the grocery checkout. Already, people without credit cards and bank accounts are generally turned away by shops and banks alike when they seek to cash checks.

In the next few decades, ordinary currency will hardly fade into oblivion, and checks will continue to be valid for commercial tender. In fact, the number of checks has grown, rather than declined, in recent years. But more and more of the economy's financial business, from paying wages to shopping, will be conducted by digital rather than "analog" means; and the analog economy may well shrink relative to the whole or even in absolute terms. The currency-based economy, while unlikely to become a financial ghetto, may be increasingly isolated from the broad range of services that more and more Americans may enjoy. Thus consumers without bank accounts and digital access may find themselves in something akin to the position of inner-city residents without cars who are constrained to one high-priced grocery store. Theirs could be a world of high payment-services fees, few and inflexible investment options, expensive (sometimes unobtainable) credit, diminished financial horizons. Like the automobile and the suburban lifestyle that the family car made possible, digital finance offers a potentially vast expansion of choice and opportunity for those who have access to it; but, also like the automobile, it may imply a widening relative gap for those who are left behind in the "inner city" of finance.

The converse is also true, fortunately. New technology has the potential to reach more people more cheaply than ever before. If that potential is tapped, it can bring services to formerly isolated constituencies at lower cost than at any time until now. "Perhaps in conjunction with product-design innovations," Comptroller Ludwig has said, "price reductions flowing from technological innovations may enable the extension of the financial service marketplace to many low income households." An automated teller machine in a shopping mall is much cheaper than a full service bank branch, and installing a computer terminal in a grocery store, McDonald's restaurant, post office, or check cashing outlet may prove cheaper still. Although traditional depository branches will continue to be essential, digital media can reduce the costs of connecting dangerous or isolated areas to financial services. Indeed, if such areas are connected and the people who live there become accustomed to using them, the result could be to bring in more capital and services.

It is certainly true that any world of "public phone" digital access remains some distance away. As the twenty-first century approaches, the goal of universal home access to a crucial nineteenth-century technology—the telephone—remains unattained. As of 1995, about a fifth of American households whose incomes were below $10,000, and almost 10 percent of households in the $10,000 to $20,000 range, still did not have a telephone at home. It can come as no surprise, then, that in low-income America a home computer is as rare as a home telephone was in the early years of this century and that access to the information superhighway is today still a disproportionately higher-income phenomenon. About a third of all householders who are under age 60 and who earn incomes over $50,000 now have personal computers with modems (and of those under age 30 in this higher-income bracket the PC-plus-modem penetration level is already above 40 percent). On the other hand, of the least affluent households (those with annual incomes below $15,000), fewer than 4 percent have computers with modems, and rural areas, which may stand to benefit disproportionately from access to electronic commerce and information, are less likely to have them than urban ones.

Yet even those small numbers are a start, and technology tends to diffuse downward and outward over time. Forecasters project that many of the new purchases of PCs will be made by older Americans and those with more modest incomes, especially if the inexpensive "Internet computer" becomes a hit. And the government can use its market power to help the diffusion process. Just as the electrification campaign in the Roosevelt era helped bring millions of rural households "on line," to the vast benefit of rural America, so efforts to help disseminate access to digital finance may help bring into the mainstream many who have felt alienated from traditional financial institutions.

And so both the need and the opportunity for governmental efforts to help extend financial opportunity are real and growing. This does not mean replacing or pushing aside markets' attempts to do so. Large though it may be, the federal government could never begin to match either the resources or the skill of the private sector in reaching out to customers, nor should it try to do so. What it can do, however, is to provide incentives so that, wherever possible, poorer and less affluent consumers are not left behind. Equality of access can never be assured. But opportunity of access can surely be broadened, if government, private companies, and new technologies work hand in hand.

Existing Remedies

In the 1970s, as it became clearer that lending practices in the inner cities and among minority and disadvantaged groups were intimately connected with a variety of social problems, the government began paying attention. The upshot was the passage of two critical financial measures, which, in conjunction with the Fair Housing Act and the Equal Credit Opportunity Act, have provided the backbone of the government's efforts to broaden access to credit.

The first, and undoubtedly most prominent, was the Community Reinvestment Act (CRA) of 1977. Proponents of the act argued, with some reason, that banks and other depositories were taking deposits from inner-city and other less affluent neighborhoods, while lending mostly in other areas and frequently, indeed, overlooking qualified loan applications in the process. CRA was designed to encourage banks to be more sensitive to providing for local communities' needs. This mandate was not imposed out of the blue: banks and thrifts, as the proponents (again with justice) noted, enjoy federal charters, granted on the basis of a showing of need in a particular community, as well as recourse to a federal safety net in the form of deposit insurance. It was not illogical, therefore, to examine such institutions' community service records when considering whether to grant applications to merge with or acquire another institution, open or relocate a branch, seek a charter, obtain deposit insurance, or otherwise expand in ways requiring normal regulatory approval. Moreover, CRA lets community groups enter protests against institutions that they believe have not served local communities adequately.

Community groups nevertheless have complained that the Community Reinvestment Act has done too little to channel investment to inner cities. And, indeed, the picture is far from perfect. But even the most conservative estimates suggest that the act has helped funnel substantial volumes of credit to less advantaged areas. Even as banks' and thrifts' share of the total mortgage market has fallen in recent years, their share of mortgage loans in low- and moderate-income areas has risen, a trend no doubt partly due to the CRA. The act's greatest contribution, surely, has been the change it has wrought in the psychology of lending. It has encouraged lenders to ask themselves, as a matter of routine business, whether they are paying attention to poor as well as wealthy neighborhoods—yet always "consistent with the safe and sound operation of [the] institution." To no small extent, the conjecture of the law's original advocates proved right, as many bankers will now attest: profitable loans were going unwritten in inner-city and poorer neighborhoods. Unquestionably, banks' affordable lending programs and (therefore) their experiences vary widely, but some report *lower* delinquency rates for low-income loans (though this is due in part to the kinds of risk-mitigation techniques, such as credit counseling and careful application of underwriting flexibility, that are part of many successful affordable lending programs). Meanwhile, administrative reforms implemented by the present administration have substantially reduced the paperwork and compliance costs of the CRA, focusing it more on effective outcomes and less on process requirements.

It should be noted that the Community Reinvestment Act is neither an antidiscrimination measure nor an antipoverty program, as such. The act specifically aims at low- and moderate-income *neighborhoods*, as distinct from low-income individuals, members of minority groups, or predominantly minority neighborhoods. No doubt it has helped direct credit to such neighborhoods; but it is not intended as a remedy for discrimination, present or past. And differential treatment by the credit markets of persons of varying racial and ethnic backgrounds remains a significant issue. In the word *persons*, however, lies a critical distinction. Many analyses have found that the mortgage markets give shorter shrift to minority neighborhoods than to predominantly white ones. However, neighborhoods' racial and ethnic compositions correlate strongly with such economic factors as income and wealth levels, age and condition of housing stock, owner occupancy rates, and so on. There is some evidence indicating that when economic factors are taken into account, lenders do not appear to discriminate against minority neighborhoods, as such. But discrimination against minority *individuals* is a different matter. Although the issue is, predictably, controversial, some careful research—most notably, perhaps, a study performed by the Federal Reserve Bank of Boston in 1992 and subsequently checked and confirmed by economists in the Comptroller of the Currency's office—has found that, even after such variables as income, employment, and prior credit experience are controlled for, minority applicants were more likely to be denied loans than were whites. Discrimination has also been found by using carefully matched applicants, one white and the other minority, to test for disparate treatment.

Several important civil rights laws address this issue more directly than does the Community Reinvestment Act: notably the Fair Housing Act, which outlaws discrimination in the sale or rental of housing and in real estate transactions (including provision of mortgage credit), and the Equal Credit Opportunity Act, which prohibits discrimination in "any aspect of a credit transaction . . . on the basis of race, color, religion, national origin, sex or marital status, or age." Publicity can also be a powerful, market-based enforcement tool, which Congress deployed in 1989 by amending the Home Mortgage Disclosure Act (HMDA) to require lenders to report each year on the race, sex, and income of mortgage applicants, including cases in which loans were withdrawn or denied. Few major companies want to become known as being in the bottom of the league on fair lending, and the disclosure act makes institutions' minority lending performance easy for the public to see and judge.

Combined with the requirements of the CRA and with lenders' increasingly vigorous search for new customers in a mature mortgage market, the new disclosure requirements seem to have made a difference. Annual mortgage originations to African Americans rose by 193 percent between 1990 (when HMDA's reporting requirements were strengthened) and 1995, and originations to Hispanics rose by 94 percent, as against 70 percent for whites. Momentum appears to have continued or even picked up in the most recent years, as banks have become more conscious of their own and each other's minority lending performance and as the economic expansion unfolded. As figure 5-1 shows, between 1993 and 1995, mortgages issued to African Americans and Hispanics grew much more rapidly than those to whites, although the trend did not extend to 1996.

Similarly, until 1996 the number of new mortgages also increased much faster for borrowers in low-income areas than those in either middle- or higher-income regions. Part of the reason for this pattern, again, was natural growth in the lower-income market as the economy expanded. But a large part, too, was the increasing involvement of banks and other lenders in voluntary programs aimed at serving borrowers in less affluent

Figure 5-1. Growth in Home Purchase Loans, by Race, 1993–95

Percent change

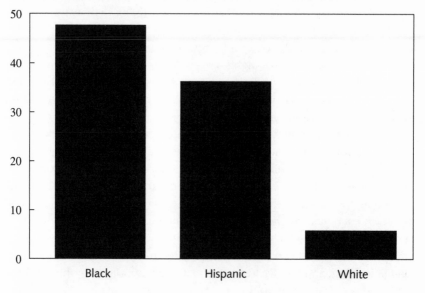

Source: Office of the Comptroller of the Currency.

regions. Many banks, including some of the largest, have announced commitments for lower-income lending, sometimes ranging into the billions of dollars over a period of years. In keeping with that trend, the number of banks given "outstanding" ratings under the Community Reinvestment Act has more than doubled in the past four years, while "needs to improve" ratings have dropped by more than half.

The matter of credit distribution in America is complex and nuanced, defying easy generalizations. Some caveats should therefore be noted. Although low-income mortgage lending has grown disproportionately quickly, it has done so from a comparatively small base. In 1993, for instance, the number of loans, measured as a share of owner-occupied housing units, was 2.7 percent in low-income census tracts, as against 7.2 percent for upper-income tracts. Moreover, the number of lenders competing in upper-income census tracts was about twice that in moderate-income tracts and four times that in low-income ones. Similarly, although

the number of loans extended to members of minorities has soared recently, it remains true that blacks are much likelier to be denied a loan
than whites and that denial rates for minorities are higher in predominantly minority neighborhoods than in predominantly white ones. To what
extent this pattern reflects additional risks, and to what extent it reflects
more insidious factors, is an unsettled question.

In any case the rise in minority lending in recent years reflects mainly
a surge in mortgage applications. It is, of course, precisely the point of
outreach programs to seek applications from worthy customers who might
previously have been overlooked. Still, the difference in approval rates
between minority and white borrowers suggests that there is more work
to be done in bringing members of minorities fully into the economic
mainstream—work not only for the financial sector, but for the government and society in general. Although credit will never be as accessible to
the poor as to the wealthy, no doubt credit democratization has a considerable distance yet to go before fully running its course. The tailing off of
the growth in loans to minority borrowers and to those living in low-
income areas in 1996 underscores this conclusion. In part, the very rapid
growth rates simply may have been unsustainable. But it is also possible
that some lenders have grown complacent in their efforts to reach out to
creditworthy borrowers.

At the same time, an important message should not be obscured:
policy appears to be working. Just as the government succeeded in helping markets democratize credit throughout the postwar period, so now it
appears to be succeeding in helping ensure that creditworthy low-income
and minority borrowers are not overlooked.

Credit Access: The Challenge Ahead

As is often the case with government policies, today's successes can
contain the germ of tomorrow's exhaustion. The Community Reinvestment Act has proved helpful and deserves its place in the federal policy
arsenal. But it is, by design, a broad-brush program. It deliberately seeks
to help expand the flow of credit to whole neighborhoods, rather than to
lower-income individuals. Indeed, most mortgage borrowers in low-income neighborhoods do not have low incomes (and, for that matter, most
low-income borrowers buy homes in moderate- or middle-income areas,

not low-income neighborhoods). Where community credit is concerned, this broad approach is appropriate: improving neighborhoods requires lending money to relatively secure people who want to buy or renovate houses on poor blocks. From a developmental point of view, *where* investment happens is at least as important as who invests.

But, inevitably, any program will have its easiest successes with the easiest cases. The CRA is good at encouraging general purpose lenders to look for customers who, while not being the simplest to cater to, nonetheless pose acceptably small risks and, indeed, can offer some handsome profits while helping bootstrap a struggling neighborhood. Finding ways to bring credit options to a more difficult, but still potentially reachable, class of borrower—who may, moreover, live in an especially rough part of town—is, by definition, a harder job. It will require not just a more inclusive attitude but whole new products offered in tandem with additional services. Poorer and very inexperienced borrowers may need counseling, smaller loans, or innovative forms of collateral. Conventional banks and thrifts often will not be particularly well adapted to this kind of business. Yet other, more specialized kinds of lenders, ranging from credit unions to nonprofit community development groups, often know how to reach the neediest and to succeed where ordinary commercial finance cannot easily thrive.

Increasingly, then, federal policy will need to *target* its attempts to extend access to credit. Specifically, it will need to operate through specialized institutions focused on needy constituencies, in addition to operating through a broad mandate placed on banks and aimed at entire neighborhoods. This does not imply backing away from the existing commitment to encouraging conventional lenders to reach out to overlooked clients. But it does imply that as the broader approach nears its limits, targeted ones will need to be added to the mix.

Community Development Financial Institutions (or CDFIs) can do much to fill this niche. A federal fund for CDFIs was created in 1994 to help existing and new community development lenders expand credit and related financial services (including brokerage and information services) to entrepreneurs in underserved and distressed communities.[1] These lenders can extend credit to residents and businesses for a wide range of purposes: to finance home ownership, rehabilitate dilapidated buildings, and finance new and existing businesses. In exchange, lenders are assisted with up-front matching federal aid.

Specialized lenders have an advantage over conventional banks and thrifts in reaching the hardest-to-qualify borrowers, for they have experience in providing the counseling and other financial assistance often needed to ensure that these borrowers remain creditworthy. America should take advantage of this experience by building on it.

The Accountless: A New Frontier for Policy

Until very recently, "access to financial services" was, in the eyes of policymakers and community activists alike, nearly synonymous with "access to credit." And this equation was natural: no community can thrive if its businesses and entrepreneurs are starved for capital. Moreover, such invidious practices as redlining, a practice dating from the 1930s, when both public agencies and private lenders used racial and demographic data to rate whole neighborhoods for credit risk, operated primarily through the home mortgage and real estate markets. No doubt it was not only understandable but proper for policy to focus first on ensuring that no class faced systematic discrimination in credit markets and that no borrower was ignored or shunted aside simply because of where he or she happened to live.

As strides have been made toward democratizing credit, however, another quite different sort of problem has surfaced, one that is intimately connected to the digitization of the American economy. That is access to depository and payment services. For making loans represents only one side of the balance sheet. The other side is also important and has been, comparatively speaking, neglected by policy until very recently.

According to the Federal Reserve's latest Survey of Consumer Finances, 15 percent of American households lacked a checking account in 1995, down from 19 percent six years before. The survey also showed that 85 percent of the accountless families had annual incomes below $25,000, and a majority of them were nonwhite or Hispanic. John Caskey of Swarthmore College notes in his pioneering research on "alternative banking" that accountless families are also more likely to be headed by someone who is single, unemployed, or female. They are less likely to own their own home, they tend to have more children living at home, and they are very unlikely to hold bank credit cards.

Many readers may be surprised to learn that almost one in six families does without a checking account. The reasons may be more surprising still, or at least more complex than expected. A first instinct may be to blame the matter on a scarcity of bank branches in poorer neighborhoods, particularly as consolidation and competition in the industry force cost cutting. In fact, many inner-city neighborhoods, such as central Los Angeles or the Bronx, contain comparatively few bank branches.

Yet when asked by the Survey of Consumer Finances why they did not keep checking accounts, only 1 percent of respondents said that no bank had convenient hours or locations. Some 23 percent of respondents (up from 15 percent in 1992) said they "do not like dealing with banks"; 27 percent said they did not write enough checks to make an account worthwhile; 21 percent said they did not have enough money, they thought, to make having an account worthwhile; and 8 percent (down from 11 percent in 1992) cited high service charges. It is worth noting that these responses are closely interrelated. Depositories typically charge fees only on small-balance checking accounts, which, for those with low savings, can discourage doing business with a bank in the first place. This problem has probably grown in recent years. As banks have come under increasing competition from other providers of financial services, they have been forced to curtail the cross-subsidies that enabled them to provide low-cost accounts at the expense implicitly of better-heeled customers.

John Caskey's own survey of low-income households in several regions (households with incomes below $25,000 in Atlanta, Oklahoma City, or any of five smaller eastern cities) supports the hypothesis that low savings is a critical reason why people do without checking accounts. Of the 900 households he surveyed in May and June of 1996, 22 percent had no deposit account of any kind; of those without accounts, more than half (53 percent) said they did not need an account because they rarely saved much.

In the modern economy, to be without any sort of bank account is no small matter. It often means, to begin with, holding savings as cash, a practice that is both dangerous and insecure. It may also discourage saving in its own right, thus increasing the vulnerabilities of the poor. Furthermore, being without a checking account requires many of the poorest Americans to pay considerably more for basic financial services than other people need ever contemplate, since not all banks will cash checks for non–account holders and some banks will charge for the service, while check-cashing outlets tend to charge much more for their services (typically 2 to 3 percent of a check's value) than do banks.

A Nudge toward the Mainstream

Federal policy can induce many more Americans to join mainstream finance by having and using a bank account. The Comptroller of the Currency, in conjunction with the Consumer Bankers Association, has convened an educational forum to learn more about people who lack banking relationships (with attention to such matters as the effects of language and cultural differences) and also about possible ways to extend the reach of the mainstream market. Further, the Comptroller's office has announced it will waive application fees for depository institutions that seek new charters and branches in low- and moderate-income census tracts that are not already served by a depository institution. As the Comptroller acknowledges, this is a small step, but one that, by reducing obstacles to serving less affluent populations, points in the right direction.

A larger opportunity, and potentially also a more serious challenge, arises in the context of electronic banking. Under a statute passed in 1996, the government is required to shift the overwhelming majority of federal payments, ranging from wages and contract payments to Social Security and veterans' benefits (but not tax refunds), to electronic funds transfer (EFT) after January 1, 1999.[2] A major question is how to integrate this electronic payments initiative with the substantial population of Americans who do not have bank accounts and who have relied on cashing paper checks. If properly implemented, the electronic payments system could help shift many lower-income Americans toward mainstream finance, while reducing fraud and saving money.

Electronic payments systems can work in a number of different ways, which are not mutually exclusive. Government payments may simply be directly deposited into recipients' bank accounts, thus saving the paperwork and processing costs of using checks. Or, for income support programs or food stamps, whose target populations often lack bank accounts, benefits may be credited to accounts held in beneficiaries' names by the government itself or by private companies who administer the program on behalf of the government. Then beneficiaries may use debit cards to withdraw money from their accounts, either by using automated teller machines (ATMs) or point-of-sale terminals, such as those at grocery checkouts or drug store cash registers. Point-of-sale transactions require telephone verification to ensure that the beneficiary's account has not been overdrawn, but smart cards (stored-value cards), whose embedded computer chip can keep account records, could obviate even that need: beneficiaries would be issued smart cards, which would be charged up at regular intervals and then used as the equivalent of cash.

Today about 43 percent of federal payments and a higher proportion of state payments are made using paper checks. All levels of government, however, are moving to electronic transfer. Fourteen states currently have electronic payments systems in place, five of them statewide, and virtually all the states have plans for electronic payments. State programs typically focus on using electronic payments for income support and other defined-benefit programs. For example, Alabama is launching electronic payment for food stamps, while many welfare recipients in Kansas receive benefits by means of the "Kansas Vision" card.

The benefits of digital payment are considerable. Electronic transfer is considerably less expensive for the federal government than issuing checks and so is expected to save the government tens of millions of dollars a year and perhaps eventually several hundreds of millions. What may be at least as important, however, is electronic transfer's power to reduce the incidence of fraud and abuse. Texas, for instance, has found that switching to electronic payment substantially reduced its food stamp rolls and wiped out the barter of food stamps for drugs. Moreover, pilot programs find these systems to be popular with users and deliverers alike. As the systems become widespread for government benefits, more merchants are likely to adopt the point-of-sale technology that lets them make electronic funds transactions. So, in all likelihood, the spread of electronic benefits payments will also help propel the broader movement away from paper-based transactions.

Electronic funds transfer has potentially broader and deeper implications at the federal level than do the state programs, since the law requires the federal government to digitize virtually *all* federal payments (except for tax refunds), not just payments for particular programs. Under the law, recipients of federal payments would designate a bank of their choice to receive payment. If payees do not designate a bank, Treasury is obligated to ensure that they have access to an account at a financial institution at reasonable cost and with the same consumer protections as other accounts at the same financial institution.

Most social security beneficiaries now receive their benefits electronically, as direct deposits into their bank accounts; new federal contracts also require direct deposit payment. A larger challenge is reaching populations that, as the above data make clear, are far less likely than average to hold deposit accounts. Although the government can use electronic payments to encourage federal beneficiaries to maintain deposit accounts, it needs to make sure that digitally paid benefits are easily and conveniently accessible to all.

State electronic benefits programs have handled this problem by hitching a ride on retail point-of-sale systems and bank-operated automated teller machines. For cash benefits, most states provide a limited number of free ATM visits a month, after which recipients pay about $1 for each use of a banking machine. Those fees, of course, are considerably lower than the ones charged by check-cashing outlets and other "fringe" banks.

In the long term, governments' movement toward electronic payments is only a first step toward a general shift to digital money, but it is an important step. The Treasury Department estimates that more than 340 million federal payments a year, involving more than $240 billion, will switch from paper check to electronic transfer. The changeover will not be without glitches, but it also offers an opportunity: it can serve as a testing ground in seeking to make sure that the maximum number of people can become participants in an age of digital payments. Though many details of the federal government's electronic payments initiative remain to be decided, some general principles may be useful.

One is to remember that for many Americans the payments system is not synonymous with traditional banks. In reaching this population, it may be useful to examine carefully the role of alternative payments system providers. Some check cashers, for instance, have expressed the desire to install ATMs for customers who wish to withdraw government benefits. Of course, the government should be careful to assess whether arrangements with such providers can be made on terms that are suitable to both the government and federal beneficiaries, at competitive prices and with acceptable safety. In the longer run, moreover, it may be possible, using the economies of digital funds transfer, to channel payments services through a host of nontraditional but close-to-home providers, ranging from post offices to fast food restaurants. In short, the government should think creatively and flexibly in seeking to expand inexpensive access to financial services without forsaking consumer protection.

Second, the government should nonetheless encourage people to use and trust mainstream financial institutions. It should also encourage mainstream institutions to extend their reach when it can do so without using coercive or heavy-handed approaches. Not only are mainstream accounts less apt to eat into low-income consumers' budgets, they may help encourage thrift and, over time, help draw more consumers into the expanding web of the digital economy. If well administered, electronic funds transfer can become a good example of how government can use its own influence in the marketplace to help make low-income consumers and mainstream financial institutions more attractive to each other.

As a general proposition, finally, as the government tries to expand access to depository services, it should look for opportunities to use incentives and market forces, rather than flat requirements or direct government account holding. In many cases, banks will find it profitable to offer accounts in which low-income consumers can receive and hold their federal benefits. Indeed, electronic payment may create a profitable new market for banks. Today people who lack bank accounts must cash their government checks in a lump sum upon receipt. But when federal money is deposited electronically into accounts held by (or for) federal beneficiaries, many of them will prefer to withdraw cash as they need it. Many will therefore maintain at least modest balances, and those balances, while perhaps too meager to support full-service checking accounts, might support low-cost, limited access accounts, whose features would depend on balances maintained.

Some people, no doubt, will be especially hard to lure into the banking system or will be unable or unwilling to maintain account balances. In fact, in May 1997 the Treasury Department proposed that banks offer a special low-cost deposit account on which customers could draw only by accessing ATMs and point-of-sale terminals through their debit cards. These "Direct Deposit Too" accounts would not require customers to hold any minimum balances. And in September 1997, Treasury announced that it would waive the electronic requirement for certain recipients of government benefits who believe that abandoning paper check delivery would cause them a financial hardship: people with disabilities, those who may not live near a bank, or who now cash their checks for free.

As a last resort, the government can secure accounts for those who do not wish to take advantage of these and other possible deposit arrangements banks might offer. But it would be far better, where possible, to encourage all types of depository service providers to reach out to this population. Moreover, incentives might be selectively available to banks doing business in low-income areas. The Comptroller's waiver of application fees for depositories opening branches in "unbanked" low-income areas is a good example of this sort of targeted localism in action.

The Other Kind of Capital

And what of the world of digital finance more broadly? Beyond matters of credit and payment, how best to ensure that all Americans can enjoy the fruits of the digital revolution? Here, at last, the circle closes: the issues of finance merge with the larger challenges for public policy in an age when the advantage of brains over muscle grows by the year. In the end, it can be taken as a given that America's most literate and numerate, its professionals and top-level businesspeople, will change the face of finance. With sophisticated financial models and vigilant computer agents reaching around the world over the Internet, they will invent countless kinds of transactions that are now undreamt of, but that tomorrow will be as ordinary as options and mutual funds have become today.

But will digital finance, in turn, change the face of America? And will its potential be fully exploited by people who wear uniforms or denim to work, as well as by pin-striped professionals? That is a much harder question. It depends, finally, less on finance itself than on the education and skill of American consumers and workers. And those depend on families, schools, and neighborhoods, all working in partnership with a government that seeks to open doors to knowledge and achievement, but that cannot push people through them.

In the end, the power of the financial system is no greater than the sophistication and ingenuity of the people who use it. Smart cards are much less important than smart people, and the Internet is, after all, nothing but a conduit for the creativity of the millions of Americans who are beginning to discover it. Money, microchips, and sound public policies are all, of course, important. But for all the promise and perils of financial capital, human capital is more important still. In finance, as in everything else, it is brainpower and imagination that will open the next American frontier.

Notes

Introduction

1. Congress also directed the Treasury Department to consult with the heads of certain other government agencies and with private sector and academic experts. It has done so. In addition, we have also met with and received valuable advice from various individuals in these different communities.

Chapter 1

1. A well-known study of the financial services industry by McKinsey Global Institute has estimated that between 1980 and 1993, overall productivity in financial services increased at an annual rate of almost 4 percent, nearly three times faster than for the rest of the economy. Within the financial services industry, bank employment was particularly hard hit during the early 1990s, but has rebounded somewhat to 1.5 million employees through the second quarter of 1997, up from 1.45 million in the first quarter of 1996.

2. Some states also placed restrictions on or discriminated against out-of-state insurers for reasons similar to those that led them to restrict the geographic scope of their banks.

3. The Fed has delegated authority to oversee margin requirements on exchange-traded futures contracts to the Commodity Futures Trading Commission (CFTC). It is important to distinguish between margins on securities and performance bonds in the futures industry. Securities margins represent an *extension of*

credit from the broker to the customer. In contrast, futures margins, or performance bonds, are good-faith deposits the customer *pays in advance* against potential losses in a futures position from one settlement cycle to the next.

4. The SEC was also given the responsibility for policing trading of securities by corporate insiders—directors, officers, or principal shareholders—to ensure the integrity of the markets. In 1984 Congress gave the SEC added authority to bring suit at the agency's discretion for civil penalties of three times the profits made on insider trading. Furthermore, in 1990 Congress gave federal courts the power to order the removal from office of any director or officer convicted of insider trading.

5. Congress also has used disclosure policy to protect consumers against lending abuses by, among other things, requiring banks and savings and loans to fully disclose their credit terms and conditions.

6. When this conversion was authorized in 1968, part of the old Fannie Mae was split off into a new government corporation, the Government National Mortgage Association (Ginnie Mae) within the Department of Housing and Urban Development. Ginnie Mae was limited to supporting the secondary market for the special housing programs (FHA and VA) and was given Fannie Mae's remaining mortgage portfolio to liquidate.

7. Interestingly, despite the deregulation of deposit interest rates, Merrill Lynch's cash management accounts have enjoyed rapid growth. In 1995 more checks were written on Merrill than on any institution except for Bank of America and Citibank.

8. Section 20 allows national banks and state banks belonging to the Federal Reserve System to have securities affiliates, provided they are not "engaged principally" in underwriting the kinds of securities mentioned above.

9. Initially, the Fed limited the revenues from securities underwriting in areas off-limits to the bank itself to no more than 5 percent of the securities affiliate's total revenues. The revenue test was subsequently increased to 10 percent, and in late 1996 the Fed raised it again, to 25 percent (with the affiliates earning the balance of the revenues primarily from underwriting federal government bonds, which banks can do in their own right).

10. Actually, regulators first arranged for other large banks to lend to Continental, but when the loans proved insufficient to halt the deposit run, the creditor banks' claims also were put at risk by Continental's demise. Accordingly, in July 1984 all the U.S. banking regulators involved—the Federal Reserve, FDIC, and Comptroller of the Currency—agreed in the name of forestalling systemic risk to extend protection beyond the insurance limit.

11. Under Section 141 of the FDICIA, failed institutions must be resolved by the method that involves the least cost to the FDIC, which as a practical matter means that the FDIC must not protect uninsured depositors against loss. Section

141 permits the least-cost requirement to be waived if it is necessary to avoid "systemic risk" (such as a run by depositors on other banks), but this can be done only if both the FDIC's Board of Directors and the Board of Governors of the Federal Reserve System recommend the action by a two-thirds vote, and if the Secretary of the Treasury, in consultation with the President, makes the same determination.

12. Actually, the FDIC did limit the growth of weak savings banks that it supervised, but this policy was not applied by federal regulators of the more numerous savings and loan associations.

Chapter 2

1. Instead, the Telecommunications Act of 1996 authorizes a system whereby universal service is achieved, not by charging some users more to allow other users to pay less, but by placing a small assessment on the revenues from *all* telecommunications services and using the proceeds to assist low-income users and those located in high-cost areas. Such a neutral means of financing does not distort competition in the way that the old system of cross-subsidies did.

2. The chart shows commissions paid by large institutional customers; separate data for retail trades were unavailable.

3. Anticipating this development, the Comptroller of the Currency issued an advisory in August 1996 to all national banks to install systems to monitor and control risks stemming from credit derivatives, which on the whole, the OCC acknowledged, should provide major benefits to banks that otherwise are too heavily exposed to particular types of risk.

4. The risks of derivatives are addressed again in chapter 4.

5. Mutual fund companies and brokerages allow their customers to gain access to their accounts by writing checks, but these are drawn on and cleared through banks.

6. Indeed, John Boyd and Mark Gertler have shown that when a number of adjustments are made in the conventional calculations of U.S. banks' market share of financial assets—notably by accounting for off-balance-sheet risks and for unreported loans to American companies by foreign banks with U.S. offices (which are counted for this purpose as American banks)—banks' decline during the past several decades largely disappears.

7. A number of academic studies have found, for example, that mergers between larger banks in particular have not improved efficiency and in some cases have detracted from it.

8. In fact, recent evidence from research conducted at the Federal Reserve Bank of New York indicates that bank efficiency improved significantly following

removal in the 1970s and 1980s of geographic restrictions on bank expansion. Moreover, the researchers have found that most of the reduced banking costs from the elimination of intrastate banking restrictions in particular were passed on to customers in the form of lower loan rates.

9. Nonetheless, the OTC markets increasingly are adopting the long-standing practice in the futures industry of requiring collateral to reduce credit risk exposure between counterparties.

Chapter 3

1. Recent studies of the Toronto Stock Exchange, which, for stocks priced at $5 or more, switched several years ago to trading in 5 cent ticks rather than in 12.5 cent units, suggest that Canadian investors are saving a little more than 1 cent per share as a result of the change, which in turn has led to an increase in the volume of trading.

2. Previously only stocks priced under $10 on NASDAQ were priced in sixteenths. The corresponding threshold for stocks traded on the American Stock Exchange is $5 and under.

3. In 1996 Congress narrowed the differences between the national thrift and bank charters by revoking special tax rules for thrifts regarding treatment of bad debts and by broadening the ability of thrifts to originate and hold credit card, student, and small-business loans.

4. Section 23A of the Federal Reserve Act, for example, says that banks belonging to bank holding companies cannot grant credit to any one affiliate in amounts exceeding 10 percent of the bank's capital, and in the aggregate exceeding 20 percent of the bank's capital. Meanwhile, under generally applicable lending restrictions, a bank cannot extend loans to any single customer in excess of 15 percent of capital, a restriction that would apply if a bank belonging to a holding company wanted to support its affiliates indirectly by lending to their customers. However, if restrictions on banks' activities were liberalized, there might be a case for placing an aggregate ceiling on the extension of bank credit to all customers of affiliates.

5. Moreover, if any subsidy provided by the federal safety net were significant, then banks would routinely conduct their nonbanking activities through subsidiaries rather than holding company affiliates. Yet many banks in fact engage in consumer and commercial finance, and data processing, through affiliates rather than subsidiaries, contradicting the supposition that any sizable federal subsidy (net of supervisory costs) exists. In any event, as discussed shortly in the text, even if a net subsidy exists, it can easily be transferred by a bank to its holding company (and from there to its affiliates) through dividend payments.

6. In other words, banks' investments in their subsidiaries should be deducted from their capital accounts in determining whether they meet regulatory capital requirements.

7. In June 1997, the Treasury Department proposed two ways to address the banking-commerce issue. Under one approach, Congress could allow a limited mixing of the two, coupled with a limit on bank affiliations with commercial firms having assets in excess of $750 million. This first approach would also meld the currently separate thrift and banking charters into a single charter. The alternative approach would restrict banks to affiliating with financial enterprises only and would retain the current distinction between the bank and thrift charters (while also continuing to allow commercial affiliations of unitary thrift holding companies).

8. Regulation E, issued and enforced by the Federal Reserve Board, limits the liability of holders of lost credit cards to $50. In March 1997 the Fed issued a report to Congress addressing to what extent, if any, Regulation E should be applied to issuers of stored value cards. The Fed's report outlined a range of alternatives without endorsing any of them. Since then, a proposal to apply a $50 liability limit on debit cards has been introduced in Congress, which could well have prompted MasterCard and Visa to announce during the summer that they were voluntarily imposing such a cap.

9. In principle, however, some smart cards might pay interest—raising, in another form, the complex question of whether the cards are like cash or like bank accounts.

10. Among the more important elements of the guidelines are the rules for defining "relevant markets" and for calculating measures of concentration of economic activity, which provide warning signals for when mergers are most likely to be challenged.

Chapter 4

1. For a similar definition, see Bartholomew, Mote, and Whalen (1997).

2. FDICIA also directed the Federal Reserve to develop a regulation limiting the credit exposure of banks to each other, which it has since done in Regulation F. This regulation restricts any bank from depositing amounts greater than 25 percent of its capital with another bank unless the bank that holds the deposit is "adequately capitalized." Given the increasingly rapid pace at which capital positions of banks, especially big ones, can change, it may be appropriate for the Fed to extend the limits of Regulation F to deposits held with all banks, regardless of their current capital positions.

3. FDICIA also provided legal certainty for multilateral netting arrangements

among banks that participate in settlement networks such as the Clearing House Interbank Payments System (CHIPS), but the act does not reach the net positions that foreign exchange participants may have with each other.

4. As noted in Chapter 1, Section 141 of FDICIA permits protection of otherwise uninsured depositors only on the approval of the Federal Reserve Board, the FDIC, and the Secretary of the Treasury, who must all find the action necessary to prevent systemic consequences.

5. Two important distinctions between even a very large issuer of commercial paper and a very large commercial bank underscore why the Fed need not consider lending to the former if it gets in financial trouble: the liabilities of nonbank issuers of commercial paper are not insured, and the issuers are not linked to the payments system. As a result, the danger to the economy from even a contagious interruption in the commercial paper market is almost certainly much lower than from a contagious run on the banking system or a breakdown of the system for clearing and settling payments among banks.

6. According to data compiled by the Investment Company Institute, at year end 1996 there were $3.54 trillion held in mutual funds (equities and bonds), of which $1.24 trillion consisted of funds held in retirement accounts. Of the latter amount, roughly 70 percent was held in equity funds, 30 percent in bond and money market funds.

7. Technically speaking, money market funds are not legally required to redeem their shares at par. But investors certainly expect them to behave this way, expectations which have been reinforced by the fact that some sponsors of money funds have voluntarily contributed funds to them to ensure that they would not "break the buck."

8. As a last resort, the SEC can order the suspension of redemptions if it is necessary to protect mutual fund investors. The SEC has used this power several times: notably, after President Kennedy's assassination in 1963, the power blackouts of New York City in 1977 and of lower Manhattan in 1990, problems in the municipal bond market in 1986, and the closure of the Hong Kong Stock Exchange in November 1987.

9. Other factors contributed to generalized panic at the time. For example, the presidential task force formed to study the cause of the 1987 stock price collapse found that a new feature of the market—so-called portfolio insurance—had aggravated selling pressure. Portfolio insurance, now discredited, consisted of strategies that caused stocks and stock index futures and options to be sold automatically after an initial price decline. The strategies may have worked in more normal times, but when investors were all running for the door at the same time, the selling they produced only made matters worse.

10. Nonetheless, NASDAQ reportedly experienced delay in completing some trades in late October, a problem that should not reappear once its handling capacity is increased in 1998.

11. Similarly, the futures industry has implemented its own circuit breakers to include related derivative markets, so that they are coordinated with the NYSE.

12. The trading halt linked to the Dow initially was to last one hour following a 250 point move, and to expand for another two hours if the Dow moved another 150 points after trading resumed. To accommodate the significant increase in stock prices since 1987, in early 1997 the NYSE revised the trading halts to one-half hour following a 350 point move in the Dow and a further one hour halt following another 200 point Dow change. In percentage terms, however, the revised triggers are well below the levels required by the original trigger.

13. The clearinghouse supporting the Chicago Mercantile Exchange also maintains a $250 million line of credit with a consortium of banks to meet liquidity needs.

14. Federal Reserve Board Chairman Alan Greenspan struck a similar theme in his address to the Federal Reserve Bank Structure Conference in Chicago in May 1997.

15. In the Fed's proposal, precommitment would apply to banks' dealings in securities, foreign exchange, and derivatives in their "trading accounts" (instruments bought to hedge the trading of the underlying securities). Derivatives related to the hedging of risks in the rest of the bank—for example, in the traditional lending activities of the "bank" proper—would not be covered by the precommitment approach (just as they are not covered by the current "market risk" amendment to the capital rules).

16. In fact, the Federal Reserve reportedly is considering a wide range of approaches for modifying the current risk-based capital standards, including an option that would extend the precommitment concept to all credit risk, as well as more finely tuning the existing risk weights on various types of loans. The Fed is also studying the capital allocation models that banks are using to apportion capital according to the risks that various instruments may present.

17. The subordinated debt requirement would apply to *banks* and not their holding companies. However, to prevent large bank organizations from splitting themselves up into many smaller banks as a way of avoiding the requirement, it would apply to all banks within a banking organization whose total assets exceeded the applicable threshold.

18. Under the risk-based capital requirements agreed to in the Basle Accord, banks must back 4 percent and 8 percent of their risk-weighted assets with "tier 1" and "tier 2" capital, respectively. Subordinated debt can count for up to 2 percent of tier 2 capital, but for none of tier 1 capital.

19. Thus, for example, banks in organizations above a certain size (the $10 billion threshold, for example) would be required, not just simply allowed, to back 1 to 2 percent of their risk-weighted assets with subordinated debt, on a quarterly basis. In addition, organizations subject to the requirement could be required to issue debt having maturity of at least a year (to ensure long-term

stability), with a certain fraction coming due each quarter, so that even if a bank chose not to expand its risk-weighted assets, it would still need to subject itself to the discipline of the market on a regular basis.

20. The General Accounting Office made a similar recommendation in late 1996, while at the same time commending bank regulators for bolstering their monitoring of bank derivatives activities and market participants themselves for improving their management of risks associated with derivatives.

21. To be sure, significant hurdles remain in implementing market-value accounting for banks, many of whose assets are not readily tradable and thus difficult to assess. This has driven accounting bodies, such as the Financial Accounting Standards Board (FASB), to adopt "partial" market-value accounting measures. For example, beginning in December 1998, the FASB will require publicly traded companies to state at their market values all derivatives greater than amounts being hedged. Critics had attacked this rule when it was proposed for, among other reasons, the impracticality of distinguishing between derivatives used for hedging and those for speculation. But this criticism highlights a more general problem with all attempts to mark only a portion of a bank's assets or liabilities to market. Such halfway measures can potentially mislead investors about the true condition of the overall institution; a far better approach is to work on adopting truly comprehensive market-value accounting for all assets and liabilities.

22. Under RTGS, every buyer would need money to cover all of its transactions on the spot. Instead of being able to wait for a few hours to come up with funds, buyers would therefore either have to maintain positive balances in their clearing accounts at all times or (if they wanted to run a negative position) have to get a line of credit from another institution or post some form of credible collateral. Either arrangement would impose potentially significant costs on member banks.

23. In a related—and welcome—initiative, banks from twenty large industrialized countries are working on creating a limited-purpose bank to clear foreign exchange transactions, one of the most important sources of risk to CHIPS. Participating banks would maintain accounts at this bank in various currencies; these accounts would be used to settle foreign exchange transactions instantaneously, thereby eliminating "Herstatt risk" (the risk of a breakdown in settlement due to the lag in clearing foreign exchange transactions).

24. The Fed also settles payment for more than 100 other small-value net-payment arrangements.

25. Banks can and do make payments to each other directly, without going through the Fed, by settling against the accounts they may hold with each other or through accounts they may hold with their correspondent banks.

26. Toward this end, the Federal Reserve has begun consolidating its data processing centers for electronic payments services to improve reliability, especially in emergencies.

27. If banks hold funds in their clearing accounts that exceed their reserve requirements, however, the Fed will designate those amounts as "clearing balances" and grant the banks credits to offset fees for Fedwire and other Federal Reserves, such as check clearing and ACH transactions.

28. In 1997 CHIPS was averaging $1.4 trillion a day in transactions. Foreign banks can belong to CHIPS only through their U.S. (New York–based) branches or subsidiaries.

29. It also explains why the average transaction on CHIPS ($6.5 million in 1994) is substantially larger than the average transaction on Fedwire ($2.9 million in 1994).

30. Major clearinghouses include the Government Securities Clearing Corporation (U.S. government bonds); MBS Clearing Corporation (mortgage-backed securities); National Securities Clearing Corporation (stocks, corporate bonds, and municipal bonds); Options Clearing Corporation (options); and the Board of Trade Clearing Corporation and Chicago Mercantile Exchange (financial futures).

31. The Chicago Mercantile Exchange, for example, marks all open positions to market at least twice a day and more often when volatility warrants.

Chapter 5

1. Qualified lenders can include community development banks and credit unions, revolving loan funds, microloan funds, minority-owned banks, and community development corporations.

2. In September 1997, Treasury announced that while it intends to have low-cost accounts for the unbanked available by that date, recipients would continue to get checks until the accounts are operational or until January 2, 2000, whichever is earlier (subject to an allowance for hardship waivers, discussed later).

Bibliography

Amel, Dean F. 1996. "Trends in the Structure of Federally Insured Depository Institutions, 1984–1994." *Federal Reserve Bulletin* 82 (January): 1–15.

August, James D., and others. 1997. "Survey of Finance Companies, 1996." *Federal Reserve Bulletin* (July): 543–56.

Avery, Robert B., and others. 1996. "Credit Risk, Credit Scoring, and the Performance of Home Mortgages." *Federal Reserve Bulletin* 82 (July): 621–48.

Baer, Herbert L., Douglas D. Evanoff, and Christine A. Pavel. 1991. "Payment System Issues in a 24-Hour Global Economy." *Research in Financial Services Private and Public Policy*, vol. 3: 1–61.

Bank Administration Institute and the Boston Consulting Group. 1995. *The Information Superhighway and Retail Banking*, vol. 1. Chicago: BAI, June.

———. 1995. *The Information Superhighway and Retail Banking*, vol. 2. Chicago: BAI, December.

Bank for International Settlements (BIS). 1997. *Bank for International Settlements: 67th Annual Report*. Basle, BIS.

———. 1996. *Settlement Risk in Foreign Exchange Transactions*. Basle, March.

———. 1995. *Cross-Border Securities Settlements*. Basle, March.

———. 1993. *Payment Systems in the Group of Ten Countries*. Basle, December. (Also known as *The Red Book*)

———. 1994. *Payment Systems in the Group of Ten Countries*. Basle, December.

Barfield, Claude E., ed. 1996. *International Financial Markets: Harmonization versus Competition*. Washington: American Enterprise Institute.

Barrett, Amy, and Nanette Byrnes. 1996. "A New S&L Mess." *Business Week*, May 13:108.

Barth, James R., Daniel E. Nolle, and Tara N. Rice. 1997. "Commercial Banking Structure, Regulation, and Performance: An International Comparison." OCC Economics Working Paper 97-6.

Bartholomew, Philip F., Larry R. Mote, and Gary W. Whalen. Forthcoming. "Systemic Risk," in *Finance Issues in Development*. Washington: American University Press.

Benston, George J. 1990. *The Separation of Commercial and Investment Banking: The Glass-Steagall Act Revisited and Reconsidered*. Oxford University Press.

Benston, George J., and George G. Kaufman. 1988. *Risk and Solvency Regulation of Depository Institutions: Past Policies and Current Options*. Monograph Series in Finance and Economics. New York University, Salomon Brothers Center for the Study of Financial Institutions, Graduate School of Business Administration.

Berger, Allen N., and Loretta J. Mester. 1997. "Inside the Black Box: What Explains Differences in the Efficiencies of Financial Institutions." Finance and Economics Discussion Series 1997-10. Federal Reserve Board, January.

Berger, Allen N., Anil K. Kashyap, and Joseph M. Scalise. 1995. "The Transformation of the U.S. Banking Industry: What a Long, Strange Trip It's Been." *Brookings Papers on Economic Activity* 2: 55–200.

Bishop, Matthew. 1996. "Corporate Risk Management: A New Nightmare in the Boardroom." *Economist*, February 10: Survey, 53–55.

———. 1996. "A Survey of Corporate Risk Management: Too Hot to Handle?" 1996. *Economist*, February 10: 1–22. Survey starts after p. 58.

Board of Governors of the Federal Reserve System. 1997. *Report to the Congress on the Application of the Electronic Fund Transfer Act to Electronic Stored-Value Products*. March.

Booz, Allen & Hamilton Inc., Financial Services Group. 1996. *Consumer Demand for Internet Banking*. Washington.

Borowsky, Mark, et al. 1995. "The Smart Card Era Dawns at Last." *Credit Card Management* (June): 57.

Boston Consulting Group. 1995. *The Information Superhighway and Retail Banking*, vols. I and II. Chicago: Bank Administration Institute.

Boyd, John H., and Mark Gertler. 1994 "Are Banks Dead? Or Are the Reports Greatly Exaggerated?" *Federal Reserve Bank of Minneapolis Quarterly Review* 18 (Summer): 2–23.

Boyd, John H., and David E. Runkle, 1993. "Size and Performance of Banking Firms: Testing the Predictions of Theory." *Journal of Monetary Economics* 31 (February): 47–67. February

Brimmer, Andrew F. 1989. "Distinguished Lecture on Economics in Government: Central Banking and Systemic Risks in Capital Markets." *Journal of Economic Perspectives* 3 (Spring): 3–16.

Browne, F. X., and David Cronin. 1995. "Payments Technologies, Financial Innovation, and Laissez-Faire Banking" *Cato Journal* 15 (Spring-Summer): 101–16.

Bryan, Lowell L. 1991. *Bankrupt: Restoring the Health and Profitability of Our Banking System*. Champaign, Ill.: Harper Business.

———. 1988. *Breaking Up the Bank: Rethinking an Industry under Siege*. Homewood, Ill.: Dow Jones-Irwin.

Canner, Glenn B., and Wayne Passmore. 1995. "Home Purchase Lending in Low-Income Neighborhoods and to Low-Income Borrowers." *Federal Reserve Bulletin* 81 (February): 71–103.

Cartellieri, Ulrich, and Alan Greenspan. 1996. "Global Risk Management." William Taylor Memorial Lecture no. 3. Washington: Group of Thirty.

Carron, Andrew S. 1982. *The Plight of the Thrift Institutions*. Brookings.

Caskey, John P. 1994. *Fringe Banking: Check-Cashing Outlets, Pawnshops, and the Poor*. New York: Russell Sage Foundation.

Chaum, David. 1994. "Prepaid Smart Card Techniques: A Brief Introduction and Comparison." *DigiCash publication*. Website: http://www.digicash.com/index_n.html.

Cole, Rebel A., and John D. Wolken. 1995. "Financial Services Used by Small Businesses: Evidence from the 1993 National Survey of Small Business Finances." *Federal Reserve Bulletin* 81 (July): 629–67.

Corzine, Jon. 1996. "Keynote Address: Financial Markets at the End of the 20th Century." *Quarterly Review of Economics and Finance* 36: 9–16. Special issue.

Dadush, Uri, and Milan Brahmbhatt. 1995. "Anticipating Capital Flow Reversals." *Finance & Development* (December): 3–5.

Deloitte & Touche Consulting Group. 1995. *The Future of Retail Banking: A Global Perspective*. Washington: Deloitte & Touche.

Eaton, Leslie. 1996. "Slow Transition for Investing: Stock Market Meets Internet." *New York Times*, November 11: A-1.

Edwards, Gerald A. Jr., and Gregory E. Eller. 1996. "Derivatives Disclosures by Major U.S. Banks, 1995." *Federal Reserve Bulletin* 82 (September): 791–801.

Ernst and Young LLP and The American Bankers Association. 1996. *Special Report on Technology in Banking: Creating the Value Network 1996*. Washington.

Ettin, Edward C. 1994. "The Evolution of the North American Banking System." Paper presented at "'Experts' Meeting on Structural Changes in Financial Markets: Trends and Practices." Paris: OECD. July 11–12.

Fancher, Carol H. 1996. "Smart Cards." *Scientific American* 275 (August): 40–45.

Federal Reserve Bank of New York. 1995. *Fedwire: The Federal Reserve Wire Transfer Service*. Monograph prepared by the Payments System Studies Staff of the Research and Market Analysis Group. March.

Freeman, Andrew. 1996. "Turning Digits into Dollars: A Survey of Technology in Finance." *Economist*, October 26. A 22-page survey following p. 66.

Gardner, Lisa, A., and Martin F. Grace. 1993. "X-Efficiency in the U.S. Life Insurance Industry." *Journal of Banking and Finance* 17 (April): 497–510.

Garwood, Griffith L., and Dolores S. Smith. 1993. "The Community Reinvestment Act: Evolution and Current Issues." *Federal Reserve Bulletin* 79 (April): 251–67.

Gates, Bill, with Nathan Myhrvold and Peter Rinearson. 1995. *The Road Ahead.* London: Viking.

Gibson, Paul. 1996. "The Technology Conundrum." *Institutional Investor* (July): 35–38.

Giles, Martin. 1996. "The Domino Effect: A Survey of International Banking." *Economist* (April 27): 59–97.

Goldstein, Morris, and Philip Turner. 1996. *Banking Crises in Emerging Economies: Origins and Policy Options.* Basle: Bank for International Settlements.

Greenspan, Alan. 1997. "Remarks at the Conference on Bank Structure and Competition of the Federal Reserve Bank of Chicago." May 1, 1997.

———. 1996. "Banking in the Global Marketplace: Remarks at the Federation of Bankers Associations of Japan, Tokyo, Japan." Washington: Federal Reserve System. November 18.

———. 1996. "Statement before the Committee on Banking, Housing, and Urban Affairs, U.S. Senate, March 26, 1996." *Federal Reserve Board Bulletin* (May): 403.

Group of Thirty. 1997. *Global Institutions, National Supervision and Systemic Risk.* Washington.

Gurley, John G., and Edward S. Shaw. 1960. *Money in a Theory of Finance.* Brookings.

Harris, Stephen L., and Charles A. Pigott. 1997. "A Changed Landscape for Financial Services." *OECD Observer* (June-July): 28–31.

Hawke, John D. Jr. 1996. "New EFT Law Presents Challenges, Opportunities." *American Banker,* November 6: 4ff.

Herring, Richard J., and Robert E. Litan. 1995. *Financial Regulation in a Global Economy.* Brookings.

Himmelstein, Linda. 1996. "This Virtual Broker Has Real Competition." *Business Week,* July 22: 91–92.

Holland, David, and others. 1996. "Interstate Banking: The Past, Present and Future." *FDIC Banking Review* 9 (Fall): 117.

Holland, Kelley. 1994. "The Poor Need Access to Digital Banking, Too." *Business Week,* November 21: 112.

Holland, Kelley, Paula Dwyer, and Gail Edmondson. 1994. "Technobanking Takes Off." *Business Week,* November 18: 52–53.

Horvitz, Paul M. 1983. "Market Discipline Is Best Provided by Subordinate Creditors." *American Banker,* July 15: 4.

Horvitz, Paul M., and Lawrence J. White. 1996. "The Challenges of the New Electronic Technologies in Banking: Private Strategies and Public Policies." Paper presented at the Western Economic Association, June 29. NYU Salomon Center Working Paper Series S-96-44.

Humphrey, David B. 1996. "The Economics of Electronic Benefit Transfer Payments." *Federal Reserve Bank of Richmond Economic Quarterly* 82 (Spring): 77–94.

Humphrey, David B., Lawrence B. Pulley, and Jukka M. Vesala. 1996. "Cash, Paper and Electronic Payments: A Cross-Country Analysis." *Journal of Money, Credit, and Banking* 28, part 2 (November): 914–39.

Javetski, Bill, and William Glasgall. 1994. "Borderless Finance: Fuel for Growth." *Business Week*, November 18: 40.

Jayaratne, Jith, and Philip E. Strahan. 1997. "Entry Restrictions, Industry Evolution, and Dynamic Efficiency: Evidence from Commercial Banking." *Federal Reserve Bank of New York Staff Reports*, no. 22. March.

———. 1996. "The Finance-Growth Nexus: Evidence from Bank Branch Deregulation." *Quarterly Journal of Economics* 3 (August): 639–70.

Juncker, George R., Bruce J. Summers, and Florence M. Young. 1991. "A Primer on the Settlement of Payments in the United States." *Federal Reserve Bulletin* 77 (November): 847–58.

Kennickell, Arthur B., and others. 1997. "Family Finances in the U.S.: Recent Evidence from the Survey of Consumer Finances." *Federal Reserve Bulletin* (January): 1–24.

Keynes, John Maynard. 1936. *The General Theory of Employment, Interest and Money.* Harcourt, Brace.

Kimelman, John. 1997. "After Years of Downsizing, Bank Jobs on the Rise." *American Banker*, August 19: 1.

Kupiec, Paul H., and James M. O'Brien. 1993. "A Pre-Commitment Approach to Capital Requirements for Market Risk." Finance and Economics Discussion Series 95-36. Washington: Federal Reserve Board, no. 95-36. July.

Lacker, Jeffrey M. 1995. "Neighborhoods and Banking." *Federal Reserve Bank of Richmond Economic Quarterly* 81 (Spring): 13–39.

Lindgren, Carl-Johan, Gillian Garcia, and Matthew I. Saal. 1996. *Bank Soundness and Macroeconomic Policy.* Washington: International Monetary Fund.

Lindsey, Richard R., and Anthony P. Pecora. 1997. "10 Years After: Regulatory Developments in the Securities Markets since the 1987 Market Break." U.S. Securities and Exchange Commission.

Litan, Robert E. 1987. *What Should Banks Do?* Brookings.

———. 1991. *The Revolution in U.S. Finance.* Brookings.

Ludwig, Eugene A. 1996. "The Democratization of Credit and the Future of Community Development," NR 96-21. Speech before the Community Development Conference, Arlington, Va. February 23.

———. 1996b. "Greater Economic Opportunity for Today and Tomorrow." *Vital Speeches of the Day,* 62 (March 1, 1996): 290–92.

———. 1996c. "Speech before the Consumer Bankers Association, September 30," NR 96-106. Washington: Office of the Comptroller of the Currency.

Marcus, Craig E. 1996. "Beyond the Boundaries of the Community Reinvestment

Act and the Fair Lending Laws: Developing a Market-Based Framework for Generating Low- and Moderate-Income Lending." *Columbia Law Review* 96 (April): 710–58.

Marshall, Chris, Larry Prusak, and David Shpilberg. 1996. "Financial Risk and the Need for Superior Knowledge Management." *California Management Review* 38: 77–101. Spring.

Mayer, Martin. 1997. *The Bankers: The Next Generation.* Truman Talley Books/ Dutton.

McKinsey Global Institute. 1992. *Service Sector Productivity.* Washington.

Mills, Edwin S., and Luan' Sende Lubuele. 1994. "Performance of Residential Mortgages in Low- and Moderate-Income Neighborhoods." *Journal of Real Estate Finance and Economics* 9 (November): 245–60.

Mishkin, Frederic S. 1995. "Comment on Systemic Risk," in George K. Kaufman, ed., *Banking, Financial Markets, and Systemic Risk,* 31–45. JAI Press.

Modahl, Mary A., and Sara H. Eichler. 1995. "The Internet Economy," in Forrester Research, Inc., *People & Technology Strategies,* vol. 2.

Moore, Richter H. Jr. 1994. "Wiseguys: Smarter Criminals and Smarter Crime in the 21st Century." *Futurist* (September 1): 33–37.

Munnell, Alicia H., and others. 1996. "Mortgage Lending in Boston: Interpreting HMDA Data." *American Economic Review* 86 (March): 25–53.

Murphy, Jamie, and Chris Lacher. 1996. "1-Mississippi, 2-Mississippi: How to Measure the Web." *New York Times CyberTimes* (August 10-11).

National Commission on Financial Institution Reform, Recovery and Enforcement. 1993. "Origins and Causes of the S&L Debacle: A Blueprint for Reform." Report to the President and Congress of the United States. Washington.

National Telecommunications and Information Administration, U.S. Department of Commerce. 1995. *Falling through the Net: A Survey of the "Have Nots" in Rural and Urban America.* July.

O'Connell, Vanessa. 1996. "On-Line Investing Flourishes as Brokers Slash Commissions on Computer Trades." *Wall Street Journal,* September 27: C1.

———. 1996. "Studies Back Using Cents in Stock Deals." *Wall Street Journal,* November 21: C1, C21.

———. 1997. "Point, Click and Buy: On-Line Investing Takes Off, But Watch Out for a 'Crash.'" *Wall Street Journal,* September 5, 1997, C1.

Office of Technology Assessment. 1990. *Trading around the Clock: Global Securities Markets and Information Technology.* Washington.

Organization for Economic Cooperation and Development. 1993. "World Securities Markets: Looking Ahead." *OECD Financial Market Trends* 55 (February): 13–41.

Parkinson, Patrick, and others. 1992. *Clearance and Settlement in U.S. Securities Markets.* Staff study 163. Board of Governors of the Federal Reserve System.

Patrikis, Ernest T. 1996. "The Controversy Continues: Gross vs. Net Settlement."

Speech before The International ACH Conference: "Making Electronic Payments a Reality," San Francisco. April 16.

Peek, Joe, and Eric S. Rosengren, 1996. "The International Transmission of Financial Shocks: The Case of Japan." Federal Reserve Bank of Boston. January.

Polonchek, John, and Ronald K. Miller. 1996. "The Valuation Effects of Insurance Company Securities Offerings." *Advances in Financial Economics* 2: 187–204.

Presidential Task Force on Market Mechanisms. 1988. *Report of the Presidential Task Force on Market Mechanisms.* January.

Purdy, Matthew, and Joe Sexton. 1995. "Bank-Poor Communities Are Forced to Improvise." *New York Times,* September 11: A-1.

Rhoades, Stephen A. 1996. "Competition and Bank Mergers: Directions for Analysis from Available Evidence." *Antitrust Bulletin* 41 (Summer): 339–64.

Saunders, Anthony, and Ingo Walter. 1994. *Universal Banking in the United States: What Could We Gain? What Could We Lose?* Oxford University Press.

Scarlata, Jodi G. 1992. "Institutional Developments in the Globalization of Securities and Futures Markets." *Federal Reserve Bank of St. Louis* 74 (January-February): 17–30. Vol. 74.

Seiberg, Jaret. 1996. "Banks Making Good Progress in Their Fair-Lending Efforts." *American Banker,* September 16: 1.

Spar, Deborah, and Jeffrey J. Bussgang. 1996. "The Net." *Harvard Business Review* 74 (May-June): 125–33.

Spiro, Leah Nathans. 1996a. "Amex Stoops to Conquer." *Business Week,* May 20: 34.

———. 1996b. "Panic in the Year Zero Zero: Can the Financial World Reprogram Its Computer in Time?" *Business Week,* August 12: 72–73.

Spiro, Leah Nathans, with Linda Himelstein. 1996. "With the World Wide Web, Who Needs Wall Street?" *Business Week,* April 29: 120–21.

Starobin, Paul. 1993. "Make 'Em Pay." *National Journal* 25 (July 24): 1856–61.

Summers, Lawrence H. 1981. "Inflation, the Stock Market and Owner Occupied Housing." *American Economic Review* 71 (May): 429–34.

———. 1991. "Macroeconomic Consequences of Financial Crises," in Martin Feldstein, ed., *The Risk of Economic Crisis.* University of Chicago Press.

———. 1991. "Planning for the Next Financial Crises," in Martin Feldstein, ed., *The Risk of Economic Crisis.* University of Chicago Press.

Teitelman, Robert, and Stephen Davis. 1996. "How the Cash Flows." *Institutional Investor* (August): 58–73.

Timmons, Heather. 1996. "Improving Minority Lending: A Hands-On Proposition." *American Banker,* September 17: 1.

U. S. Congressional Budget Office. 1996. *Emerging Electronic Methods for Making Retail Payments.* June

U.S. Department of the Treasury. 1991. *Modernizing the Financial System: Recommendations for Safer, More Competitive Banks.* February.

U.S. General Accounting Office. 1996. *Financial Derivatives: Actions Taken or Proposed since May 1994.* November.

———. 1994. *Financial Derivatives—Actions Needed to Protect the Financial System.* Report to Congressional Requesters. May.

U.S. Securities and Exchange Commission. 1994. *Market 2000: An Examination of Current Equity Market Developments.* Washington. January

U.S. Securities and Exchange Commission and Booz, Allen & Hamilton. 1996. *Internet Banking Study.* Washington.

Wachter, Susan, and Michael Schill. 1995. "Uses and Limitations of HMDA Data in Identifying Discrimination and Redlining." Discussion paper 237. University of Pennsylvania, Institute for Law and Economics.

Wall, Larry D. 1993. "Too-Big-to-Fail after FDICIA." *Economic Review of the Federal Reserve Bank of Atlanta* (January-February): 1–14.

Wallman, Steven M. H. 1996. "Technology and Our Markets: Time to Decimalize." Speech before the Center for the Study of Equity Markets (Pace University). September 25.

Warner, Joan, and David Lindorff. 1996. "Developing Markets Have a Life of Their Own." *Business Week,* June 17: 104–05.

Warther, Vincent. Forthcoming. "Has the Rise of Mutual Funds Increased Market Instability?" Paper prepared for the first annual issue of the *Brookings-Wharton Papers on Financial Services.*

Weiss, Gary. 1996. "The New Grapevine is Online." *Business Week,* May 27: 132–33.

Wells, Kirstin E. 1996. "Are Checks Overused?" *Federal Reserve Bank of Minneapolis Quarterly Review* 20 (Fall): 2–12.

Werner, Ingrid M., and Linda L. Tesar. Forthcoming. "The Internationalization of Securities Markets since the 1987 Crash." Paper prepared for the first annual issue of the *Brookings-Wharton Papers on Financial Services.*

Whalen, Gary. 1997a. "Bank Organization Form and the Risks of Expanded Activities." Economics working paper 97-1. U.S. Office of the Comptroller of the Currency. January.

———. 1997b. "The Competitive Implications of Safety Net-Related Subsidies." (OCC) Economics working paper 97-9. U.S. Office of the Comptroller of the Currency. May.

Wilke, John R. 1996. "Giving Credit: Mortgage Lending to Minorities Shows a Sharp 1994 Increase." *Wall Street Journal,* February 13: A1.

Wilmarth, Arthur Jr. 1995. "Too Good to Be True? Unfulfilled Promises behind Big Bank Mergers." *Stanford Journal of Law, Business and Finance* 2 (Fall): 1–88.

Winston, Clifford. 1993. "Economic Deregulation: Days of Reckoning for Microeconomists." *Journal of Economic Literature* 31 (September): 1263–89.

Woodall, Pam. 1995. "Who's in the Driving Seat: A Survey of the World Economy."
    Economist, October 7.
Woolley, Suzanne. 1996. "What's Next, Bridge Tolls?" *Business Week*, September
    2: 64–65.
Yuengert, Andrew M. 1993. "The Measurement of Efficiency in Life Insurance:
    Estimates of a Mixed Normal-Gamma Error Model." *Journal of Banking and
    Finance* 17 (April): 483–96.
Zagorin, Adam. 1996. "Sub-Prime Time." *Time*, November 4: 67–68.

"All of a Sudden Every Banker Is a World Banker." 1996. *Economist*, July 27: 61–
    62.
"America's Financial Reform; Breaking Glass-Steagall." 1995. *Economist*, March 4:
    77.
"Artificial Intelligence: The Model Fund Manager." 1995. *Economist*, September 9:
    75–76.
"Digitizing Dollars." 1996. *Economist*, March 3: 68.
"Disastrous Bonds." 1996. *Economist*, August 31: 60.
"Electronic Benefits Transfer Update." 1996. *Checklist* (Fall): 36.
"The Future of Financial Services." 1995. *Banking World* (January): 21–37.
"How Does Your Stockmarket Grow?" 1996. *Economist*, July 27: 66.
"Look Out Below." 1996. *Economist*, July 6: 23–25.
"Managing Risk." 1996. *Wharton Alumni Magazine* (Spring): 24.
"Networks Play The Price Is Right on EBT." 1996. *Bank Network News*, October
    11: 1.
"Old Lady, New Problems." 1996. *Economist*, July 27: 63–64.
"The Seismic Shift in American Finance." 1995. *Economist*, October 21: 75–77.
"The Smart Card Era Dawns at Last." 1995. *Credit Card Management* (June).
"A Smoother Ride, But Less Fun." 1996. *Economist*, February 24: 77–78.
"Those Damned Dominoes." 1995. *Economist*, March 4: 78.
"The Train Now Stranded in the City of London. . . ." 1996. *Economist*, August 3:
    61–62.
"Trimming Hedges." 1996. *Economist*, June 22: 71–72.
"Where Next?" 1996. *Euromoney* (January): 36–46.

Index

Acknowledgments

The preparation of this report would not have been possible without the help of numerous individuals. The Advisory Commission on Financial Services, appointed by the Secretary of the Treasury under the Riegle-Neal Interstate Banking and Branching Efficiency Act of 1994, gave thoughtful consideration to the subject and provided valuable insights into the issues addressed in this paper. The members of that commission are Stephen J. Brobeck, John G. Heimann, Beth Hodges, Mary A. Houghton, Glenn H. Hutchins, Orin S. Kramer, Donald A. Moore Jr., John F. Sandner, and Rachel F. Robbins. Franklin D. Raines also served as a member of the commission until his appointment as Director of the Office of Management and Budget in September 1996.

In addition, Treasury staff members made important contributions through their consultations with the authors and comments on earlier drafts. In particular, Under Secretary for Domestic Finance John D. Hawke Jr., Assistant Secretary for Financial Institutions Richard S. Carnell, former Assistant Secretary for Economic Policy Joshua Gotbaum, Daniel Sichel, Robert Gillingham, Joan Affleck-Smith, Mark Bender, David Icikson, Victoria P. Rostow, and David Fischer made important contributions to the report.

Anita Whitlock provided secretarial help for this project. Steve Baron and Elaine Simerman provided research assistance. James Schneider and Brenda Szittya edited the manuscript, Carlotta Ribar proofread the pages, and Robert Elwood compiled the index.